PRINCETON COLLEGE

DURING THE

EIGHTEENTH CENTURY.

BY

SAMUEL DAVIES ALEXANDER,

AN ALUMNUS.

NEW YORK:

ANSON D. F. RANDOLPH & COMPANY,

770 BROADWAY, COR. 9th STREET.

INTRODUCTORY NOTE.

ON account of the many sources from which I have derived my information, and not wishing to burden my page with foot-notes, I have omitted all authorities. I have drawn from printed books, from old newspapers and periodicals, and from family records, and when the words of another have suited me, I have used them as my own. As Dr. Allen says, "Compilers seem to be licensed pillagers. Like the youth of Sparta, they may lay their hands upon plunder without a crime, if they will but seize it with adroitness."

Allen's Biographical Dictionary, Sprague's Annals, and Duyckinck's Cyclopædia of American Literature, have been of the greatest service; but in many instances I have gone to the original sources from which they derived their information. I have also used freely the Centennial Discourses of Professors Giger and Cameron of the College.

The book does not profess to be a perfect exhibition of the graduates. But it is a beginning that may be carried nearer to perfection in every succeeding year. Its very imperfection may lead to the discovery of new matter, and the correction of errors which must unavoidably be many.

My object has been to give brief sketches of the Alumni *after* their graduation, yet often stating the place of birth and name of parents. Out of 894 graduates during the 18th Century, I have noticed 646. The remaining names may be sketched hereafter in a supplement, and it is hoped that this publication will stimulate those who possess information of any of those whose names are omitted to send the same to the compiler.

I return my sincere thanks to those persons who have assisted me in this work.

S. D. A.

PREFACE.

THE history of a College is best read in the lives of her sons. The history of the changes which occur in her government and instruction is too contracted in its nature. To take in the grand sweep of her influence, we must follow her sons as they go forth into the world to mould and direct the elements that surround them.

The biographical notices which are here given of the graduates of Princeton, are something more than mere personal memoranda, or a table of necrology; they are the *facts* of a grand generalization, which will demonstrate that Princeton has had much to do in *securing the liberties of our country;* in *founding the Presbyterian Church in this land;** and in *introducing and stimulating the higher forms of Academic and Collegiate learning.* These Sketches are not selected from the great body of graduates; but it is the whole number, just as they stand in the Catalogue, so far as their history could be traced.

The mutterings of the storm which afterwards broke upon the country, was faintly heard by the early graduates who left the College; but their lives were passed amidst the most tremendous struggles of Liberty against Oppression; and the facts to be presented will leave no doubt as to the side upon which the sons of Princeton

* Other Churches besides the Presbyterian are well represented by Princeton graduates. James Manning, that bright light in the Baptist Church, and the founder and First President of Brown University, was an Alumnus of Princeton; and no less than five Bishops of the Episcopal Church were graduates of Princeton, viz., Clagget, Hobart, Meade, McIlvaine and Johns; while some of the most distinguished laymen among our graduates have been members of that Church.

arrayed themselves; they but carried into practice the immortal principles instilled into them by those noble men who guided the affairs of the College.

I have been deeply impressed, while gathering these memorials, that the Alumni of Princeton, with but few exceptions, as far as I can discover, stood shoulder to shoulder on the side of their country. Ministers and laymen vied with each other who should lead the van.

When we examine the first movements which resulted in Independence, we shall find that the graduates of Princeton were among the earliest as their originators or their most hearty promoters.

Let a few facts tell the story: The first bloodshed of the Revolution was not at Lexington, but several years earlier, on the Alamance, in North Carolina, in an engagement between Governor Tryon's troops and the "Regulators," on the 16th of May, 1771. And who were these Regulators? Not a set of adventurers, but the sturdy members of three Presbyterian Congregations, who had as their pastors three graduates of Princeton; one of whom had been for days endeavouring to procure peace, and, on the day of battle, was on the ground, still hoping to avert the blow.

When the party of patriots went aboard the "Tea Ship" in Boston Harbour, THOMAS MELVILLE, a graduate of the class of 1769, was among the number; and the only specimen of that historic tea that escaped the destruction of that night was found the next morning in the shoes of Melville, and, being placed in a vial, is extant at this day.

When the heavy hand of arbitrary power became almost unbearable, and before the country was aware that relief was possible, a little band of brave souls in North Carolina were at their secluded homes laying the foundations for the Temple of Liberty. And who were these men who conceived and published the Mecklenburg Resolutions—who consecrated "life, fortune and sacred honour" (their own words) to the country's deliverance?

The man who penned these Resolutions, and who was the Secretary of the Convention which adopted them, was EPHRAIM BREVARD, a graduate of Princeton of the class of 1768. Next to him, and perhaps the most influential man who signed the immortal paper, was HEZEKIAH JAMES BALCH, a graduate of the class of 1766; and, to form a trinity of Princeton Heroes, we add the name of WAIGHTSTILL AVERY, of the class of 1766. Here, then, was the first impetus given to the cause of Liberty by men who had so lately come forth from the cradle of freedom and learning. When one of the graduates of Princeton was rudely aroused from sleep by the owner of the house in North Carolina, where he had stopped to rest, entering his room and saying, "I allow no man to sleep under my roof but a Whig;" he answered, "Let me rest in peace, then, for I graduated at Princeton under Dr. Witherspoon, a Signer of the Declaration of Independence;" that is a sufficient pass-word for him. A single incident in the life of this great man will show the influence which pervaded Princeton. When the Declaration of Independence was on its passage in the Continental Congress, and the result was doubtful, the scale was turned, in a great measure, by a speech of Dr. Witherspoon. In the course of that speech (when he perceived the House to be wavering) he said: "There is a tide in the affairs of men—a nick of time. We perceive it now before us. To hesitate is to consent to slavery. That noble instrument on your table, which insures immortality to its author, should be subscribed this very morning by every pen in this House. For my own part, of property I have some—of reputation more. That reputation is staked upon the issue of this contest—that property is pledged; and although these gray hairs must soon descend into the sepulchre, I had infinitely rather they should descend thither by the hands of the public executioner than desert, at this crisis, the sacred cause of my country." No wonder his name was a pass-word throughout the American lines.

When the Continental Congress met, and throughout its many dark and desponding, yet heroic sessions, Princeton was present during different times, in the person of twenty-four of her sons; and when that Congress was called upon on the 4th of July, 1776, to sign the Declaration of Independence, Princeton answered by her President and two of her Alumni.

Every department of the army found her well represented. Almost every Presbyterian clergyman who had come forth from her walls was, at one time or another, either a chaplain, an officer, or in the ranks. In the last letter which one of these wrote to his wife before he was barbarously murdered, after he had surrendered, are these touching words: "We are going over to attack the enemy. You would think it strange to see your husband, an old man, riding with a French fusee slung at his shoulder. This may be the last letter you shall ever receive from your husband."

Let the sketches that follow prove the assertion, that the Alumni of Princeton were ever the staunchest, bravest, most self-sacrificing, most persevering friends of American Liberty.

Not only were the graduates of Princeton unanimous in their patriotic work, but the Presbyterian Church owes a stupendous debt of gratitude to these men, which she should, even at this late day, begin to repay. Of the six graduates of the first class, five became Presbyterian ministers, and the sixth was RICHARD STOCKTON, a strong Presbyterian, as his Will conclusively proves. Of the second class of seven, six became Presbyterian ministers, and the seventh was WILLIAM BURNET, an Elder in the Presbyterian Church during life. And how remarkable has the work of these men, and of those who followed them, been in laying the foundations of the Presbyterian Church in those forming communities of Western Pennsylvania, Delaware, Maryland, Virginia, North Carolina, Kentucky and Tennessee—the very strongholds of Presbyterianism at this day!

When Samuel Davies left his work in Virginia to assume his place at Princeton, he left as his successor JOHN TODD, a graduate of Princeton of the class of 1749; and although at first he stood alone, he was soon reinforced from the same old Halls by men of like mind and like holy purpose; and their works do follow them. JOHN TODD, and WILLIAM GRAHAM, and SAMUEL STANHOPE SMITH, all of Princeton, will ever be honoured for their foundation work in behalf of the Presbyterian Church in Virginia. North Carolina early felt the power of Princeton; and HUGH MCADEN, HEZEKIAH JAMES BALCH, JOSEPH ALEXANDER, and DAVID CALDWELL, fresh from College, gathered the scattered families into permanent Presbyterian Churches. Western Pennsylvania, the home of bloody savage warfare, but now the very fountain of Presbyterian power, welcomed from Princeton those noble, self-sacrificing pioneers, THADDEUS DOD, JOHN MCMILLAN, and others of kindred spirit; and Tennessee and Kentucky tell the same story. All these men, with hardly an exception, were graduates of Princeton.

The testimony of General Joseph Reed, that eminent patriot, in reference to the influence of the Presbyterian Church on our great struggle for Liberty, is worth remembering. Of that Church he wrote: "When I am convinced of its errors, or ashamed of its character, I may perhaps change it; till then I shall not blush at a connection with a people who, in this great controversy, are not second to any in vigorous exertions and generous contributions, and to whom we are so eminently indebted for our deliverance from the thraldom of Great Britain."

But the influence of the Alumni of Princeton on the higher forms of education in our country, is more remarkable than all. By the side of the Church they planted the Classical School, out of which grew many of our most important colleges. What breadth of views these men must have possessed; what a foresight into the future of the country, which prompted them to inaugurate these higher schools of learning in the very wilderness, and amidst the very clangor of savage war! But they were men mighty in faith, mighty in prayer, and mighty in work, and we this day humbly and gratefully acknowledge their wisdom and their heroism. But let me adduce a few facts to establish the claim that Princeton graduates have ever fostered the higher educational interests of our country.

The man chosen to visit Great Britain and collect funds for an Indian Mission School in Connecticut, which afterwards grew into Dartmouth College, was NATHANIEL WHITAKER, a graduate of the class of 1752. The College of Rhode Island (afterwards Brown University) had its origin in the conception and personal exertions of JAMES MANNING, a graduate of the class of 1762; and he became its first President. Union College, New York, owes its existence in a great measure to the persevering exertions of THEODORE DIRCK ROMEYN, a graduate of the class of 1765, and its first President was JOHN BLAIR SMITH, a graduate of the class of 1773, and its second President was JONATHAN EDWARDS of the class of 1765. Hamilton College, New York, owes its existence to SAMUEL KIRKLAND, a graduate of the class of 1765, through whose influence Hamilton Oneida Academy was incorporated, and to which he conveyed a large landed estate, and which became, under a new charter, Hamilton College. The first Medical College in America, at Philadelphia, was founded by WILLIAM SHIPPEN, a graduate of the class of 1754. He also delivered the first course of lectures that had ever been given in this country on Anatomy; and the first medical degree ever conferred in this country was by this college and to John Archer, a graduate of Princeton, of the class of 1760. The second Medical College established in this country was at New York, and the men who had the chief hand in it, and who became its professors, were JAMES SMITH, a graduate of the class of 1757, and JOHN V. B. TENNENT of the class of 1758. The first Provost of the

University of Pennsylvania after its reorganization, was JOHN EWING, a graduate of the class of 1754. When Queens College (Rutgers) was revived in 1808, Dr. Livingston became the nominal President, but the Vice-President and the acting President, the man who had done more than any other in its revival, was IRA CONDICT, a graduate of the class of 1784. In 1776 JOHN BROWN, a graduate of the class of 1749, started a Grammar School at Timber Ridge, Virginia, at which Dr. Archibald Alexander attended among the first scholars. This school grew into Liberty Hall, and that into Washington College, over which we find as first President WILLIAM GRAHAM, a graduate of the class of 1773. About 1776 SAMUEL STANHOPE SMITH, a graduate of the class of 1769, through his eloquence and energy, was the means of founding Hampden Sidney College in Virginia, and he was elected the first President. The second President was JOHN B. SMITH, a graduate of the class of 1773. The first meeting of the Trustees to take measures for founding Dickinson College in Pennsylvania, was held in 1783, and the leading man in the Board was BENJAMIN RUSH of the class of 1760.

In 1789, THADDEUS DOD, a graduate of the class of 1773, established in Western Pennsylvania an Academy which was called Washington Academy, of which he was the first Principal; this under a new charter became Washington College. A school in the same neighbourhood, called the Log Cabin, was started about 1790 by JOHN McMILLAN, a graduate of the class of 1772. Under a new charter it became Jefferson College, and JOHN WATSON, a graduate of the class of 1797, became the first President, and James Dunlap, of the class of 1773, the second President. The first Classical School in North Carolina was founded by JOSEPH ALEXANDER, a graduate of the class of 1760, and a charter was obtained from the Colonial Legislature in 1770, under the name of Queen's Museum. This charter was repealed by the King; but a new charter was granted by the Legislature in 1771, and again repealed by Proclamation, as being too liberal. But still the College flourished without a charter. It was in the halls of this College that the Mecklenburg Convention held its sessions. After the Revolution, this College became Liberty Hall under a new charter, and *thirteen* of its fifteen Trustees were graduates of Princeton. In the course of a few years, this College was transferred to Winnsboro, South Carolina, and merged in Mount Zion College, over which THOMAS H. McCAULE, a graduate of Princeton of the class of 1774, presided. Soon after the Revolution, there were six admirable Classical Schools in North Carolina, five of them being under the direction of graduates of Princeton. In 1796, JOSEPH CALDWELL, a graduate of the class of 1791, became Professor of Mathematics in the University of North Carolina. He found the College in a state of disorganization, but by his faithful labour and energy, it was saved from ruin, and the foundation of its future usefulness laid. Mr. Caldwell became its first President in 1804. In 1811 he resigned, and ROBERT HETT CHAPMAN, a graduate of the class of 1789, succeeded him, but he remained only a few years, when Mr. Caldwell was recalled. In Georgia, the second Presidents of Franklin College and Oglethorpe University were both graduates of Princeton. In 1810, HENRY KOLLOCK, a graduate of the class of 1794, was elected President of the University of Georgia, but he declined the honour. In 1785, Martin Academy, the first literary institution ever established in the great valley of the Mississippi, was founded by SAMUEL DOAK, a graduate of the class of 1775; afterwards it received a charter under the name of Washington College, and Mr. Doak became the first President. In 1793, the Territorial Legislature of Tennessee granted a charter to Greenville College, and HEZEKIAH BALCH, a graduate of the class of 1776, who had conceived and matured the whole plan, was elected the first President. In 1785, the Legislature of North Carolina granted a charter to Davidson Academy, located in Davidson County (what is now Tennessee), THOMAS B.

CRAIGHEAD, a graduate of the class of 1775, being the main agent in securing it. In course of time this Academy became the University of Nashville, and Mr. Craighead was elected the first President. In 1783, Transylvania Seminary (afterwards University) was established in Kentucky, through the influence of CALEB WALLACE, a graduate of Princeton; and DAVID RICE, a graduate of the class of 1761, became the President of the Board of Trustees, and its virtual manager. And the last class of the century furnished two Presidents; Jacob Lindly, the first President of Ohio University, and James Carnahan of our own venerable college.

Have we not, then, in these facts, which I have drawn from my biographical notices, overwhelming evidence of the influence of Princeton, in originating and fostering the higher forms of education in the formative state of our country?

Read the sketches that follow, and the conviction will be irresistible, that *the Country*, the *Presbyterian Church*, and the cause of *high Christian Culture*, owe their present exalted position in the land to the noble men who went forth from Princeton during the last century.

BIOGRAPHICAL SKETCHES.

PRINCETON COLLEGE

DURING THE EIGHTEENTH CENTURY.

1748.

Enos Ayres, the first on this illustrious catalogue, was probably a native of Elizabethtown, New Jersey. If not, he was certainly residing there before he entered college, as his correspondence with Dr. Bellamy shows. Mr. Ayres was ordained by the Presbytery of New York about 1750, and settled as the pastor of the Churches at Bethlehem and Blooming Grove, Orange County, New York. In a few years he relinquished the charge at Bethlehem, and continued the pastor of Blooming Grove, until his death, which occurred in 1765.

Benjamin Chestnut came to this country from England. He was licensed by the Presbytery of New York in 1749, and was immediately transferred to the Presbytery of New Brunswick, by whom he was ordained, October 30, 1751, and settled at Woodbury and Timber Creek, New Jersey. In May, 1753, he resigned his charge, but for a time continued to supply the congregations. After preaching at a number of places, he was finally, in 1756, settled as the pastor of Charleston and Providence Churches, Pennsylvania. In 1765, Mr. Chestnut visited the South on a missionary tour. At one time he taught a school about twenty miles from

Philadelphia. Mr. Chestnut was a laborious and faithful minister: besides his regular duties, he was untiring in fulfilling the appointments of the Presbytery, in missionary work, extending as far as Egg Harbour, New Jersey, and the adjacent country on the Atlantic Coast. He died in 1775.

Hugh Henry, having studied theology, was ordained by the Presbytery of New Castle in 1751, and settled as pastor of the Churches of Rehoboth, Wicomico and Monokin, in Maryland. President Davies spoke of him as promising great usefulness. He was a laborious and highly esteemed minister. Mr. Henry died in 1763.

Israel Reid, a licentiate of the Presbytery of New York, was ordained by the Presbytery of New Brunswick, March 7, 1750, and settled as pastor of the Presbyterian Church at Bound Brook, New Jersey. He was the first graduate of Princeton who became a member of the Synod of the Presbyterian Church.

Mr. Reid, besides his charge at Bound Brook, took charge at an early day of the Church at New Brunswick. He died after a life of great usefulness, November 28, 1793.

Richard Stockton. No name stands higher among the Lawyers and Statesmen of America, than that of Richard Stockton. He was the son of John Stockton, and was born in Princeton, New Jersey, October 1, 1730. After graduating, he studied law with David Ogden, of Newark, and soon became prominent in his profession.

In 1766 he visited Europe, where he was received with flattering marks of friendship and respect by many eminent noblemen, gentlemen, and men of letters. During this visit, his life was in imminent peril on two occasions: once he was attacked at night in the city of Edinburgh by a desperate robber, and after a severe contest, in which he successfully defended himself with a small sword, now in possession of the family, he repelled the attack without receiving any material injury.

The second escape was of a different character. He had engaged his passage in a packet for the purpose of crossing the Irish Channel, but his baggage being accidentally detained, did not arrive before the vessel had sailed. Although greatly disappointed, it proved the cause of his preservation, for the vessel in which he intended to embark was wrecked in a violent storm, and every soul on board perished.

In 1774 Mr. Stockton was appointed Judge of the Supreme Court of New Jersey, and in 1776 was offered the Chief Justiceship, which he declined. The same year he was elected to the Continental Congress, and was one of the Signers of the Declaration of Independence. While a member of Congress, during a visit to the house of a friend in Monmouth County, New Jersey, he was captured by a party of royalists and thrown into prison in New York city. His confinement and the barbarity of his treatment seriously and permanently affected his health. He obtained his release through the interference of Congress.

Mr. Stockton had an unrivalled reputation at the bar; and it is said that he always refused to engage in any cause which he knew to be unjust. From 1757 till his death he was a Trustee of the College; and for many years a member and Trustee of the Presbyterian Church in Princeton. An estimate of the high tone of his Christian character can be formed by reading the following extract from his last Will: "As my children will have frequent occasion of perusing this instrument, and may probably be peculiarly impressed with the last words of their father, I think proper here, not only to subscribe to the entire belief of the great leading doctrines of the Christian religion, such as the being of a God, the universal defection and depravity of human nature, the divinity of the *Person*, and completeness of the redemption purchased by the blessed Saviour, the necessity of the divine Spirit, of divine faith accompanied with an habitual virtuous life, and the universality of divine Providence; but also in the bowels of a father's affection to charge and exhort them to remember that 'the fear of God is the beginning of wisdom.'"

Mr. Stockton was a man of great coolness and courage. His bodily powers, both in relation to strength and agility, were of a very superior grade, and he was highly accomplished in all the manly exercises peculiar to the period in which he lived; his skill as a horseman and swordsman was peculiarly great. In person he was tall and commanding, approaching nearly to six feet in height.

What a noble example to lead the van and stimulate the energies of all future graduates! Mr. Stockton died in Princeton, February 28, 1781.

Daniel Thane came to this country from Scotland. He was ordained by the Presbytery of New York, and settled as pastor of the Presbyterian Church at Connecticut Farms, New Jersey, August 29, 1750. In 1754, he was sent by the Synod on a three months' tour to Virginia and the Carolinas, where he did good service preaching under the forest trees. In 1757, he was dismissed from his charge in New Jersey, and removed to Delaware, where he became pastor of the Presbyterian Churches at New Castle and Christina Bridge. In 1763, he left his charge in an irregular manner. His name disappears from the roll of Synod after 1763. He is said to have died in 1764.

1749.

John Brown was born in Ireland, in 1728. He was licensed by the Presbytery of New Castle, and sent as a missionary to the Valley of Virginia. In 1753, he was called to the united Churches of Timber Ridge and New Providence, Virginia. This call he accepted. In addition to his pastoral work, he established a grammar school near his residence, which afterwards was merged in Liberty Hall, and finally grew into Washington College. It was in this congregation that the Alexander family resided. In 1796, Mr. Brown, weighed down under the infirmities of age, resigned his charge, and soon after followed his children to Kentucky. The following is the inscription on his tomb at Frankfort: "The tomb of the Rev. John Brown, who, after graduating at Nassau Hall, devoted himself to the ministry, and settled at New Providence, Rockbridge County, Virginia. At that place he was stated pastor forty-four years. In the decline of life he removed to this county, to spend the feeble remainder of his days with his children. He died in the 75th year of his age, A. D. 1803." The sons of Mr. Brown all became distinguished men. One was a United States Senator from Kentucky; another was a Senator from Louisiana and Minister to France, and the third became an eminent physician and Professor in Transylvania University.

William Burnet was the son of Ichabod Burnet, a distinguished physician of Elizabethtown, New Jersey. After graduating, he studied medicine with Dr. Staats, of New York; but the trouble with the mother-country coming on, he relinquished a lucrative practice, and entered actively into the political movements of the day. Dr. Burnet was Chairman of the "Committee of Public Safety" at Newark, which met daily. In 1775, he was superintendent of a military hospital, established on his own responsibility, in Newark. In the winter of 1776, he was elected a member of the Continental Congress; but early in the session Congress divided the thirteen States into three military districts, and Dr. Burnet was appointed Physician and Surgeon-General of the Eastern District; he accordingly resigned his seat in Congress, and entered upon his office, the arduous duties of which he continued to discharge till the close of the war, in 1783. At one time Dr. Burnet was stationed at West Point, and on a certain occasion, he was dining with a party of gentlemen at the house of Gen. Arnold,* when the officer of the day entered, and reported that a spy had been taken below, who called himself John Anderson. It was remarked by the persons who were at the table, that this intelligence, interesting to the general as it must have been, produced no visible change in his countenance or behavior—that he continued in his seat for some minutes, conversing as before—after which he arose, saying to his guests, that business required him to be absent for a short time, and desiring them to remain and enjoy themselves till his return. The next intelligence they had of him was, that he was in his barge, moving rapidly to a British ship of war, the *Vulture*, which was lying at anchor a short distance below the Point.

At the close of the war Dr. Burnet returned to his family, and devoted himself to agricultural pursuits. Soon after he was appointed presiding Judge of the Court of Common Pleas by the Legislature of New Jersey, and was also elected President of the State Medical Society. Being a fine classical scholar, on taking the chair, he read an elaborate essay in Latin, on the proper use of the lancet in pleuritic cases. Dr. Burnet died October 7, 1791.

* This is on authority of his son, the Hon. Judge Jacob Burnet, of Ohio.

1749.

John Hogg (or Hoge) was the son of William Hoge, "an exile for Christ's sake" from Scotland. He was licensed by the Presbytery of New Brunswick, October 10, 1753. In 1755, he was ordained by the Presbytery of New Castle, and became the first pastor of the Churches of Opecquon and Cedar Creek, Virginia. In 1760, we find him the pastor of Tuscarora, Opecquon and Back Creek Churches. About 1762, Mr. Hoge, on account of the remissness of his people in giving him a support, resigned his charge, and removed to Pennsylvania.

Thomas Kennedy. I can learn nothing of Mr. Kennedy. As accurate a historian as Richard Webster has confounded him with Samuel Kennedy, who was licensed by the Presbytery of New Brunswick, and installed at Baskingridge, N. J., in 1751. But this Samuel Kennedy was educated at Edinburgh, according to an extended memoir of him by Rev. Isaac V. Brown, appended to his Life of Robert Finley, and published in 1819. This must be a different man from our graduate, who was probably not a clergyman.

John Moffat, a Scotchman by birth, was ordained by the Presbytery of New York in 1751, and installed as pastor of the Presbyterian Church at Wallkill, Orange Co., New York. In 1795, he joined the Associate Church. In 1773, he was residing in Delaware, but returned and engaged in teaching in Litttle Britain, Orange County, New York. De Witt Clinton was one of his pupils. He died April 22, 1788.

John Todd is said to have been a weaver before he joined college. He was licensed to preach by the Presbytery of New Brunswick, November 13, 1750. Immediately after his licensure he went to Virginia, and became an assistant to the Rev. Samuel Davies in Providence Church. After the removal of Mr. Davies to Princeton, Mr. Todd became the leading Presbyterian preacher in that region. During the Revolution, he was a staunch Whig. While pastor in Virginia he taught a classical school, and the Rev. James Waddel, who was at that time reading divinity with Mr. Davies, assisted him in teaching. Col. Gordon, of Lancaster County, on hearing him preach, said: "I never heard a sermon, but one I heard from Mr. Davies, that I heard with more attention and delight. Oh, if the Lord would be pleased to send us a minister of as much piety as Mr. Todd!" He died suddenly, July 27, 1793.

Eleazer Whittlesey, when he came to college, brought a letter of introduction from Dr. Bellamy to President Burr, from which we judge that he was a native of Connecticut. He was licensed by the Presbytery of New Castle in 1750, and labored faithfully in Hartford County, Maryland, and was the means of establishing a number of congregations. He was a man tenderly loved for his zeal and integrity. His health was infirm, and he was subject to seasons of melancholy. Mr. Whittlesey died December 21, 1751. There is no record of his ordination.

1750.

Hugh Bay became a physician and practiced at Herberts Cross Roads, Hartford County, Maryland. He was a brother of Rev. Andrew Bay, one of the early Presbyterian ministers in this country, at one time settled in Albany. I know nothing further of Dr. Bay's history.

Alexander Clinton, the eldest son of Charles Clinton, the ancestor of the family of Clintons in New York, became a physician, and practiced in the city of New York.

Daniel Farrand, a native of Connecticut, after spending two years at Yale, transferred his relation to Nassau Hall. In 1752 he was ordained and settled over a Congregational Church at South Canaan, Connecticut, where he continued in the faithful discharge of his duties till near the close of life. He died on the 28th of May, 1803, in the eighty-first year of his age, and the fifty-first of his ministry.

Mr. Farrand was of a medium stature, with a large head, and a heavy clumsily-formed body; his features were uncommonly large, and his countenance altogether indicative, not of refinement, but of much mental strength and solidity. His scholarship, especially in classical learning, was very great. In religious matters he was always grave and dignified, and yet was not wanting in wit. On one occasion, at a meeting of ministers, a certain Dr. W. had set up a vigorous defense of the ideal system of Bishop Berkeley. The next morning when they were about separating for their respective homes, the horse of Dr. W. was missing, under such circumstances as to induce the apprehension that he had been stolen; and it was proposed by some one that he should advertise him; upon which Mr. Farrand, with much apparent gravity, asked the Doctor whether he had a perfect idea of his horse,—such as would enable him to *give* a perfect idea of him. He replied that he had. "Well, then," said Parson Farrand, "why don't you fit your saddle and bridle on it and ride home. You surely can want no better mode of travelling."

It was a perilous matter to attempt to extort a compliment from Mr. Farrand. He was travelling on horseback in a part of the country where he was an entire stranger. Noticing a considerable gathering at a private house, he concluded that it was some religious meeting, and being willing to rest himself and his horse, he dismounted and went in, and remained till the close of the service. The man who officiated turned out to be a very illiterate, self-conceited preacher. He took for his text the account given by the Evangelist of the evil spirits entering into the herd of swine. Immediately on the close of the service, Mr. Farrand left the house and proceeded on his journey; but he had not gone far before the preacher, who had eyed him during the lecture, and happened to be going the same road, overtook him. He remarked to him directly that he had seen him at the lecture and presumed from his appearance that he was a clergyman. Mr. Farrand having replied that he was, the preacher very unceremoniously requested his opinion of the sermon. Mr. Farrand declined expressing his opinion, remarking at the same time that he was not in the habit of dealing in compliments. This increased the preacher's anxiety to hear his opinion, and he repeated his request with still greater energy. "Well," said Mr. Farrand, "if you insist on hearing my opinion, I must say I think you made worse work with the Scriptures than the devil did with the swine."

Mr. Farrand was admitted to an *ad eundem* Master's degree at Yale in 1777.

1750.

Jacobus Frelinghuysen was the son of the Rev. Theodorus Jacobus Frelinghuysen. He died at sea, on his return from Holland, in 1754, whither he had gone for ordination. At the time of his death he was pastor elect of the Reformed Dutch Church at Kinderhook, New York.

1751.

Samuel Clark studied theology, and was ordained and installed pastor of the Second Congregational Church at Farmington (now Kensington), Connecticut, in July, 1756. Mr. Clark appeared well in the pulpit; and the epitaph on his tombstone mentions among other estimable qualities of the man, that he was, "in the gift of preaching, excellent, laborious and pathetic." Mr. Clark continued in his charge until his death, November, 1775.

He received the degree of Master of Arts from Yale, in 1757.

Alexander Gordon was a tutor in the college from the time of his graduation until 1754, in which year he died.

Robert Henry was born in Scotland. After leaving college he studied theology, and was licensed by the Presbytery of New York. In 1752, he was sent by the Synod to Virginia, at the request of the Rev. Samuel Davies. In 1753, he was ordained by the Presbytery of New Castle, and on the 4th of June, 1755, was installed as pastor of Cub Creek, in Charlotte County, Virginia, and Briary, in Prince Edward County, both then in Lunenburg County. After his installation, Mr. Davies and Mr. Todd preached five days in his congregation, and many were awakened. The success of Mr. Henry was most remarkable. He was a man of eccentric manners, but most devotedly pious. He was not in the habit of reading his sermons or even of writing. Short notes of preparation were all he used, and not always those. It is said of him, that on a certain occasion, he thought he ought to prepare himself with greater care than usual, and having written a sermon, he commenced reading from a small manuscript. A gust of wind suddenly swept the paper from the Bible. He watched its progress as it sailed along to an old elder's seat. The old gentleman had been listening seriously, and as the paper fell at his side, he deliberately put his foot upon it. Mr. Henry waited for him to bring it back to him. The old gentleman looked up as if nothing had happened; and Mr. Henry finished his sermon in the best way he could. It was the end of his written preparation to preach. There is nothing left as the production of his pen. Dr. Archibald Alexander was the second successor of Mr. Henry in his charge. Mr. Henry was called to the Steel Creek Church in North Carolina, in 1766, but never entered upon the charge, dying May 8, 1767.

Samuel McClintock, after graduating, studied theology, and was ordained, and settled as pastor over the Congregational Church at Greenland, New Hampshire, in 1757. President Burr had offered him a tutorship in the college, which he declined. During the Revolution he was a strong Whig, and repeatedly acted as chaplain in the army, and his patriotic exhortations animated the soldiers in the conflict. Five of his sons were in the American army.

In 1791, the honorary degree of Doctor of Divinity was conferred upon him by Yale. His ministry lasted forty-eight years, during which period the last Sunday of his life was the only one in which he was disabled for the performance of his usual public duties. He died in 1804.

Dr. McClintock was regarded among the churches in his neighborhood as pre-eminent for practical wisdom, and many cases of casuistry were referred to him as an umpire.

The following is a list of his publications:

A Sermon on the Justice of God in the Mortality of Man. 1759.

A Sermon entitled, "The Artifice of Deceivers detected, and Christians warned against them." 1770.

Herodias, or Cruelty and Revenge. The Effects of Unlawful Pleasure. A Sermon. 1772.

A Sermon at the Commencement of the New Constitution of New Hampshire. 1784.

An Epistolary Correspondence with Rev. John C. Ogden. 1791.

A Sermon entitled, "The Choice," occasioned by the drought, the fever, and the prospect of war. 1798.

An Oration Commemorative of Washington. 1800.

Henry Martin received his license to preach from the Presbytery of New York. In 1752, he supplied the pulpits of Maidenhead and Hopewell, in New Jersey, and on the 9th of April, 1753, he was ordained, and installed as pastor of the Presbyterian Churches in Newtown and Salisbury, Bucks County, Pennsylvania. He died about 1763.

Benjamin Youngs Prime was the son of the Rev. Ebenezer Prime, of Long Island. After graduating, he studied medicine and pursued the practice for several years. In 1756 he was appointed tutor in the College, which position he held for about a year. In 1762 he visited Europe for the purpose of pursuing his medical studies to more advantage; he remained there for two or three years, and took his degree of Doctor of Medicine at the University of Leyden. Dr. Prime became a highly accomplished scholar, eminent for his mathematical, philosophical and classical attainments. He was in the habit of writing with great facility both prose and poetry in the Hebrew, Greek, Latin, French and Spanish languages; and in the opening of the Revolutionary struggle, his patriotic and popular songs spread like wild-fire over the land, and helped to kindle the sparks of liberty into a flame.

After his return from Europe in 1764, he became a practitioner of medicine and surgery in the city of New York; but after a few years, his father becoming infirm, he returned to Huntington, Long Island, and resumed his residence with his father, and occupied his time in the pursuit of elegant letters. Dr. Prime was the grandfather of the Drs. Prime of the *New York Observer*. He died October 31, 1791.

In 1764 an 8vo pamphlet of 94 pages was published in London, under the following title: "The Patriot Muse, or Poems on some of the Principal Events of the Late War; together with a Poem on the Peace. Vincit amor patriae. By an American gentleman." The author was Dr. Prime. In 1791 he published "Columbia's Glory, or British Pride Humbled; a Poem on the American Revolution; some part of it being a Parody on an Ode entitled, Britain's Glory, or Gallic Pride Humbled, composed on the capture of Quebec, 1759."

Robert Ross became a Congregational minister, and in November, 1753, was ordained and installed pastor of the First Church in Bridgeport, Connecticut. Mr. Ross is said to have been a man of great dignity, and had a commanding influence over his people. He wore the ancient dress of cock-hat, wig and small clothes. He remained in this charge until his death, in August, 1799.

Nathaniel Scudder belonged to an old family in Monmouth County, New Jersey. After leaving college, he studied medicine and practiced in his native county until the opening of the Revolution, when he entered actively into public life. He was Colonel of the Battalion of the Monmouth Militia; and from 1777 to 1779 represented New Jersey in the Continental Congress. He was also a member of the Committee of Safety. Colonel Scudder was an earnest Christian, and was an Elder in Mr. Tennent's Church at Freehold. For many years he was a Trustee of the College.

Colonel Scudder was the grandfather of the distinguished missionary, Rev. John Scudder, M. D. He was killed in a skirmish against the "Refugees" at Black Point, Monmouth County, New Jersey, in 1781. At the time of his death Dr. Scudder was a Trustee of the College.

1751.

David Thurston became the pastor of the Second Congregational Church in Medway, Massachusetts, on the 23d of June, 1752. In consequence of ill health and difficulties in the congregation, on the 22d of February, 1769, he resigned; and in the spring of 1772, he removed to Oxford, Massachusetts, where he purchased and cultivated a farm.

1752.

George Duffield, a native of Pennsylvania, acted as tutor in the College from 1754 to 1756. He was licensed to preach by the Presbytery of New Castle, March 11, 1756, and in 1759 he was settled over a Presbyterian Church in Carlisle, Pennsylvania. In 1766, by order of the Synod, in company with Rev. Charles Beatty, he made a missionary tour through Pennsylvania, Maryland and Virginia. Soon after his return he was called to the Third Presbyterian Church in Philadelphia.

Dr. Duffield was a strong Whig, and was at one time, in connection with Bishop White, Chaplain of the Continental Congress. During the dark and almost hopeless period of the Revolution, he acted as chaplain in the retreat of the army through New Jersey, and was at the battle of Princeton.

He remained pastor of the Third Church in Philadelphia until the day of his death, February 2, 1790. The honorary degree of Doctor of Divinity was conferred upon him by Yale in 1785.

Dr. Duffield was an eminently devoted Christian and a most faithful minister. He took an active part in the organization of the Presbyterian Church after the Revolution, and was the first Stated Clerk of the General Assembly. He was for thirty years a Trustee of the College.

Dr. Duffield published an account of his tour with Dr. Beatty, and a Thanksgiving Sermon on the Restoration of Peace, 1783.

Jeremiah Halsey held the office of tutor in the college from 1757 to 1767, longer than any other individual.

In 1766, the Trustees voted a sum of money to him, "in consideration of his extraordinary and faithful services." On the retirement of Mr. Halsey from the tutorship, the Trustees gave him a certificate with the corporation seal attached, certifying his faithful services, and recommending him as "a gentleman of genius, learning and real merit." Dr. Green testifies that Mr. Halsey was one of the best scholars that was ever educated in the institution. In 1767, he was ordained by the Presbytery of New Brunswick, and sent on a missionary tour to the South; afterwards was settled as a pastor, but the place of his location I have not been able to discover. He was for eleven years a Trustee of the College. Mr. Halsey died in 1780.

Samuel Livermore, descended from one of the ancient New England families, was born at Waltham, Massachusetts, near Boston, in May, 1732. There is a diary of Mr. Livermore, published in *Putnam's Magazine*, for June, 1857, written on the eve of his journey to college. It is interesting to know what was the outfit of a New England boy going to a distant college, and here we have it. He sailed from Boston in the sloop *Lydia*, September 10, 1751. For this voyage he laid in, according to his diary,

	£	s.	d.
5 quarts of West Ind. rum	£1	17s.	6d.
¼ lb. of tea *a* 48s.		12	0
Canister		6	0
1 doz. fowls	2	10	0
2 pounds loaf sugar *a* 8s.		16	0
1 doz. and 8 lemons	1	9	0
3 pounds butter		12	0
Box		5	0

His stock of clothes might well suit a collegian of the present day; it consisted of two close coats, one great coat, two jackets, thirteen shirts, seven pairs of stockings, six caps, four cravats, three handkerchiefs, one pair of breeches.

His library was not as complete as his wardrobe; his books were, Bible, Latin and Greek Testaments, and Grammar, Latin Dictionary and Lexicon, Ward's Introduction to Mathematics, Gordon's Geography, Virgil and Tully. Mr. Livermore carried letters of introduction to Governor Belcher and President Burr, giving him the highest character for sobriety and studiousness.

All such facts are valuable when we consider the eminence to which this young man afterwards attained.

On returning to New England, after due preparation, he entered upon the practice of the law. Before the Revolution, he was Judge Advocate of the Admiralty Court. He was a member of the Continental Congress from 1780 to 1783, and from 1786 to 1787; and from 1782 to 1790 he was Judge of the Superior Court; and from 1793 to 1801 he was a member of the United States Senate from New Hampshire, after which he was Chief Justice of New Hampshire. Judge Livermore was one of the first trustees of Dartmouth College. He died in May, 1803.

Cornelius Low was probably a son of Cornelius Low, of Newark, New Jersey. The Low family did not sympathize with the country in the Revolutionary War, and now are almost forgotten, though prominent formerly. What became of Mr. Low I have no means of discovering.

Nathaniel Whitaker prepared for the ministry and was ordained and settled over a Presbyterian Church in the State of New York about 1753. In 1759 he became pastor of a Church near Norwich, Connecticut. In 1766 he was sent to Great Britain with the Rev. Samson Occom, a Mohegan Indian, to solicit funds for a school for the Indians at Lebanon, Connecticut. Lady Huntingdon, Romaine and Venn warmly advocated his cause. While abroad he received the honorary degree of Doctor of Divinity from the University of St. Andrews. After eighteen months' absence he returned, having been perfectly successful in his mission. And thus he prepared the way for the founding of Dartmouth College, which grew out of this school.

While in England he published several sermons on "Reconciliation to God."

In July, 1769, he was installed pastor of the Second Congregational Church of Salem, Massachusetts, but in 1773 he withdrew and formed a Presbyterian Church. At the opening of the war Mr. Whitaker espoused warmly the cause of Independence, and engaged largely in the manufacture of saltpetre for the army. On the occasion of the Boston Massacre in 1771, he preached a sermon on the "Fatal Tragedy in King Street;" and on the proclamation of Independence, another entitled "An Antidote to Toryism." After the peace he reprinted the latter with another, "On the Reward of Toryism."

Being too strong a Presbyterian for his neighbors, he was compelled to leave Massachusetts, and removed to Virginia, where he died in poverty near Hampton, January 26, 1795, aged 65.

John Wright. Jonathan Edwards writes to Rev. John Erskine, of Scotland, under date of July 7, 1752, "Mr. John Wright, a member of New Jersey College, who is to take his degree of Bachelor of Arts the next September, is now at my house. He was born in Scotland; has lived in Virginia, and is a friend and acquaintance of Mr. Davies; and has a great interest in the esteem of the religious people of Virginia, and is peculiarly esteemed by President Burr; has been admitted to special intimacy with him; and is a person of very good character for his understanding, prudence and piety."

Mr. Wright was licensed the year after his graduation, and ordained by the Presbytery of New Castle. In 1755 he was installed pastor of the Presbyterian Church in Cumberland, Virginia. His work was specially among the negroes, many of whom were converted under his ministry.

1752.

It is melancholy to record that a man of such promise should fall. In the weakness of body, and the melancholy of which he complains in one of his letters, he sought relief in stimulants. His morning of expectation went down in clouds.

1753.

Daniel Isaac Brown was probably the son of Rev. Isaac Brown, the loyalist, who left Trinity Church in Newark, New Jersey, during or at the commencement of the Revolution, because he "could not pray for the king in peace and quietness and undisturbed."

The son became a physician, and in 1758 was admitted to a Master's degree at King's College, New York. Both father and son left New York for Nova Scotia, with many others, about 1783.

Israel Canfield was probably the son of Israel Canfield of Morris County, New Jersey, who was a friend and companion of good men, as in his will he gives £10 to the Presbyterian ministry or fund. The son died the year after his graduation, August 2, 1754, aged 26

John Harris came from Wales, while a child, with his father's family, who settled in Maryland. In 1754 he was licensed by the Presbytery of New Castle; and in 1756 he was ordained and installed as pastor of Indian River Church, in Delaware. This charge he resigned in 1759, and removed to the South; and in 1772 we find him pastor of Long Cane and two other Churches in South Carolina, where he remained until 1779, when forced by declining health, he resigned his charge.

Mr. Harris was acknowledged by all to have been a pious, judicious and exemplary minister of the Gospel. Bold, enthusiastic and independent, he was peculiarly fitted for the stirring times in which he lived. It was his boast that every man in his congregation was a Whig. Such a man was especially obnoxious to the Tories, and he had many narrow escapes. It is asserted that he often preached with his gun in the pulpit and his ammunition suspended from his neck, after the fashion of the times.

An anecdote is told of him evincing his determination and his insight into character. Colonel A—, a worthy man, but of a pliant temper, lived far down on the Savannah river, in a region much subject to Tory aggressions. He was a personal friend of Mr. Harris, and a member of one of his congregations, but having held a commission under the royal government, it was feared he would compromise his principles for British protection. The suspicion no sooner entered the mind of his friend Harris, than he mounted his horse, and taking his saddle-bags for a long visit, determined not to leave him till he took a decided stand on the right side. He stayed with him several days, and on his return, reported that "all is right." Mr. Harris was at one time a member of the Provincial Congress of South Carolina. He died about 1790.

Robert Harris, after graduating, became a physician in Philadelphia. He was elected a Trustee of the College in 1761, at the same meeting at which Dr. Finley was chosen President, and continued in that office until his death in 1815; having been a trustee for fifty-four years. For a large part of the time, Dr. Harris was the oldest trustee in the "Board." He was present at the meeting in August, 1768, when Dr. Witherspoon took the oath of office as President of the College; and at the meeting in May, 1795, at which Dr. Smith was chosen President, Dr. Harris was present, and presided at the opening of the session of the Board.

John Houston became a Congregational minister, and settled at Bedford, New Hampshire, September 28, 1757, and was dismissed from his charge in 1778. He died February 4, 1798.

1753.

Hugh McAden was born of an humble but pious parentage, in Pennsylvania. After graduating, he studied theology with the Rev. John Blair, and was licensed by New Castle Presbytery in 1755. He was immediately sent on a missionary tour through the South. On his journey through Pennsylvania and Virginia, he witnessed the greatest distress caused by a severe drought, and the alarm created by Braddock's defeat. On reaching Carolina he entered upon his missionary work with zeal and ardour. Returning to the North, he was ordained by the New Castle Presbytery, in 1757, and became pastor, soon after, of the congregations in Duplin and New Hanover, North Carolina. Here he remained about ten years, when, believing that the influence of the climate upon his health was too unfavorable to justify his remaining longer in the lower part of the State, he removed to Caswell County, and there finished his days. He died January 20, 1781. Mr. McAden left a manuscript journal extending through a number of years. This journal shows with what untiring zeal these early missionaries prosecuted their work. The journal has been preserved in "Foote's Sketches of North Carolina." Mr. McAden was systematic in study, in visiting and in labour, and faithfully fulfilled his ministry. He was truly one of the chief founders of the Presbyterian Church in the Southern States.

John McKesson sprang from an old Scotch family, who moved to Antrim, in Ireland, in 1665. John was the son of Alexander McKesson, and was born at Fagg's Manor, Pennsylvania, March 20, 1734. After graduating, he took up his residence in the city of New York. Throughout the Revolution Mr. McKesson was Clerk of the Provincial Congress of New York. He died of yellow fever, in a house which stood on the spot where the *Herald* office now stands, September 7, 1798. Mr. McKesson was a bachelor, and left a large fortune for the times. He was admitted to a Master's degree at King College, New York, in 1758.

1753.

Nathaniel Potter became a minister, and was settled as pastor of the Congregational Church at Brooklyne, Massachusetts, in 1755. He left this charge in 1759, and died in 1768. Harvard admitted him to the degree of Master of Arts in 1758.

Mr. Potter published a Discourse in 1758, entitled, "New Year's Gift."

Nathaniel Sherman, a brother of the celebrated Roger Sherman, of Connecticut, was ordained and settled as pastor of the Congregational Church at Bedford, Massachusetts, February 18, 1756. This charge he resigned December 17, 1767. In May, 1769, he was installed as pastor of the Church at Mount Carmel, Connecticut; where, having preached until August, 1772, he retired to East Windsor, Connecticut, and there died July 18, 1797.

Joseph Shippen. There is an interesting letter of Mr. Shippen extant, written while he was a junior in college, in which he informs his father of President Burr's marriage. He writes: "In the latter end of May, he [Mr. Burr] took a journey into New England, and during his absence, he made a visit of but three days to the Rev. Mr. Edwards' daughter, at Stockbridge; in which short time, though he had no acquaintance with, nor indeed ever seen the lady these six years, I suppose he accomplished his whole design; for it was not above a fortnight after his return here, before he sent a young fellow, who came out of college last fall, into New England, to conduct her and her mother down here. . . . I think her a person of great beauty, though, I must say, that in my opinion, she is rather too young (being only twenty-one years of age) for the President. This account you 'll doubtless communicate to mammy, as I know she has Mr. Burr's happiness much at heart."

Mr. Shippen was the son of William Shippen, M.D., of Philadelphia. Immediately after graduating, he entered the Provincial Army, in which he soon rose to the rank of Colonel, and served in General Joseph Forbes' expedition in 1758, which resulted in the capture of Fort Du Quesne. After the troops were disbanded, he went to Europe, partly on a mercantile adventure, but especially for the advantage of foreign travel. He returned to Philadelphia in December, 1761, and was shortly after appointed Secretary to the Province. About 1773, he removed to the country, in the neighborhood of Philadelphia. In 1789, he was appointed Judge of Lancaster County. Colonel Shippen was esteemed by all who knew him, as an eminently just and upright man. To his service as a soldier, he added the accomplishments of a scholar and a man of taste, and was not destitute of some talent in versification. The only reason why he did not enter the revolutionary army was feeble health. He died February 10, 1811.

Benjamin Woodruff was the son of Samuel Woodruff, an eminent merchant of Elizabethtown, New Jersey, and for nearly twenty years a Trustee of the College. After graduating, he pursued the study of theology, probably with his pastor, Elihu Spencer. In due time he was licensed to preach, and on March 14, 1759, was ordained pastor of the Presbyterian Church of Westfield, New Jersey. During the forty-four years of his ministry at Westfield, he greatly endeared himself to his people, by his preaching and pastoral intercourse.

Mr. Woodruff is described as small in person, dignified and precise in his manners, social in his habits, scrupulously exact and fastidious in his dress, with small-clothes, silk hose, buckles, cock-hat and ruffles, everywhere the same and always commanding profound respect.

He died quite suddenly April 3, 1803.

Joseph Woodruff, a brother of the preceding, after graduating, returned to Elizabethtown and entered into business with his father, who was largely engaged in the West India trade.

1754.

Moses Barrett. From the time of his graduation until 1757, Mr. Barrett was the first preceptor of Moor's Indian Charity School, at Lebanon, Connecticut. This school was afterwards removed to New Hampshire, and became the nucleus of Dartmouth College, although the school itself was never merged in the college. What became of Mr. Barrett after leaving this school, I have not been able to discover.

Benjamin Chapman was ordained on the 17th of March, 1756, and settled over the Congregational Church at Southington, Connecticut. He was dismissed from his charge, September 28, 1774, but continued to reside in Southington until his death, which occurred June 22, 1786. Mr. Chapman was admitted to a Master's degree at Yale in 1761.

John Ewing. The parents of Mr. Ewing were early emigrants from Ireland, and settled in Maryland. After graduating, he remained three years as tutor in the college. At the age of twenty-six he was employed as instructor of the Philosophical classes in the University of Pennsylvania, during the absence of Dr. Smith, the Provost, in Europe. In 1758 Mr. Ewing became pastor of the First Presbyterian Church in Philadelphia. In 1773 he visited Europe, but at the opening of the Revolution, in 1775, he returned to this country, notwithstanding the most tempting offers which were made to induce him to remain in England. During this visit he received the honorary degree of Doctor of Divinity from Edinburgh. While abroad he visited Dr. Samuel Johnson, nobly defending the cause of his country, which was violently assailed. After liberally applying the terms "rebels" and "scoundrels" to the people of America, Johnson turned rudely to Dr. Ewing, demanding, "What do you know in America? You never read; you have no books there." "Pardon me, sir," said Dr. Ewing, "we have read the *Rambler*." The graceful blending of retort and compliment pacified the savage essayist, and till midnight he sat with Dr. Ewing in amiable and genial conversation.

In 1779 Dr. Ewing was appointed Provost of the University of Pennsylvania. He was one of the most remarkable scholars of his day. In classical learning and natural science, he stood without a rival. His Hebrew Bible was constantly at his side, and was used from choice for devotional purposes. At an hour's notice, he was ready and fully competent to supply the place of any professor who might chance to be absent. In the pulpit, he was eminently popular among the more cultivated. He died September 8, 1802.

Dr. Ewing published, Part of a Sermon on the Death of Dr. Alison. A Sermon on the Death of George Bryan, 1791. The Design of Christ Coming into the World, in the "American Preacher," Vol. II. And several communications in the Transactions of the American Philosophical Society. His Lectures on Natural Philosophy were published in 1809.

Benjamin Hoit, (or Hait,) while a student, paid a visit, in company of President Davies, to New York. Mr. Davies writes of him: "A promising young man; I had an agreeable conversation with him on original sin, and the influence of the flesh upon the spirit to incline it to sin." Mr. Hait (which is his true name) was licensed by the Presbytery of New Brunswick, October 25, 1754, and sent to the Forks of Delaware. He was ordained December 4, 1755, and installed pastor of the Presbyterian Church at Amwell, New Jersey. While settled here, by order of Synod, he visited and supplied the southern vacancies. He gave up his charge in Amwell in 1765. In

1766 he was settled at Connecticut Farms, New Jersey, and died there June 27, 1779.

Ezra Horton became a Congregational minister, and settled at Union, Connecticut, in June, 1759, where he remained until June, 1783. Mr. Horton was admitted to an *ad eundem* Master's degree, at Yale, in 1772. He died in 1789.

Hugh Knox came to this country from Ireland, in 1751. Dr. Rodgers, of New York, then of Delaware, becoming interested in him, established a school, of which Mr. Knox became the head. While thus engaged, an event happened which moulded the whole of his life. He had become associated with a number of young men who were accustomed to meet on Saturday afternoons for a frolic. On one of these occasions, some one of the company cried out to Knox: "Come parson" (a title which they gave him on account of his being the gravest of their number, and withal a great admirer of Dr. Rodgers' preaching), "come parson, give us a sermon!" At first he declined, but being pressed, gave an exact imitation of Dr. Rodgers, and almost verbatim, the sermon that he had preached on the previous Sabbath. As he proceeded, his auditors, who began to listen in merriment, became deeply serious, and the speaker himself was overwhelmed with a sense of his sin. The next morning, overcome with remorse, he fled from the place. Soon after, he went to Newark, and applied to President Burr for admission to college. He related his whole previous course, and his repentance, and was admitted. His course in college was all that could be desired. After his graduation, he studied theology with President Burr, and was ordained by the Presbytery of New York, in 1755, and was sent to the Reformed Dutch Church in the Island of Saba, of which he became pastor. At his ordination, he preached a sermon on "The Dignity and Importance of the Gospel Ministry," which was published by the unanimous request of the Presbytery. In 1772, he resigned his church at Saba, and settled at St. Croix, where he spent the remainder of his days.

The celebrated Alexander Hamilton was placed in early boyhood under the instruction of Mr. Knox, and formed a strong attachment for him; while Mr. Knox in return, watched and assisted with the utmost fidelity, the development of the wonderful powers of his pupil. They kept up an active correspondence in after life; and two of Mr. Knox's letters are preserved in the first volume of Hamilton's works. Both were written during the Revolution, and breathe a spirit of earnest devotion to the American cause. Mr. Knox was admitted to a Master's degree at Yale, 1768, and the degree of Doctor of Divinity was conferred upon him by the University of Glasgow.

Dr. Knox published (according to Dr. Miller) five or six volumes, chiefly sermons. Two volumes of his sermons, printed in Glasgow, in 1772, are in the Library of the College, at Princeton.

David Matthews, one of the few disloyal graduates of Princeton, was a native of Orange County, New York. After leaving college, he studied law, and entered upon the practice in New York City, where, for twenty years, he acted as Crown Officer. In 1775, he succeeded Mr. Hicks as Mayor of the city, but being a decided royalist, his name was entered on the list of the suspected as early as May, 1776. In 1779, he was arrested by order of the Committee of Safety, and lodged in jail, whence he was soon removed to Connecticut. The charge against him was that he was cognizant of, or concerned in, Governor Tryon's plot to assassinate General Washington and blow up the fort, but the evidence against him was far from being conclusive. By the Act of 1779, he was attainted, and his property confiscated. After the war, Mr. Matthews removed to the Island of Cape Breton, where he was appointed Commander-in-Chief and President of the Council, and Attorney-General. He died in

July, 1800; it is said of a broken heart, on account of the treatment received in this country. Mr. Matthews is represented to have been a cheerful and instructive companion, a sincere and faithful friend. He was charitable and hospitable to a fault. His judgment was clear and accurate in the administration of the laws and constitution of the British Colonies.

Jonathan Odell, a grandson of President Dickinson, was from Connecticut Farms, New Jersey. After graduating, he entered the ministry, but I can discover no facts as to his place of settlement, or of his after life.

Sylvanus Osborne studied theology, and was ordained, and settled as the first pastor of the Congregational Church at East Greenwich, Connecticut, June 29, 1757. Mr. Osborne continued in this charge until his death, in 1771. He was admitted to an *ad eundem* Master's degree at Yale, in 1757.

Mr. Osborne was a successful pastor, and during his ministry there was continued harmony, and a constant attention to the things of another world, which resulted in members being added to the church every year.

David Purviance was probably the son of Samuel Purviance, who was at this very time a leading merchant in Philadelphia, an elder in the Presbyterian Church, and a warm and active friend of the college. Of the son I can learn nothing.

William Ramsay was a brother of the Historian, David Ramsay, of South Carolina, a graduate of the class of 1765. He was licensed by the Association of Fairfield East, Connecticut, November 25, 1755, and was received into the Abingdon Presbytery and ordained, and settled as pastor of the Fairfield Church, May 11, 1756. He died November 5, 1771. His character may be learned from the inscription on his tomb:

"Beneath this stone lie interred the remains of the Rev. William Ramsay, M. A., for sixteen years a faithful pastor in this place, whose superior genius and native eloquence shone so conspicuously in the pulpit as to command the attention and gain the esteem of all his hearers. In every situation of life he discharged his duty faithfully. He lived greatly respected and died universally lamented."

Benajah Root (the name is commonly spelled Roots) was ordained and installed pastor of a Congregational Church at Simsbury, Connecticut, August 10, 1757. In 1773 he became pastor of a Church at Rutland, Vermont. Here he remained until his death in 1787. Mr. Root was a faithful preacher of the Gospel, ardently attached to the doctrines of religion as they are expressed in the Westminster Catechism, and much interested in revivals. He was admitted to a Master's degree at Dartmouth in 1784.

Mr. Roots published a Sermon preached at the Organization of his Church in 1773.

Josiah Sherman was a brother of Nathaniel Sherman of the class of 1753. In 1755 he was licensed by the Litchfield South Association of Connecticut, and in 1756 was ordained pastor of the Congregational Church at Woburn, Massachusetts. Mr. Sherman remained here until April 11, 1775, when he removed to Connecticut, and in August of the same year was installed pastor of the Plymouth Church, Milford, Connecticut. In June, 1781, he resigned this charge, and in June, 1783, was settled at Goshen, Connecticut. In February, 1789 he resigned, having been called to a Church in Woodbridge, Connecticut, but died a few months after his arrival there, November 24, 1789.

Mr. Sherman wore a large white wig, and was very imposing and winning in his appearance. He had popular talents, and on his settlement at Goshen was at first very acceptable. But alienation arose in consequence of his avowing, in his preaching, Arminian sentiments, and he was compelled to resign.

Mr. Sherman received a Master's degree from Harvard in 1758, and from Yale and Dartmouth in 1765.

He published A Discourse Addressed to Infidels. A Discourse, Redemption by Christ. The History of Melchisedec.

William Shippen, a brother of Joseph Shippen, of the class of 1753, after his graduation, entered upon the study of medicine with his father in Philadelphia, and completed his course in Edinburgh. In 1764 he commenced a course on Anatomy in his native city, which was the first ever pronounced in the world on that subject. He was one of the founders of the Medical College connected with the University of Pennsylvania, and was elected the first professor in 1765.

In the Revolutionary war he proved himself to be an ardent patriot, and represented his State in the Continental Congress. Dr. Shippen was for more than thirty years a Trustee of the College. He died in 1808.

Thomas Smith. I have not been able to discover with absolute certainty, but I think there is little doubt that Mr. Smith was a brother of William Smith the Chief Justice of the Province of New York, and of Charles Smith of the Class of 1757. After graduating he was admitted to the New York Bar, and became eminent in his profession. During the Revolution he removed to Haverstraw, New York, and in 1781, while residing there, Aaron Burr became a student of law in his office. Mr. Smith died in Haverstraw after 1800.

Noah Wadhams, a native of Goshen, Connecticut, received ordination and was settled over the Congregational Church at New Preston, Litchfield County, Connecticut, in 1757, where he remained until 1768. He was admitted to a Master's degree at Yale in 1764. He died in 1806.

1755.

Jonathan Baldwin, after graduating, removed from New Jersey, his native State, to New York city, and became Steward of King's College, just organized. Afterwards he occupied the same position at Princeton. How long he held this post, I have not discovered. Mr. Baldwin, after leaving Princeton, retired to Newark, New Jersey, where he died in 1816.

Benoni Bradner was a son of the Rev. John Bradner, of Goshen, New York. After his licensure, he preached at Jamaica, Long Island, from 1760 to 1762. Afterwards he was settled at Nine Partners, in Dutchess County, New York, and in June, 1786, became the minister of the Independent Church in Blooming Grove, Orange County. Consumptive, and troubled with shortness of breath, he lived to the age of seventy-one, and died January 29, 1804. He was a Trustee of the Morris County Society for Promoting Religion and Learning from its formation. Yale admitted him to the degree of Master of Arts in 1758.

Thaddeus Burr was a son of Henry Burr, who died in New Jersey, in 1742. It is uncertain whether this Henry Burr was a cousin or a brother of President Burr. Henry Burr is said to have been the brother of President Burr, in the Massachusetts Historical Collection, vol. vii., p. 187. If this is true, then Thaddeus was a nephew of President Burr. But others, with apparent good reason, think that Henry was a cousin of President Burr, and that would make Thaddeus his second cousin.

Thaddeus Burr became a lawyer in Fairfield, Connecticut, and rose to eminence and wealth. John Hancock, President of the Continental Congress, was married in his house, to Miss Dorothy Quincy, of Boston, in 1775. During the Revolution Mr. Burr was the High-Sheriff of the county. In 1779, his splendid mansion was burned by the forces under General Tryon. Mrs. Burr made a personal application to Governor Tryon, but he refused to protect her or the house. The house of Mr. Burr was the mansion of his ancestors: it was a house where elegant hospitality reigned, and where refined enjoyments were daily felt and distributed to the friend and the stranger. Mr. Burr was admitted to a Master's degree at Yale, in 1758.

Wheeler Case was licensed to preach by Suffolk Presbytery, and settled as first pastor of Pleasant Valley Church, Dutchess County, New York, in November, 1765. Poughkeepsie for some years formed a part of his charge, but during the war it became so enfeebled as to be virtually extinct. Mr. Case continued in the pastorate of Pleasant Valley for more than twenty years. In 1778, an anonymous pamphlet was published at New Haven, entitled, "Poems occasioned by several circumstances and reminiscences in the present grand contest of America for Liberty." The author was Wheeler Case. He states in the preface, that some of the pieces were written merely for amusement, and with the design to promote the cause of Liberty, into whose treasury he casts his mite in publishing them. These Poems were re-published by M. W. Dodd, of New York, in 1852.

Mr. Case probably died April 8, 1793.

Benjamin Conklin became a Congregational minister, and was settled November 23, 1763, over a church in Leicester, Massachusetts. He resigned his charge June 30, 1794, and died January 30, 1798. Mr. Conklin was a laborious minister. He was pleasing and interesting, without being brilliant; useful and instructive, without being great. He performed the duties of his station honorably and acceptably, and among the patriots of the Revolution, he deserved a very high place. In one of the towns bordering upon his parish, it was thought by some of the people that their clergyman did not preach strongly enough in favor of the cause of liberty; "then," said he, "I will exchange with Mr. Conklin, and he will satisfy you, I am sure."

John Hanna received his license to preach from the Presbytery of New Brunswick, about 1760. In April, 1761, he was ordained by the same Presbytery, and settled as pastor of Alexandria, Kingwood and Bethlehem Churches, New Jersey, where he remained until his death, in 1801. Mr. Hanna was also a physician, and practised quite extensively, but it never interfered with his duties as a pastor or as a member of the various church courts. Dr. Hanna was a warm-hearted patriot, and ever true to the American cause.

Garret Leydecker, spelled also Lydekker, was licensed by Conferentie in 1765. In 1767, he preached as a supply; and from 1770 to 1776, he was pastor of the Reformed Dutch Church at English Neighborhood, New Jersey. At the opening of the Revolution he took the side of the British, and fled to New York, and finally to England, where he died in 1794.

Joseph Montgomery received his license from the Presbytery of Philadelphia about 1759, and was ordained by the Presbytery of Lewes about 1761, and settled as pastor of the Presbyterian Churches of New Castle and Christiana Bridge, Delaware. The Presbytery of New Castle reported to the Synod in 1785, "that in consequence of Mr. Joseph Montgomery's having informed them that, through bodily indisposition, he was incapable of officiating in the ministry, and having also accepted an office under the civil authority, they have left his name out of their Records." From 1784 to 1788, Mr. Montgomery represented Pennsylvania in the Continental Congress. He was admitted to a Master's degree at the Philadelphia College, and Yale in 1760.

Isaac Smith served as a tutor for one year after his graduation. He afterwards studied medicine and began to practice; but the troubles with Great Britain commencing, he soon became distinguished for his patriotic services, and in 1776 was in command of a regiment. At the close of the war he was appointed a Judge of the Supreme Court of New Jersey, which position he held for eighteen years. He was also a member of the House of Representatives after the present Constitution was formed, from 1795 to 1797, and was highly esteemed by Washington and Adams. Mr. Smith united the characters of a Christian, scholar, soldier and gentleman. He died in 1807, in hope of mercy through the Redeemer.

1756.

Stephen Camp was a son of John Camp, of Newark, New Jersey. He was a brother-in-law of the Hon. Isaac Tichenor, of the Class of 1775, and encouraged by him, went with him or followed him into Vermont. He was a lawyer, but not very successful in his profession, and died young, according to tradition. Mr. Camp was a nephew of Dr. William Burnet, of the Class of 1749.

Alexander Martin. The family of Mr. Martin moved from New Jersey to Virginia, and from thence to North Carolina, from which State the son came to college. In 1772, he represented his State in the Colonial Assembly. In 1774, he was a member of the first Assembly of the people in North Carolina, met to vindicate their rights. He was a member of the Legislature in 1775 and 1776. At the breaking out of the war he became a Colonel in the Continental line, and participated in the battles of Brandywine and Germantown. In the last he was near Gen. Lafayette when he was wounded.

After the war, Mr. Martin was Speaker of the Senate of North Carolina. In 1782, he was elected Governor of the State, and again in 1789. He left several manuscripts in prose and verse. An ode on the death of Gen. Francis Nash, and one on Gov. Caswell were published in the *North Carolina University Magazine.* From 1793 to 1799, Mr. Martin represented his State in the Senate of the United States. In 1793, Gov. Martin received the Honorary degree of Doctor of Laws from Princeton. He died in 1807.

From the omission in the Triennial Catalogue of any honorary designations, I have felt some doubt whether our graduate was the Gov. Martin sketched above. But as we know that Gov. Martin's brother graduated in 1762, and, as Wheeler in his history of North Carolina says that he was, "at Princeton for a time," I conclude that I am right in my conjecture.

William Mills, a native of Long Island, was ordained by the Presbytery of Philadelphia in 1762, and became pastor of the Presbyterian Church at Jamaica, Long Island. He died in New York, March 18, 1774, where he had gone to get medical advice for a chronic disease under which he was suffering.

Mr. Mills was admitted to a Master's degree at Yale in 1771. A New York paper of that day says that "His amiable disposition, his peaceful and prudent conduct, his unaffected piety and rational devotion, remarkably endeared him to those acquainted with him." Mr. Mills appears to have been a man of wealth, as "three improved farms," constituting a part of his estate, were advertised for sale shortly after his death.

Josiah Ogden. The father of Mr. Ogden resided in Newark, New Jersey, and was a member of the Presbyterian Church; but some trouble arising from his gathering in his hay on the Sabbath, he went over to the Episcopalians, and was one of the founders of old Trinity Church in that town. Our graduate died young. He had two brothers who were prominent men in their day, Dr. Jacob Ogden, of Long Island, and Judge David Ogden, a graduate of Yale, and a noted loyalist. There is a notice of him in "Sabin's Loyalists."

Joseph Peck was licensed by Fairfield East Association, in Connecticut, on May 29, 1758. In 1762 I find him settled over a Presbyterian Church at Phillippi, in what was called Phillips' Precinct, lying between Fishkill and South Salem, New York. On October 27, of the same year, he, in connection with Solomon Mead and Elisha Kent, met and organized what was long known as Dutchess Presbytery. Mr. Peck remained in this charge until 1769, when in June of that year he was installed pastor of a Congregational Church in New Fairfield, Connecticut, where he remained until 1775. I can trace him no further.

Azel Roe came to College from Long Island. He was licensed by the Presbytery of New York in 1760, and two years after was ordained. In 1763 he became pastor of the Presbyterian Church at Woodbridge, New Jersey, afterwards connected with Metuchin. During the Revolutionary war Mr. Roe proved his patriotism in many ways. The part of New Jersey in which he resided, was much annoyed by marauding parties sent out from the British troops stationed on Staten Island. On one occasion, a brave Continental Captain, who had done great execution in driving off or annoying these predatory bands, was very anxious to attack a party which had encamped near the Blazing Star Ferry, but could not induce his men to follow him. As many of them belonged to Mr. Roe's congregation, he thought he would put in requisition *his* influence over them. Accordingly he called and stated his difficulty, and found Mr. Roe more than willing to second his efforts. The good minister accompanied the Captain to the place where his men were, and addressed a few words to them, exhorting them to their duty, and enforcing his exhortation by telling them that it was his purpose to go into the action himself. And into the action he went—every man following readily. But when the bullets began to fly among them, they promised that if he would keep out of harm's way, they would do the business for the enemy. And seeing that their spirits were sufficiently excited, he did retire, and, as he afterwards acknowledged, very much to his own comfort.

One night the Tories united with the British and seized Mr. Roe while he was with his family, and carried him off as a prisoner to New York, where they shut him up in the "Sugar House." As they were on their way to New York, they were obliged to ford a small stream. The officer in command, who seemed to have taken a fancy to Mr. Roe, and treated him politely, insisted that the captured minister should allow him to carry him over on his back. When they were about the middle of the stream, Mr. Roe, who relished a joke, and was not wanting in ready wit, said to the officer, "Well, sir, if never before, you can say after this, that you was once priest-ridden." The officer was so convulsed with laughter, that he had well nigh fallen under his burden into the water. When they arrived in New York, an excellent breakfast was sent to Mr. Roe by the father of Washington Irving, who had been informed of his imprisonment.

Mr. Roe was a Trustee of the College twenty-nine years—from 1778 to 1807. In 1800 the honorary degree of Doctor of Divinity was conferred on him by Yale. Dr. Roe was about the medium height and well proportioned. His manners were more than ordinarily graceful and dignified. His preaching was distinguished for substantial excellence, rather than those qualities which attract the multitude. He was universally and highly esteemed as a pastor, and was in charge of the same flock for fifty-four years. He died in November, 1815.

Jesse Root came to College from Massachusetts. After preaching for three years, on account of family circumstances he studied law, and was admitted to the Bar in 1763. In 1777 he raised a company in Hartford and joined General Washington; he was made Lieutenant-Colonel soon after. From May, 1779, till the close of the war, he was a member of the Continental Congress. In 1789 he was appointed a Judge of the Superior Court of Connecticut, and was Chief Justice from 1796 until his resignation in 1807.

He was, as a judge, learned and dignified—a man of

warm and undoubted piety. At the age of eighty-five he was always seen in his place in the prayer-meeting and conference. On the evening of his death, he said, "I set out on a pleasant journey in the morning, and I shall get through to-night. He died March 29, 1822. In 1800 Yale conferred the honorary degree of Doctor of Laws upon Judge Root.

His publications are: Report of Cases adjudged in the Superior Court and in the Supreme Court of Errors of Connecticut from 1789 to 1798, Hartford, 1798–1803. 2 vols. 8vo. Illustrated by notes on adjudged points and rules of practice.

1757.

Moses Baldwin. The Commencement of 1757 was the first, after the removal of the College to Princeton; made sadly memorable by the death of President Burr, two days before. At the head of the roll and of the Class of this year stood Moses Baldwin, a native of Newark, New Jersey. After graduating, he studied theology, and was licensed probably by Suffolk Presbytery. On the 17th of June, 1761, he was ordained, and settled over a Congregational Church in Palmer, Massachusetts. He remained as pastor of this church until June 19, 1811, when he resigned. He died in 1813. As a minister, Mr. Baldwin was faithful and diligent in discharging the duties of his office. His great ambition was to live to the glory of God. His preaching was impressive, for Christ and his Cross was all his theme. He was admitted to a Master's degree at Dartmouth, in 1791.

Caleb Barnum, a native of Danbury, Connecticut, was licensed by the Fairfield East Association, May 30, 1759, and was ordained, and settled pastor of the Congregational Church at Franklin, Massachusetts. He remained here about eight years, when on account of difficulties in the congregation he resigned. Soon after the opening of the Revolutionary War, Mr. Barnum was appointed Chaplain in the Western Army, but died in camp in 1776. Mr. Barnum's successor at Franklin was the celebrated Dr. Nathaniel Emmons. Mr. Barnum was admitted to an *ad eundem* Master's degree at Harvard, in 1768.

Nicholas Bayard was probably the son of William

Bayard, a leading merchant in New York before and during the Revolution. The family was distantly connected with Col. John Bayard, of Philadelphia, whose sons afterwards graduated at Princeton. After graduating, Mr. Bayard returned to New York. There is in *Holt's Gazette* of November 10, 1763, a long account of disorderly people doing mischief and pilfering on Sundays, in the Bowery, particularly that a great number surrounded the orchard of Mr. Nicholas Bayard, where a large quantity of apples "lay on heaps for making cider," and Mr. Bayard being from home, the overseer was abused, who then ordering a gun to be brought kept them off till dark; when the orchard was attacked, and he fired at the legs of one, and wounded him. The family sent another gun, and a reinforcement of another white man. The loafers came on again, supposing the garrison out of ammunition, but received another shot in the legs of one of the party, who then retreated. Mr. Bayard, on returning, kept watch with his neighbors all night. All this occurred near the present Grand Street and Bowery. Mr. Bayard was at one time an Alderman of the city.

Noah Benedict was born in Danbury, Connecticut. He was ordained, and installed pastor of the Congregational Church at Woodbury, Connecticut, October 22, 1760, where he preached for fifty-three years. He died in September, 1813. In 1760, he was admitted to a Master's degree in Yale, and from 1801 to 1812, was a Fellow of Yale College.

Mr. Benedict published a Sermon on the Death of Dr. Bellamy, 1790. Memoirs of Dr. Bellamy, 1811.

Abner Brush after graduating, studied theology, and in 1758 was ordained by the Presbytery of New York, and installed as pastor of the Presbyterian Church at Goshen, New York. Mr. Brush remained in this charge until 1766, in which year he probably died.

1757.

Caleb Curtiss studied theology, and was ordained, and settled as pastor of the Congregational Church at Charlton, Massachusetts, in 1761. He was dismissed from this charge in 1776, after which he represented the town in the Provincial Congress, and served in other public capacities. He died March 21, 1802.

Timothy Edwards, the eldest son of Jonathan Edwards, after his graduation, became a merchant in Elizabethtown, New Jersey; but in 1770, he removed to Stockbridge, Massachusetts, and was a leading citizen for forty-three years. He was a member of the State Council from 1775 to 1780; was Judge of Probate from 1778 to 1787; declined the nomination of member of Congress in 1779. He died October 27, 1813, aged 75.

Peter Faneuil. If I am right in my conjecture, Mr. Faneuil was the youngest child of Benjamin Faneuil, and a nephew of the well-known Peter Faneuil of Boston. He entered the celebrated Latin school of John Lovell of Boston, in 1746, and, after graduating at Princeton, entered into mercantile life in Montreal. Failing in business, he resorted to the West Indies, and, after the death of his father in 1785, he returned to Boston, where he probably died.

Elnathan Gregory studied theology and was licensed to preach by the Fairfield East Association, Connecticut, May 29, 1758. He died in 1816. I have not been able to find the place of Mr. Gregory's settlement.

William Kirkpatrick received license from the Presbytery of New Brunswick, August 15, 1758, and passed several months in missionary work in New Jersey. He was ordained and appointed a supply to the Presbyterian Church in Trenton, New Jersey, July 4, 1759, where he preached until 1766, but was never settled as their pastor. During this time he had many calls, but declined them all. In 1766 he accepted a call to the church in Amwell, New Jersey. In 1767 he was elected a Trustee of the College.

Mr. Kirkpatrick was above the ordinary size, but not corpulent; grave, dignified and commanding in his aspect, and of most engaging address. He died in Amwell, September 8, 1769.

Alexander McWhorter was born in New Castle Co., Delaware, July 15, 1734. After graduating, he studied theology with Rev. William Tennent of Freehold, and was licensed by the Presbytery of New Brunswick, August 3, 1758. On July 4th of the same year, he was ordained with a view to a mission in the South, but, receiving a call from the Presbyterian Church in Newark, he accepted, and was installed the same summer. In 1764 he visited North Carolina by order of the Synod, and was very efficient in establishing churches in that region, but came near losing his life by a violent attack of fever.

In 1775, he was appointed by Congress to visit North Carolina, and use every effort to bring over the enemies of independence to the American cause.

In 1776, Yale conferred upon him the honorary degree of Doctor of Divinity.

In 1777, he was at the battle of Trenton, having gone to headquarters to confer with General Washington about the defence of the State.

In 1778, at the solicitation of General Knox, he acted as chaplain while the army lay at White Plains. In 1779 he left Newark, that he might accept a situation in North Carolina, but was soon obliged to fly before the army of Cornwallis, losing almost all that he possessed. Returning to Newark, he resumed his old charge, which he retained until the day of his death.

In 1783, Dr. McWhorter was elected President of Washington Academy in Maryland (afterwards St. John's College), which offer he declined.

In 1802, at the advanced age of sixty-eight, he was appointed by the College of New Jersey to solicit funds in New England, for the rebuilding of the College which had just been destroyed by fire. He succeeded in collecting more than seven thousand dollars. He was a Trustee of the College for thirty-five years. Dr. McWhorter was one of the leading spirits in the organization of the Presbyterian Church. In 1789 his name stands second on a Committee, of which Dr. Witherspoon was Chairman, to whom was committed "the Book of Discipline and Government," with powers to digest such a system as they shall think to be accommodated to the state of the Presbyterian Church in America.

Dr. McWhorter was remarkably a man of order and method. He was also an accomplished teacher; and in the dearth of text-books, he wrote with his own hand for his pupils treatises on several of the sciences. As a preacher he was plain, instructive and practical; his language was correct, expressive, and often pathetic. He was among the most successful and popular preachers of his day. Of his influence in Church Courts, Dr. Griffin wrote: "His voice was listened to with profound respect, and the counsels suggested by his superior wisdom enlightened and swayed our public bodies." Dr. McWhorter died in the triumph of a rapturous faith, July 20, 1807.

He published, A sermon on The Blessedness of the Liberal, 1796. Two volumes of Sermons, 8vo, 1803.

Samuel Parkhurst was licensed by the Presbytery of New Brunswick in 1761, and ordained the next year. He was never permanently settled, but died March 11, 1768.

Joseph Reed was born in Trenton, New Jersey, August 27, 1741. He studied law with Richard Stockton, and was admitted to the Bar in 1763. He then went to London and studied in the Middle Temple until 1765, when he returned and commenced practice in Trenton. In 1770 Mr. Reed re-visited London, and on his return took up his residence in Philadelphia. In 1774 he was President of the State Convention. In 1775 he accompanied Washington to Cambridge as his Aid and Secretary, and remained with him during the campaign. In 1776 he was an adjutant-general, and was highly esteemed as an officer. By direction of Washington, he co-operated in the affair at Princeton by attacking the neighboring British posts. In 1777 he was elected a member of the Continental Congress, and at one time acted as President pro-tem. About this time he was approached by British officials, offering him great honour and emolument to use his influence for the restoration of harmony. The same year he received the offer of ten thousand pounds sterling and the best office in the gift of the crown in America, if he could effect the re-union of the two countries. To this offer he replied that "he was not worth purchasing; but such as he was, the king of Great Britain was not rich enough to do it."

In 1778 he was chosen President of Pennsylvania, and held the office till 1781.

Mr. William Rawl said of him, "His mind was perspicuous, his perceptions quick, his penetration great, his industry unremitted. Before the Revolution he had a considerable share of the current practice. . . . . When he had the conclusion of a cause, he was formidable. I have heard an old practitioner say that there was no one at the Bar he so little liked to have behind him as Joseph Reed."

Mr. Reed was a Trustee of the Presbyterian Church, both in Trenton and Philadelphia, and in one of his publications he said of that Church, "When I am convinced of its errors, or ashamed of its character, I may perhaps change it; till then I shall not blush at a connection with a people who, in this great controversy, are not second to any in vigorous exertions and generous contributions, and to whom we are so eminently indebted for our deliverance from the thraldom of Great Britain."

Colonel Reed was a Trustee of the College from 1781 until his death, which occurred in Philadelphia, March 5, 1785.

He published, Remarks on Governor Johnstone's Speech in Parliament, etc., 1779, 4to. Remarks on a Late Publication in the Independent Gazetteer, with an Address to the People of Pennsylvania. Phila. 1783, 8vo.

Stephen Sayre, a native of Long Island, became an eminent merchant in the city of London, and was at one time High Sheriff of the city. But the odour of patriotism which he carried with him from Princeton still clung to him, as we may learn from the following incident: On October 23, 1775, Mr. Sayre was arrested on a charge of high treason made against him by a sergeant of the guard (also a native American) named Richardson. He charged Sayre with having asserted that he and others intended to seize the king on his way to Parliament, to take possession of the town, and to overthrow the present government. Sayre was known to be a friend to the patriots, and on this charge Lord Rochford, one of the Secretaries of State, caused his papers to be seized and himself to be arrested. Sayre was committed to the Tower, from which he was released by Lord Mansfield, who granted a writ of *habeas corpus*. He was subsequently tried and acquitted. He prosecuted Lord Rochford for seizing his papers, and the court awarded him a conditional verdict of five thousand dollars damages. The conditions annexed proved a bar to the recovery of the money, and Sayre was obliged to suffer a heavy pecuniary loss in costs, besides the personal indignity. The whole case is reported in "State Trials." Mr. Sayre returned again to his native land, and died in Virginia in 1818.

James Smith was a brother of William Smith, the

distinguished Historian, of New York. He received his medical education chiefly in Europe, and was graduated Doctor of Medicine at Leyden. He became prominent in his profession in New York city. He is admitted to have been eminently learned, but too theoretical and fanciful, both as a practitioner and in his course of public instruction. He, in connection with John V. B. Tennent, of the class of 1758, and a few others, founded the New York Medical College, the second medical school in the United States. Dr. Smith became Professor of Chemistry and Materia Medica.

He was a writer of plays and verses, and was the author of the drama entitled, "The Male Coquette." Dr. Francis, of New York, describes him at the age of seventy, as attired in a velvet coat, with his gold snuff-box in one hand, pressing forward with his vast projecting shirt-frills discolored with the drippings of his box, and his little brochure of poetry in the other hand, tottering through the streets engaged in distributing to the chosen fair his rhyming products.

Dr. Smith died in 1812.

David Smith settled in Charleston, South Carolina, where he became a distinguished instructor of youth. He superintended the education of Edward Rutledge, one of the Signers of the Declaration of Independence.

John Strain was licensed by the Presbytery of New Castle, May 29, 1759, and ordained in 1761. He settled in York County, Pennsylvania. Dr. Archibald Alexander says of him, that he was a preacher of uncommon power and success, and his manner awfully solemn. He was called to succeed Gilbert Tennent in Philadelphia, but declined the call. He died May 21, 1774.

Joseph Treat acted as tutor for two years after his graduation. He was licensed by the Presbytery of New Brunswick in 1760. In October, 1762, he was installed as colleague of Rev. Dr. Bostwick in the First Presbyterian Church, New York City. When the Revolutionary War began, the congregation was scattered, and all the ministers left the city. Mr. Treat never returned, but supplied the Churches of Lower Bethlehem and Greenwich, in Sussex County, New Jersey, until his death, in 1797.

Henry Wells, a native of New York City, after graduating, studied medicine, and commenced practice in New York. After a short residence there, he removed to Brattleborough, Vermont, where he lived for eighteen years. In 1782, he removed to Montague, with a view of obtaining a more central situation as to business, and perhaps to diminish somewhat his labors in advancing life. Dr. Wells attained the most distinguished rank in his profession. His natural powers were good, and his medical reading was extensive and judicious. He professed a firm belief in the gospel, and was much attached to the moral and religious institutions of the country. Dr. Wells dressed somewhat like the Quakers, and wore to the last, velvet or buck-skin small-clothes, a long vest with flaps and pockets, and a broad-brimmed hat. He was a man full of cheerfulness and facetiousness. He died August 22, 1814.

1758.

Jacob Ker was a grandson of the well-known Walter Ker, of Freehold, New Jersey, who was banished from Scotland in 1685, "for his faithful adherence to God and his truth as professed by the Church of Scotland."

The subject of this sketch, after graduating, acted as tutor from 1760 to 1762. In 1763, he was licensed by the Presbytery of New Brunswick, and was ordained by the same Presbytery in 1764. On the 29th of August in the same year, he was installed as pastor of the Churches of Monokin and Wicomics, Maryland, where he remained until his death, which occurred July 29, 1795. Mr. Ker was a man of fervent piety, and a good preacher. He used manuscripts in the earlier part of his ministry, but in the latter part of his life he preached without notes. The following testimony to his worth is from the Records of the Presbytery of Lewis: "The loss of this great and good man was sensibly felt by the Church in general, and by this Presbytery in particular. He was a bright luminary in the Church, who lived exemplarily, preached warmly, and prayed fervently—a pattern truly worthy the imitation of his brethren."

Philip Peter Livingston. The Livingston family have no knowledge of any one of this name among their ancestors. I therefore suppose him to be the same as Peter Robert Livingston, who was a student in the college at this time, as proved by the following certificate, which I find in the Documentary History of New York:

"New York, May 8, 1759.—This is to certify that Mr.

1758.

John Ewing was Tutor of the New Jersey College at Princeton last year, I, the subscriber, being his pupil.

"PETER RT. LIVINGSTON."

If I am right in this conjecture, then he was a son of Robert, third proprietor of the Manor of Livingston. He was elected to represent the Manor in the Provincial Assembly in 1761 and 1768, and again in 1774. At the breaking out of the Revolution, he adhered, with other members of the family, to the side of American liberty, and in 1776, was chosen President of the Provincial Convention, as well as Chairman of the Committee of Safety, and was employed in other departments of the public service. He died November 15, 1794.

Philip Phils Livingston was the eldest son of Philip Livingston, a signer of the Declaration of Independence, and a nephew of Gov. Livingston, of New Jersey. What became of him after his graduation, I cannot discover.

John Milner became an Episcopal clergyman, and in 1764, was chosen Rector of the Episcopal Church at East Chester, New York, in which position he remained until his death.

Ralph Pomeroy was probably the son of Rev. Dr. Benjamin Pomeroy of Connecticut. After graduating, he became the third preceptor of Moor's Indian Charity School, of which Moses Barrett, of the Class of 1754, was the first. In 1786 Mr. Pomeroy was admitted to a Master's degree *ad eundem* at Dartmouth College.

Thomas Smith studied theology after graduating, and was ordained by the Presbytery of New Brunswick, and installed pastor of the Church at Cranberry, New Jersey, October 19, 1762, and died at his post December

23, 1789. Mr. Smith is represented to have been a good man, but very inefficient.

John Van Brugh Tennent studied medicine and settled in New York City. Here he soon became eminent as a physician and a man of science. In connection with James Smith, M. D., of the Class of 1757, and others, he founded the Medical College of New York, in connection with King's College, and became one of its Professors. This was the second Medical School established in the United States; the Philadelphia College, established by Dr. William Shipping of the Class of 1749, preceding it but a short time. Dr. Tennent died in 1770.

William Tennent, a son of Rev. William Tennent of Freehold, New Jersey, was licensed by the Presbytery of New Brunswick in 1761, and ordained the next year. Soon after he went to Virginia on a Missionary tour by order of the Synod, where he remained six months. In 1765, he became pastor of a Congregational Church at Norwalk, Connecticut, but retaining his connection with the Presbytery. In 1772 he accepted a pressing call to an Independent Church in Charleston, South Carolina, having been previously invited to be colleague with Dr. Pemberton in Boston. He was received in Charleston with great favor, and soon wielded a commanding influence both in the pulpit and out of it.

Mr. Tennent could not look with unconcern at the great political movements of the day. It early took firm hold of all his powers, and to it he devoted no small share of his energies, putting forth in its behalf some of his most eloquent efforts. He was early elected a member of the provincial Congress, and was also a member of the Committee of Intelligence.

In July, 1775, with Hon. W. H. Drayton, he was appointed by the Committee of Safety to go through the country and explain to the people the causes of the difficulties with Great Britain. The effect of this commission was to rouse the whole people in behalf of independence.

We find Mr. Tennent after this, employing his pen from time to time, in the public prints, in the cause of civil freedom, and on the 11th of January, 1777, he delivered an eloquent speech in the House of Assembly, Charleston, advocating a petition, penned by himself, to which had been attached the signature of many thousands, against the Church establishment of the Church of England.

Dr. Ramsay, the historian, states, that in the different hours of the same day, Mr. Tennent was occasionally heard both in his church and the State House, addressing different audiences, with equal animation, on their spiritual and temporal interests.

Mr. Tennent was not only an active and flaming patriot, but a noble preacher. A lively imagination added to a careful study of the Scriptures, enabled him to bring forth out of his treasury things new and old; yet he never entertained his audience with scholastic niceties or subtle questions. Elegance of style, majesty of thought and clearness of judgment, appeared in his discourses and concurred to render them both pleasing and instructive.

In the summer of 1777, Mr. Tennent went to Freehold to bring to his own home his widowed and aged mother. He had reached within ninety miles of Charleston on his way home, when he was attacked with a nervous fever which terminated his life August 11, 1777.

Two Sermons of Mr. Tennent were published. One entitled "God's Sovereignty no Objection to the Sinner's Striving." New York, 1765.

Jeremiah Van Rensselaer became distinguished as a patriot of the Revolution. He was at one time Lieutenant-Governor of the State of New York, and a Member of Congress from 1789 to 1791. He died in Albany, February, 1810.

1758.

William Whitwell became pastor of the first Congregational Church in Marblehead, Massachusetts, in 1762. In his preaching he was concise and pertinent, instructive and pathetic. He was admitted to a Master's degree at Harvard in 1762. He died in 1781.

Mr. Whitwell published A Sermon to Mariners, 1769; A Sermon on the death of Mr. Barnard.

1759.

James Caldwell was of French origin, his ancestors being driven over into Scotland by the fierce persecution against the Huguenots. In the reign of James I. a branch of the family removed to Antrim in the North of Ireland. It was from this family that Mr. Caldwell descended. He was born in Lancaster County, Pennsylvania, April, 1734. After graduating, he studied theology, and was ordained by the Presbytery of New Brunswick, in 1761, and installed pastor of the Presbyterian Church at Elizabethtown, New Jersey. Soon after his settlement the Revolutionary war broke out, and Mr. Caldwell entered with all his heart into the controversy. He joined the regiment of his friend and parishioner Colonel Dayton in 1776, and marched to the Northern frontier. His influence upon the troops caused the enemy to offer high rewards for his capture. In 1780 his wife was shot by a refugee, through the window of a room where she had retired with her children for safety.

Mr. Caldwell was at one time Assistant Commissary-General, where his services were of immense value. His end was sudden and violent—he was shot by an Irishman named James Morgan, who was acting as sentinel, and who is supposed to have been drunk at the time.

Mr. Caldwell was a man of unwearied activity, and of wonderful powers of both bodily and mental endurance. Feelings of the most glowing piety, and the most fervent patriotism occupied his bosom at the same time without interfering with each other.

A beautiful monument was erected over his grave in Elizabethtown in 1845; an address being made by Rev. Dr. Miller of Princeton.

Mr. Caldwell was a Trustee of the College at the time of his murder, November 24, 1781.

Jabez Campfield, a son of Benjamin Campfield, of Newark, New Jersey, after graduating, studied medicine and settled in Morristown, New Jersey. When the Revolutionary war commenced, Dr. Campfield entered the American army as a surgeon. His journal, written while acting as a surgeon under General Sullivan in his expedition against the Indians in 1779, is in possession of Edward D. Halsey, Esq., of Morristown, New Jersey.

John Carmichael emigrated to this country from Scotland. He studied theology with President Davies, and was licensed by the Presbytery of New Brunswick, May 8, 1760. On the 21st of April, 1761, he was ordained and installed pastor of the Presbyterian Church at the Forks of the Brandywine, Delaware. He remained the pastor of this Church until his death in 1785.

Like the vast majority of the graduates of Princeton, Mr. Carmichael took the side of his country; and in 1775 preached a sermon to the Militia of Lancaster County, Pennsylvania, in which he endeavoured to establish the lawfulness of self-defence. This sermon was published, and soon a second edition was called for. So effectually did he succeed in instilling into the minds of his people his own patriotic spirit, that whenever they were called into service, it is said that not a man of them hesitated or faltered.

Mr. Carmichael was a man of an eminently devout and Christian spirit.

John Clark received his license from the Presbytery of New Brunswick, May 9, 1760, and was ordained and settled at the Forks of the Delaware, October 13, 1762. In 1767, on account of bodily infirmity, he resigned his charge and removed to Maryland, where he became pastor of two churches in Baltimore County. In 1775 his pastoral relation was again dissolved, but he continued to preach to one of his churches until 1781. In this year he removed to Western Pennsylvania, and became pastor of the united churches of Bethel and Lebanon in that region. At this time he was past the meridian of life, and in very feeble health; but in appearance, grave, sedate and venerable; and as a preacher, solemn and impressive. Mr. Clark was accustomed to wear a big white wig, which sometimes excited prejudice against him. He died July 13, 1797.

James Hunt was the son of James Hunt, conspicuous in the scenes of a religious nature in Hanover County, Virginia, during the times of the Rev. Samuel Davies. He was ordained by the Presbytery of New Brunswick in 1760. In 1761 he made a missionary tour through North Carolina, being at this time a member of Hanover Presbytery. On his return he preached for some time in Lancaster County, Virginia; but the people preferring James Waddel, he sought another location. Mr. Hunt passed the greater part of his ministerial life in Montgomery County, Maryland, where for many years he was at the head of a flourishing classical school. William Wirt was for some years one of his pupils, and for two years a member of his family. Mr. Hunt took special pains to encourage his pupil in composition and for improvement in elocution.

A son of Mr. Hunt graduated in the class of 1786.

Mr. Hunt died at Bladensburg in 1793.

John Huntington was a native of Norwich, Connecticut. After graduating he became preceptor in Moore's Indian Charity School at Lebanon, Connecticut, where he remained during the years 1761 and 1762. He was ordained and installed over the Third Congregational Church in Salem, Massachusetts, September 28, 1763. His early ministry gave much promise of future usefulness and eminence, but the hopes of his people and friends were soon disappointed. He died of a quick consumption, May 30, 1766. Though he had scarcely made proof of his fine talents, yet he had won a generous confidence in his great abilities, and still more in his fervent piety.

James Leslie became a merchant in New York. In his will he left a fund for the education, in the College, of poor and pious youth for the Gospel ministry.

James Lyon was licensed to preach by the Presbytery of New Brunswick in 1762, and ordained by the same body, December 5, 1764, to go to Nova Scotia, where he laboured in the ministry for several years. In 1771 he removed to the State of Maine and began preaching at Machias, and in 1782 a Congregational Church was organized, and Mr. Lyon became its pastor. During the stormy period of the Revolution, Mr. Lyon endured great suffering and hardship. The lumbering trade, on which his people chiefly depended for subsistence, was for a season almost suspended, and they were reduced to extremity for want of provisions. The pastor might then be often seen forsaking his study, and his half-written sermon, and going to fish and dig clams to furnish food for his children. About 1782 or 1783 he removed to Newtown, Long Island, where he supplied the Presbyterian Church until the spring of 1785. He died October 12, 1794.

Mr. Lyon published a small Manual of Devotion, a few copies of which are still preserved, and serve to give a favorable impression of his piety and talents.

Ebenezer Noyes, a native of Newbury, Massachusetts, after graduating, studied medicine and practiced in Dover, Massachusetts, where he died August 11, 1767, aged 28.

Joshua Noyes was also from Newbury, Massachusetts. He wàs either a cousin or a twin brother of the above. He became a Congregational minister, and in 1759 was pastor elect of the Church in Kingston, New Hampshire. He died July 8, 1773, aged 36.

Nathaniel Noyes was born in Newbury, Massachusetts. In 1760 he was ordained as a Congregational minister, and spent his life chiefly in labouring among the destitute in New England. He died in December, 1810.

Thomas Pierce, a native of Newbury, Massachusetts, after graduating, studied theology, and in 1762, was ordained as a Congregational minister, and settled as pastor of a church at Scarborough, Maine. He died in 1775.

Henry Sherburne was a son of Henry Sherburne, of Portsmouth, New Hampshire. The father was a friend of Gov. Belcher, and intimate with the Rev. Samuel McClintock, of the Class of 1751, and it is probable that through their influence the son was sent to Princeton. He never accomplished anything after graduating, but became a spendthrift, and ended his days in the Portsmouth Almshouse, retaining a ridiculous aristocratic family feeling to the last moments of existence.

Samuel Spencer. On returning to North Carolina, his native State, soon entered upon the practice of the law. In 1775, he was appointed with Waightstill Avery, of the Class of 1766, on the Provincial Council of Safety. Under the Colonial Government, he was a member of the Legislature, and Clerk of Anson County. In 1777, he was one of the three Judges of the Superior Courts first elected under the Constitution. In 1788, he was in the State Convention assembled to deliberate upon the Federal Constitution. His talents were fully appreciated by the country. Judge Spencer died in 1794. His death was caused by a most singular circumstance. He had been in ill-health, and was sitting in his yard in the sun, when a large turkey-cock, attracted by some part of his clothing, which was red, attacked him most furiously, and before he could be rescued, was so severely wounded that he died in a short time from the injuries.

1760.

Joseph Alexander, one of the Alexander family of North Carolina, was licensed by the New Castle Presbytery in 1767. The same year he was ordained and installed as pastor of the Sugar Creek Presbyterian Church in his native State. At this place he established a classical school, which soon attained a high reputation. In a few years he removed to South Carolina.

The school established by Mr. Alexander in North Carolina, became a college under the title of Queen's Museum; but it was refused a charter by George III. After the Revolution it received a charter from the North Carolina Legislature; and is known as Liberty Hall. In the course of a few years, this college was removed to South Carolina, and became incorporated with Mount Zion College at Winnsboro, the Rev. Thomas H. McCaul, a graduate of Princeton, being the President.

Mr. Alexander on his removal to South Carolina became pastor of Union Church, where he remained until 1773, when he was installed pastor of Bullock's Creek Church. In this charge he remained until 1801, when, at his own request, the connexion was dissolved; and he remained without a pastoral charge until the close of life.

Mr. Alexander was as active in the cause of education in South Carolina, as he had been in North Carolina; and in 1797 the Legislature bestowed a charter upon Alexandria College, named after him.

In 1807, the College of South Carolina conferred the honorary degree of Doctor of Divinity upon Mr. Alexander.

Dr. Alexander was a man of small stature, and quite

lame. He was endowed with fine talents and accomplishments, and was an uncommonly animated and popular preacher. He was an ardent patriot throughout the Revolution. He died July 30, 1809.

A small volume of Dr. Alexander's sermons was published in Charleston, in 1807.

John Archer. After leaving college Mr. Archer studied divinity, but an affection of the throat led him to turn his attention to the medical profession, and he received from the College in Philadelphia, the first medical diploma ever issued in America, which is still in possession of the family. At the beginning of the Revolution, he had command of a military company, and was also a member of the Legislature of Maryland, his native State. At the conclusion of the war, he returned to his profession. As a medical man, he commanded great influence, and several discoveries were made by him, which were adopted by the profession. Dr. Archer was a member of the House of Representatives of the United States from 1801 to 1807. He died in 1810.

Samuel Blair was a son of Rev. Samuel Blair, of Faggs' Manor, Pennsylvania. After graduating, he acted as tutor in the college from 1761 to 1764. In 1764, he was licensed by the Presbytery of New Castle. In 1766, he was ordained, and installed pastor of the Old South Church in Boston. He remained in this position only a year, his health giving way. After leaving Boston, he retired to Germantown, Pennsylvania, where he passed the remainder of his life.

The estimation in which Mr. Blair was held may be judged by the fact, that when Dr. Witherspoon declined the first invitation to Princeton, the Trustees elected Mr. Blair President of the College, although not over twenty-six years of age. Hearing that a change had taken place in Dr. Witherspoon's feelings, Mr. Blair, with remarkable self-sacrifice, declined the appointment.

Mr. Blair was of medium size, of fair and ruddy complexion, and decidedly a fine-looking man. The University of Pennsylvania honored him with the degree of Doctor of Divinity in 1790. He died in 1818.

He published two sermons ; one of which was on the death of the Rev. John Blair Smith, D.D. Philadelphia, 1799.

Enoc Green was ordained by the Presbytery of New Brunswick, in 1762, and installed as pastor of the Presbyterian Church at Deerfield, New Jersey, June 9, 1769. While pastor of this church, he was abundant in missionary labor on the Coast of New Jersey. During the Revolution, he acted as chaplain, and died November 20, 1776, from camp fever, contracted while in the discharge of his duty.

Alexander Houston received his license from the Presbytery of Lewes, about 1763, and was ordained in 1764, and installed as pastor of Murderkill and Three Runs Churches in Delaware, where he remained until his death, January 3, 1785. Mr. Houston was a man greatly beloved, and a most earnest and laborious minister. Many tears were shed at his early decease.

Enos Kelsey, a native of New Jersey, after his graduation settled as a merchant in Princeton, where he lived until the close of his life. During the Revolution, he held a responsible office in the Clothier-General's office, under the State government. There is a letter of his preserved in the Revolutionary Correspondence of New Jersey, addressed to the Speaker of the Assembly, dated October 4, 1779, in which he makes an estimate of the cost of clothing the Jersey troops. He proposes to go himself to Boston and make the purchases, and thinks that by the proposed scheme, he can save the State ten thousand pounds in the purchase.

Mr. Kelsey was for many years Treasurer of the college. He was a quiet, highly respected citizen. He died in Princeton, in 1809 or 1810.

Benjamin Rush, after graduating, studied medicine with Dr. Shippen of Philadelphia. From 1766 to 1768 he was pursuing his studies in Edinburg, where he received the degree of Doctor of Medicine. On his return to Philadelphia in 1769, he received the appointment of Professor of Chemistry in the Philadelphia College. In 1776 Dr. Rush was a member of the Continental Congress and signed the Declaration of Independence.

In 1777, he was appointed Physician and Surgeon-General in the Middle Military District. Dr. Burnet, also a graduate of Princeton, holding the same position in the Eastern District. In 1787, Dr. Rush was a member of the Convention for framing the Constitution of the United States. He was connected with many scientific, literary and charitable societies, and was an eloquent advocate for the universal establishment of Free Schools. In 1811, the Emperor of Russia sent him a gold ring, as a testimony of respect for his high medical character. Dr. Rush was one of the most eminent physicians and learned medical writers that our country has produced. In 1789, Dr. Rush was transferred to the Chair of Theory and Practice of Medicine; and in 1791, the College having been elevated to the University of Pennsylvania, he was elected Professor of the Institutes and Practice of Medicine and of Clinical Practice—to which, in 1796, he added the Professorship of Physic.

Dr. Rush collected his occasional writings into seven octavo volumes.

Volumes I., II., III., IV., contain Medical Observations.

Volume V., Medical Inquiries and Observations upon the Diseases of the Mind.

Volume VI., Sixteen Introductory Lectures to Courses on Medicine, with two Lectures upon the pleasures of the Senses and of the Mind. 1811. 8vo.

Volume VII., Essays, Literary, Moral and Philosophical.

Besides these, Dr. Rush edited many medical works.

1760.

John Slemmons was licensed by the Presbytery of Donegal in 1763, and ordained by the Presbytery of Carlisle in 1766, and installed as pastor of the Presbyterian Churches of State Ridge and Chanceford, Maryland. He resigned his charge previous to 1798, and died in 1814.

Jonathan Bayard Smith, a Philadelphian by birth, after graduating, returned to Philadelphia, and pursued the study of law. At the opening of the Revolution he became a prominent friend of Independence. In 1776, Mr. Smith was one of the Secretaries of a Conference called to consider the subject of a new Constitution for Pennsylvania, and was one of the Committee (Dr. Benjamin Rush being another) to draft an Address to the People, which resulted in a convention and a new Constitution. He was a Member of the Continental Congress from Pennsylvania in 1777 and 1778.

Mr. Smith made a large donation of books to the library of the College, which fact should be kept on record, since so few of the Alumni thus remember their *Alma Mater*. He died in 1812.

Josiah Thatcher was installed pastor of a Congregational Church at Gorham, Maine, October 28, 1767, where he remained until April, 1781, when he resigned his charge. Without changing his residence, Mr. Thatcher immediately entered into public life, doing a large business as a Justice of the Peace—representing the town of Gorham for eleven years, and as Senator, the County of Cumberland, in the General Court of Maine, and holding the office of Judge of the Court of Common Pleas from 1784 to 1799.

Mr. Thatcher experienced fierce opposition during much of his ministry, but was subsequently greatly respected and honored.

He was admitted to a Master's degree at Yale in 1765. He died December 25, 1799.

1760.

Amos Thompson was a native of Connecticut, and was ordained by the Presbytery of New Brunswick in 1764. Soon after being ordained, having heard that the Rev. Samuel Hopkins had adopted some novel opinions in theology, he took horse and travelled to Newport to converse with this celebrated man, and, if possible, to convince him of his errors. The result was, that after discussing the disputed points for several days, he came away a thorough convert to Dr. Hopkins' system, to which he tenaciously adhered until his dying day, and which he preached on all occasions.

Soon after this, he removed to Virginia, and settled in Loudon County. The following story is told of him by Dr. A. Alexander. Mr. Thompson was a man of gigantic frame, but not in the least inclined to corpulency. His bodily strength was also prodigious. Upon one occasion an old Baptist clergyman named Thomas, residing in the same part of Virginia, had been threatened with personal violence by a set of rough men, if he should ever show his face in a certain pulpit. The old man took a journey of thirty miles to get the help of Amos Thompson. Thompson being fearless and fond of adventure, at once agreed to go and preach for him. When they arrived, great multitudes had gathered, some to hear and some to see the sport. While Mr. Thompson was at prayer, a company of men armed with bludgeons entered the house and took their position just before the pulpit; but when they saw the brawny arm and undaunted appearance of the preacher, they became very quiet. At the close of the discourse, Thompson addressed himself directly to these men—expostulated with them, and declaring that he would spend all the little property he possessed in seeing that justice was done. He concluded by saying that, although he was a preacher, and a man of peace, he held it to be right, when attacked, to defend himself, which he was ready and able to do.

When the meeting was ended, he went out of the house and enquired for the captain of the band. Being led to the spot where they were collected, he approached this man, and asked him to go aside with him. A stout, bold-looking man walked off with him towards the wood, on entering which he appeared to be panic-struck, stopped and raised his club. Thompson said, "Fie, man! what can you do with that?" and in a moment wrested it out of his hand, adding that he intended no violence, but that if so disposed, he could hurl him to the earth in a moment.

The old Baptist minister was never troubled afterwards by these men. It is said that Mr. Thompson was never seen without a pipe in his mouth. He died suddenly in 1801.

1761.

David Caldwell, the son of a respectable farmer in Lancaster County, Pennsylvania, was a carpenter by trade; but on being converted, he earnestly desired an education, that he might preach the Gospel. His thirst for information became a passion, and he resolved to sacrifice time, labour, and all the money that he possessed, in order to attain his end.

He graduated the year that President Davies died, being about thirty-six years old. He was licensed to preach by the Presbytery of New Brunswick, June 8, 1763, and the same summer visited North Carolina as a missionary. But it was not until 1768 that he became the pastor of the united Churches of Buffalo and Alamance, in North Carolina. Here he commenced a classical school in connection with his charge, it being the second school of permanence in North Carolina; the first being the school of Rev. Joseph Alexander, already noticed. Many of his pupils became eminent in after life. Five were governors of States; a number were promoted to the Bench; about fifty became ministers of the Gospel; a large number were physicians and lawyers. Amidst his many duties he found time also to practice medicine. Dr. Rush, who was in the class before him, was his lifelong correspondent.

Mr. Caldwell was a warm and firm friend of Independence, and he had his full share of the sufferings of the times. His house was plundered, his library and valuable papers destroyed, his property stolen, and he himself, watched for as a felon, passed whole nights in the forest.

The first blood-shed of the Revolution was not at Lexington, but on the Alamance in North Carolina, May

16, 1771, in an engagement between Governor Tryon's troops and the Regulators, as they were called. These Regulators were not adventurers, but the sturdy patriotic members of three Presbyterian congregations, all of them having as their pastors graduates of Princeton. Mr. Caldwell was one of them, and on the morning of the battle was on the ground going from one side to the other endeavouring to prevent the catastrophy.

When the University of North Carolina was established, Mr. Caldwell was fixed upon as the first President, but he declined the honour. He received the honorary degree of Doctor of Divinity from the University of North Carolina in 1810. Dr. Caldwell was a member of the Convention of 1776, which formed the State Convention, and also a member of the Convention to consider the Constitution of the United States in 1778. These were the only representative offices he ever held. After a long life of usefulness and honour, he died, August 25, 1824.

Isaac Handy was born December 19, 1743. He was the son of Colonel Isaac Handy, of Princess Anne, Maryland, a man of extensive landed possessions and great prominence in the community in which he lived. After his graduation, Mr. Handy studied law, and was admitted to practice, and continued to practice his profession in Princess Anne until his death in 1773. He married Esther Winder, the daughter of Captain William Winder, a man of fortune, and an Elder in the Wimico Presbyterian Church. Her brother was Governor of Maryland from 1812 to 1815.

Thomas Henderson, a native of Monmouth County, New Jersey, studied medicine and practiced in his native State. He was early appointed a Judge of the Court of Common Pleas. From 1779 to 1780 he was a Delegate to the Continental Congress from New Jersey; two out of the three delegates of that session from New

Jersey being graduates of Princeton. Mr. Henderson was in the House of Representatives, under the Constitution, from 1795 to 1797. He was a man of sterling worth, and of unblemished reputation. For many years he was an Elder in Mr. Tennent's Church at Freehold.

William Jauncey was a son of James Jauncey, of New York city, a leading importer before the Revolution, and a noted royalist. The son, after graduating, became a merchant, and from 1797 to 1802 he was governor of the New York Hospital.

Nathan Ker came to Princeton from the congregation of William Tennent, of Freehold, New Jersey. He was licensed by the Presbytery of New Brunswick, in 1762, and ordained August 17, 1763, and in 1766 was settled as pastor of the Presbyterian Church in Goshen, New York, where he remained until his death, which took place December 14, 1804. Mr. Ker was a zealous Whig in the Revolution, and served for some time as a volunteer Chaplain in the army. He was a man of well-balanced and cultivated mind, enlarged and liberal views, earnest piety, and extensive influence.

Mr. Ker published a Sermon in the *American Preacher* (vol. iv.) entitled "God's Sovereignty in conferring Means and Grace." 1793.

Thomas McCracken was ordained by the Presbytery of Lewes, in 1768, and died in 1770.

David Rice. The fund which supported Mr. Rice failed while he was in College, and his wardrobe became so shabby that he meditated leaving; but this coming to the ears of Richard Stockton, Esq., he sent for the young man and said to him, " I have in a literal sense ventured my bread on the waters, having a ship at sea. If it founders, you must repay me the sum I advance you; if it returns safe, I will venture in the figurative sense." Two years after Mr. Rice offered to repay him, but he refused, affirming that he had been repaid long ago.

Mr. Rice studied theology with John Todd, a graduate of the College, and was ordained by Hanover Presbytery, December, 1763. He laboured for some years in Virginia, his native State, and during the Revolution took a warm and decided stand in favour of his country. He took also an active part in the establishment of Hampden Sidney Academy, which afterwards became a college.

In 1783 he removed to Kentucky, and there organized and took charge of the congregation of Concord at Danville, Cane Run, and the Forks of Dick's River. Mr. Rice may be considered the father of the Presbyterian Church in Kentucky. In 1785 a general meeting for Conference was held, for the purpose of introducing and completing a regular Presbyterian organization in the State. Nothing so tended to the firm establishment of that Church in the far West as this Conference; and Mr. Rice was the mover and master spirit of the whole, and was Chairman of the meeting—Mr. Caleb Wallace, another graduate of Princeton, being the clerk. He was also the founder, or one of the founders, of Transylvania Academy, which afterwards became Transylvania University. In 1792 he was a member of the Convention to frame a State Constitution. A complete biography of this man would necessarily embrace the most interesting events in the literary, political, and religious movements of Kentucky in its early days. He died honoured and lamented in 1816.

The publications of Mr. Rice are, A Circular Letter to his Ministerial Brethren on the Example of Paul. An Essay on Baptism; 1789. A Lecture on the Divine Decrees; 1791. Slavery Inconsistent with Justice; 1792. A Sermon on the Opening of the Synod of Kentucky. An Epistle to the Citizens of Kentucky professing Christianity, especially those that are, or have been, denominated Presbyterians; 1805. A Second Epistle of the same nature; 1808. Letters on the Evidences, Nature, and Effects of Christianity, published in the *Weekly Recorder*, at the age of 81; 1814.

John Rosbrough came from Ireland in 1735, and

having learned a trade, he married; but losing his wife, his thoughts were turned to serious things, and after his conversion he entered the college, although advanced in life. He was licensed by the Presbytery of New Brunswick, August 18, 1762. On the 11th of December, 1764, he was ordained, and installed as pastor of Greenwich, Oxford and Mansfield Churches, New Jersey. In April, 1769, he removed to the Forks of Delaware, and October 28, 1772, was installed pastor of the Presbyterian Church in that locality; where he remained until his death, in 1777.

He was a warm friend to the country's liberties. In the dark days of the retreat through New Jersey, he joined a company of his neighbours as a private soldier, but received a commission as Chaplain soon after. One day in the neighbourhood of Trenton, he was out looking for his horse, when he was taken prisoner by a body of Hessians under British command. He begged for the sake of his dear wife and children, that they would spare his life. He quickly found, however, that his request was to be denied, and that the bloody deed was to be performed without delay. He instantly knelt down, and in imitation of his blessed Master, prayed for the forgiveness of his murderers. And scarcely had this prayer passed from his lips before a deadly weapon pierced his body, and he lay struggling in death.

The last letter his wife received from him is as follows: "My dear, I am still yours. I have but a minute to tell you that the company are all well. We are going over to attack the enemy. You would think it strange to see your husband, an old man, riding with a French Fusee slung at his back. This may be the last you shall ever receive from your husband. I have committed myself, you, and the dear pledges of our mutual love, to God. As I am out of doors I can write no more. I send my compliments to you, my dear, and to the children. Friends pray for us. I am your loving husband."

Mr. Rosbrough was above the medium size, a portly,

noble, fine-looking man. He was a good preacher, able and eloquent, though a defect in his speech caused him sometimes to stammer.

James Thompson served as tutor from 1762 to 1770. By whom he was licensed, I have no means of discovering. In 1767, he occasionally supplied the Presbyterian Church at Trenton, New Jersey.

Lawrence Van Derveer belonged to one of the old Dutch families of the county of Somerset, New Jersey. After graduating, he studied medicine, and settled in the vicinity of Baskingridge, New Jersey, and acquired a high reputation for skill in his profession. He was the father of Henry Van Derveer, who graduated in 1811. Dr. Van Derveer died in 1815.

Jahleel Woodbridge, a son of Timothy Woodbridge, was born in Stockbridge, Massachusetts. After graduating, he returned to his native town, and entered upon the practice of the law. He soon became a prominent man, and was the incumbent of many town offices. He served in both branches of the State Legislature from 1780 to 1784. From 1781 to 1787, he was Assistant Judge of the Court of Common Pleas; and Presiding Judge from 1787 to 1795; he was also Judge of Probate from 1787 to 1795. Mr. Woodbridge married Lucy, daughter of President Edwards. He died April 13, 1796, having been esteemed for his good sense, integrity and piety.

1762.

Hugh Alison, a native of Pennsylvania, after his graduation, was for some time engaged as a teacher in Charleston, South Carolina. He married, and removed to James Island, taking with him a number of young men, with a view to superintend their education. He also became pastor of the Presbyterian Church on that island. Just before the Revolution he returned to Charleston, where he died of consumption, in 1781.

Absalom Bainbridge was a native of Hunterdon County, New Jersey. After graduating, he studied medicine, and practiced for a number of years in Princeton, New Jersey. He then removed to the city of New York, where he practiced for more than twenty years. Dr. Bainbridge was the father of Commodore Bainbridge, of the United States Navy, and the maternal grandfather of the Rev. John Maclean, D.D., LL.D., Ex-president of the College. He died in 1807.

Ebenezer Davenport became a Congregational minister, and settled over the First Church at Greenwich, Connecticut, in 1767, where he remained until his death, in 1773.

Edward Gantt, a native of Prince George County, Maryland, after graduating, studied medicine, and practiced in Somerset County, Maryland. In 1770, while in full practice, he went to England, and received Holy Orders. He officiated for a while in his native parish, and in 1776 went to All Hallows Parish, Worcester County. At the end of four years, he returned to his native parish again, became its Rector, and sustained himself on his estate by the practice of medicine. In 1795, he removed to Georgetown, after it had become a part of the District of Columbia, and there exercised his ministry. He was repeatedly chosen Chaplain to the United States Senate after 1800. About 1807, he removed to Kentucky. In 1836, he was living with his daughter near Louisville, a hale, healthy old man of ninety.

Ebenezer Hazard returned to Philadelphia, his native city, after graduating. He was Postmaster-General of the United States from 1782 until the adoption of the Constitution, in 1789.

He died June 13, 1817.

Mr. Hazard published a valuable historical work, which is often quoted, entitled, Historical Collection: consisting of State papers and other authentic documents, intended as materials for a history of the United States. The first volume was published in Philadelphia, in 4to, in 1791, and the second volume in 1794. He also published, Remarks on a Report concerning the Western Indians, in the Massachusetts Historical Collection.

John McCrea, if I am not mistaken, was a son of the Rev. James McCrea, the pastor and founder of the Presbyterian Church at Lamington, New Jersey. After his father's death, he removed in 1773 to the neighbourhood of Fort Edward, New York. He was a brother of Miss Jane McCrea, whose tragical murder by the Indians, in 1777, made such a noise at the time. After her death, Col. McCrea, removed with his family to the city of Albany. His nephew, Col. James McCrea, was living at Saratoga in 1823.

James Manning shortly after leaving college was ordained as a Baptist minister, and settled in Morristown, New Jersey, near to the place where he was born. Towards the close of the year 1763, he became pastor of the Baptist Church at Warren, Rhode Island. Soon after settling here, he established a Latin school. Feeling the need of an institution of a higher character, he proposed to several influential gentlemen of the Baptist denomination, assembled at Newport, the establishment of "a seminary of polite literature, subject to the government of the Baptists." A charter was granted by the Legislature of the Colony in 1764, to "Rhode Island College," and in 1765, Mr. Manning was elected President and Professor of Languages. In 1770 the college was removed from Warren to Providence.

From the first, President Manning took a deep interest in the affairs of the country, and was actively engaged throughout the Revolution. In 1786, he was chosen to represent Rhode Island in the Continental Congress. In 1785, he received the honorary degree of Doctor of Divinity from the University of Pennsylvania.

Dr. Manning was a laborious and faithful minister of Christ, and it is wonderful that he could have performed such an amount of labour; and it is only to be accounted for from the fact, that he was gifted with a versatility and readiness of mind, which enabled him to preach admirably with but little preparation, and to accommodate himself with great facility to every variety of circumstances. He died suddenly, July 24, 1791.

Thomas Martin was a brother of Gov. Alexander Martin, of North Carolina, of the Class of 1756. After leaving Princeton, he taught school in Virginia, and President Madison was one of his pupils. At one time he was an inmate of the family of Madison's father. Mr. Martin about this time took orders in the Episcopal Church, and in 1767, became Rector of a church in Orange County, Virginia, but his labours were of short duration, as he died soon after entering upon the duties of his parish, towards the close of 1769 or the beginning of 1770.

Francis Peppard received ordination about 1764, from the Presbytery of New York, and was installed pastor of the Presbyterian Church at Mendham, New

Jersey. In 1766, he removed to Orange County, New York, and succeeded Enos Ayres as pastor of the Church at Bethlehem, having also charge of a church at New Windsor. A few years later, Mr. Peppard became pastor of the churches at Allen's Township, Pennsylvania, and Hardwick, New Jersey. He died while in this charge in 1797.

Joseph Periam, after graduating, became tutor in the College. While in this position he embraced Bishop Berkeley's theory, denying the existence of the Material Universe. Samuel Stanhope Smith, who was intimate with him, was in great danger of making shipwreck of his religious principles. After leaving the College, Mr. Periam taught school for several years, and then studied theology, and was licensed by the Presbytery of New York in 1774. In 1775, his license was withdrawn by the Presbytery. Soon after, he was appointed Quarter-master in the First Battalion of the New Jersey Brigade. In 1778, he taught an academy in Elizabethtown, New Jersey. He died October 8, 1780.

It is thought that the withdrawal of Mr. Periam's license by the Presbytery, was not on account of his peculiar views, as we find Dr. Bellamy writing of him in 1773: "Mr. Periam has become a very serious man since you saw him." And Dr. Jedediah Chapman wrote in 1772: "He is a very ingenious young gentleman—I trust a truly humble and pious Christian."

Thomas Ruston studied medicine in Philadelphia, Benjamin Rush being his fellow student. He afterwards went to Edinburg, where he received the degree of Doctor of Medicine, and in 1767 published, in Edinburg, a work on Innoculation, which was probably his *thesis* on receiving his degree.

Jonathan Dickinson Sergeant a grandson of President Dickinson, studied law and was admitted to the bar in New Jersey, his native State. But the Revolution coming on, his patriotic zeal and eminent talents soon recommended him to the confidence of the people for public employment. He was elected to the Continental Congress, and took his seat a few days after the Declaration of Independence was signed. He was afterwards repeatedly elected to the same position. Before the close of the war, he transferred his residence to the City of Philadelphia, and soon became a conspicuous member of the Bar of that city. Mr. Sergeant was the first Attorney-General of Pennsylvania, after the Declaration of Independence. He resided in Philadelphia until 1793, when he fell a victim to the yellow fever.

Mr. Sergeant was endowed with a powerful and active mind, and his moral qualities were not less distinguished and estimable than his intellectual.

Hezekiah Smith. Soon after his graduation, Mr. Smith visited the Southern States for the benefit of his health. While at Charleston, he was ordained as a Baptist Minister. On November 12, 1766, Mr. Smith was recognized as the pastor of the Baptist Church of Haverhill, Massachusetts, of which he remained the honoured pastor for a period of forty years. He was a life-long friend of his class-mate Dr. Manning, and did much for the endowment of Brown University. Mr. Smith was a native of Long Island. In 1776, he was appointed Chaplain in the Continental Army, which post he held for four years. While in this position, he became the intimate friend of Washington, and possessed the confidence and esteem of the officers and men of the whole army. He repeatedly exposed his life in battle, and was ever among the foremost in encouraging the soldiers, and in soothing the sorrows of the wounded and dying.

Dr. Smith was a man of commanding presence, large and well proportioned inspiring respect by his dignity, and winning affection by his affability and grace. He was admitted to a Master's degree at Yale in 1772, and received the honorary degree of Doctor of Divinity from Rhode Island College in 1797. He died suddenly, January 22, 1805.

1763.

James Boyd was ordained by the First Presbytery of Philadelphia in 1770, and installed pastor of the Presbyterian Churches of Newtown and Bensalem, Pennsylvania where he remained for forty-three years. His influence was widely felt, In 1781, he was elected a Trustee of the College at Princeton, which position he resigned in 1800. He died in 1813.

John Close was licensed by Suffolk Presbytery soon after his graduation and immediately visited the South, where he did good service in North and South Carolina as a Missionary. Returning to the North he was called and ordained as colleague to Rev. Ebenezer Prime at Huntington, Long Island, October 30, 1766. He was dismissed from this charge, April 4, 1773, and took charge of a church at New Windsor, New York, where he remained until 1796. He was admitted to a Master's degree at Yale in 1771. The few last years of his life were spent at Waterford, New York, where he died in 1813.

Robert Cooper came from Ireland. There is a tradition among his descendants that he learned the business of plough-making to assist him in getting an education. He was licensed by the Presbytery of Carlisle, February 22, 1765. The same year he was ordained and installed pastor of the Presbyterian Church at Middle Spring, Pennsylvania. Here he laboured faithfully for thirty years. The degree of Doctor of Divinity was conferred upon him by Dickinson College in 1792. His pastoral relation was dissolved April 12, 1797, on account of ill health.

During the American Revolution, Dr. Cooper was a zealous Whig, and often visited the army to exhort them to activity and fidelity. Indeed he is said to have been the captain of a company at one time. He preached "before Colonel Montgomery's battalion under arms," near Shippensburg, Pennsylvania, August 31, 1775, a sermon entitled "Courage in a Good Cause." This discourse was published. Dr. Cooper was a short, spare man, with a trace of melancholy in his face. He died April 5, 1805.

Beside the sermon noticed above, Dr. Cooper published "A Tract," entitled "Signs of the Times."

David Cowell was born in Trenton, New Jersey, and was a nephew of the Rev. David Cowell, that long and active friend and Trustee of the College. After graduating, he studied medicine in Philadelphia, took his degree, and returned to Trenton, where he practiced until his death. For two years he was senior physician and surgeon in military hospitals. Dr. Cowell undertook to draft an outline of his will while suffering under an attack of quinsey, and within a few hours of its fatal termination. Unable to articulate, he hastened to make a rough outline of his intentions, which he doubtless hoped to have had put into form by another hand; but he was compelled by the force of the disease to have the paper copied in the incomplete terms in which he had drawn it. It began: "I, Doctor David Cowell, being of sound judgment, but not able to talk much." In his will he left one hundred pounds to the College of New Jersey; and "to the Congress of the United States of America, one hundred pounds, if they settled themselves at Lamberton," a suburb of Trenton. His death occurred December 18, 1783.

John Craighead received ordination from Donegal Presbytery, about 1767, and was settled as pastor of Rocky Spring Church, Pennsylvania. It is said that he fought and preached alternately. At the commencement of the war he raised a company from the members of his charge, and joined Washington's army in New Jersey. Mr. Craighead was a humourist, and a good many good jokes are told of him. One day going into battle with his friend and class-mate, Robert Cooper, a cannon ball struck a tree near him, a splinter of which nearly knocked him down. "God bless me!" exclaimed Mr. Cooper; "you were nearly knocked to staves." "Oh, yes," was his reply; "and, though you are a *cooper*, you could not have set me up."

Mr. Craighead remained at Rocky Spring until 1798, when he resigned his charge, and died April 20, 1799. The Rev. Francis Herron, D. D., was his successor.

Samuel Eakin was ordained by the Second Presbytery of Philadelphia, in 1770. From 1773 to 1777, he was settled at Penn's Neck Presbyterian Church in West Jersey. But rendering himself obnoxious to the Tories by his zeal in the cause of American liberty, he was obliged to withdraw. He was the idol of the soldiers. Wherever there was a military training, or an order issued for the soldiers to march, he was, if in his power, always there to address them, and by his eloquence, would excite their emotions of patriotism to the highest pitch. It is related of him, that he was so warm a Whig that he never entered the pulpit without imploring the Lord "to teach our people to fight and give them courage and perseverance to overcome their enemies." Mr. Eakin was an extraordinary man, and next to Mr. Whitefield, esteemed the most eloquent preacher who had ever been in the country. He died in 1784.

Ezekiel Emerson, a native of Uxbridge, Massachusetts, was ordained pastor of a Congregational Church in Georgetown, Maine, July 3, 1763. He retired from the ministry in 1810, on account of infirmity, and died November 9, 1815, aged 80.

1763.

James Jauncey, a brother of William Jauncey, of the Class of 1761, became a prominent merchant in New York City. At first he took the side of the Colonies, and was an associate of Jay on the Committee of Fifty. In 1775, he was a member of the Colonial Assembly of New York. At the beginning of the Revolution he took the side of the king. Mr. Jauncey was a leading member of the Presbyterian Church in New York, and a warm friend of the Rev. Dr. Rodgers, who was greatly grieved at his taking sides against the country. Mr. Jauncey retired to England, and died in 1790.

John Lathrop, a native of Norwich, Connecticut, was for some months after his graduation engaged as an assistant teacher with the Rev. Dr. Wheelock, in Moore's Indian Charity School at Lebanon, Connecticut; and for several months he was a missionary among the Indians. On the 18th of May, 1768, he was ordained, and installed pastor of the Old North Church in Boston. At the opening of the Revolution, in 1775, he was compelled to leave his charge, but returned to it in 1776. In the meantime their house of worship had been destroyed, he therefore accepted an invitation to preach in the New Brick Church as an assistant to the Rev. Dr. Pemberton. After Dr. Pemberton's death, the two societies were united, and Mr. Lathrop became their pastor—this was in June, 1779. Here he continued till the close of his life. Dr. Lathrop adopted Unitarian views, but at what period is not certain. His preaching was practical rather than doctrinal. He was an ardent patriot. In 1778, he became a Fellow of the Corporation of Harvard, which he held during life. He was an officer in many public and charitable institutions. In 1785, he was honoured with the degree of Doctor of Divinity by the University of Edinburg. He died January 4, 1816.

Dr. Lathrop's publications are: A Sermon occasioned by the Boston Massacre, 1770. A Sermon to a Religious Society of young men at Medford, 1771. An Artillery Election Sermon, 1774. A Thanksgiving Sermon, 1774. A Sermon on the 5th of March, 1778. A Sermon on the death of his wife, 1778. A Sermon at the Ordination of William Bentley, 1783, A Discourse occasioned by the return of Peace, 1783. A Discourse before the Humane Society of Massachusetts, 1787. A Catechism for the use of children (two editions), 1791 and 1813. The Dudleian Lecture at Harvard College, 1793. A Discourse addressed to the Charitable Fire Society, 1796. A Sermon on Fires in Boston, 1797. A Fast Sermon occasioned by the yellow-fever, 1798. A Sermon on the National Fast, 1799. A Sermon on the Commencement of the Nineteenth Century (in two parts), 1801. A Sermon before the Society for Propagating the Gospel in Foreign Parts. 1804. A Sermon before the Boston Female Asylum, 1804. A Sermon at the dismission of the Rev. Joseph McKean, at Milton, 1804. A Sermon at the interment of the Rev. Samuel West, D. D., 1808. A Thanksgiving Sermon, 1808. A Sermon on the death of his wife, Mrs. Elizabeth Lathrop, 1809. A Sermon at the interment of the Rev. Dr. Eckley, 1811. A Thanksgiving Sermon, 1811. A Discourse delivered on the Author's Birthday, 1812. Two Fast Sermons occasioned by the war of 1812–1815; 1812. A Sermon on the death of the Rev. John Eliot, D. D., 1813. Biographical Memoir of Rev. John Lathrop, 1803. A Sermon at the Dedication of a church at Dorchester, 1813. A Sermon on the Law of Retaliation, 1814. A Sermon preached at Weymouth, at the interment of Miss Mary P. Bicknell, 1814. A Thanksgiving Sermon on the return of Peace, 1815. A Compendious History of the late War, 1815. Besides the above, may be mentioned, several Charges, etc., at Ordinations, delivered at different periods of his ministry; and some valuable Communications to the American Academy, which are embodied in their Collections.

Joseph Lyon. I can discover no reference to Mr. Lyon, except the record upon his tombstone: that he died at Elizabethtown, New Jersey, in 1821, in his 81st year. He was of the numerous race inhabiting Newark, Elizabeth, and Lyons Farms lying between the two.

Obadiah Noble entered the ministry and settled as pastor of a Congregational Church at Orford, New Hamsphire, November 9, 1771. He was released from this charge, February 16, 1829, and removed to Vermont, where he died the same year. He was admitted to a Master's degree at Dartmouth in 1773.

William Paterson read law with Richard Stockton, and commenced practice in Hunterdon County, New Jersey. But the troubles with Great Britain arising, he entered into public life, and soon obtained a commanding position. In 1775 he was a member of the Provincial Congress of New Jersey, and the same year was elected Treasurer of the Province. On the organization of a State Government, under the new State Constitution, Mr. Paterson was appointed Attorney-General, which position he held till the close of the war. After the war he devoted himself to his profession in the county of Somerset. In 1783 he removed to Trenton. Mr. Paterson was a delegate to the Convention which framed the Federal Constitution; six of the delegates being graduates of Princeton. Mr. Paterson took a prominent part in the deliberations of that body, and on the adoption of the Constitution was elected a member of the United States Senate—three of that body being graduates of Princeton: Paterson, of New Jersey; Elsworth, of Connecticut; and Henry, of Maryland. On the death of Governor Livingston, Mr. Paterson was chosen Governor of New Jersey, and continued in this office until March 4, 1793, when he was elevated to the Bench of the Supreme Court of the United States. He held this high office until the end of life. Judge Paterson received the honorary degree of Doctor of Laws from Dartmouth, in 1805, and from Harvard, in 1806. He was a Trustee of the College for fifteen years. He died at Albany, September 9, 1806.

He was a profound lawyer, and in every position which he held, stood conspicuous for integrity and high Christian character.

Tapping Reeve was the son of the Rev. Abner Reeve, of Long Island, and afterwards of Vermont. He entered upon the practice of the law in 1772, at Litchfield, Connecticut. Mr. Reeve was a firm and warm friend of his country during the Revolution. In 1792 he opened a law school, and continued to give lectures to students at law for nearly thirty years. In 1798 he was appointed Judge of the Superior Court of Connecticut, and afterwards was Chief Justice. His first wife was the only daughter of President Burr. Judge Reeve was a profound lawyer, and Chancellor Kent said of him: "He everywhere displays the vigour, freedom, and acuteness of a sound and liberal mind." He was also an eminent Christian, and employed much of his time in private devotion. He was accustomed to pray for the conversion of individuals among his acquaintances. He died December 13, 1823.

The Publications of Mr. Reeve are, The Law of Baron and Femme; of Parent and Child; of Guardian and Ward; of Master and Servant. New Haven. 1816. A Treatise on the Law of Descents in the several United States of America. New York. 1825.

John Simpson, a native of New Jersey, was licensed by the Presbytery of New Brunswick, in 1770, and for the two following years he preached at Easton, Pennsylvania. In 1772 he was appointed by the Synod of New York and Philadelphia to visit Virginia and North Carolina. He spent seven months in this missionary work, and in 1774 was ordained and settled as pastor of Fishing Creek Church, South Carolina. Until the stormy times of the Revolution, his life was peaceful and uneventful, except a little stir occasioned by his introducing Watts's Psalms and Hymns into his congregation; but these troubles gradually subsided. Mr. Simpson was a bold and ardent advocate of independence, and was in many conflicts and skirmishes, in some of which he was regarded as the leader and adviser. He had many narrow escapes, and in the course of the war his house, his library, his sermons, and indeed all that he possessed, were destroyed by the enemy. After the war, he gathered his scattered flock, and for ten years preached to them the Word; but from the removal of families to new settlements, he was at last obliged to seek another home.

In 1790 Mr. Simpson became pastor of Roberts and Good Hope Congregations in Pendleton County, South Carolina. In 1802 his churches were visited with a most remarkable revival. Mr. Simpson continued his labours here until his death, which occurred February 15, 1808.

William Mackay Tennent was a son of Rev. Charles Tennent, of Delaware, and a nephew of William and Gilbert Tennent. He was ordained June 17, 1772, as pastor of the Congregational Church in Greenfield, Connecticut. In December, 1781, he resigned his charge and accepted a call to the Presbyterian Church at Abington, Pennsylvania, where he continued till his death, December, 1810. He was a Trustee of the College at Princeton from 1785 till 1808. He received the Degree of Doctor of Divinity from Yale College, in 1794.

Dr. Tennent married a daughter of the Rev. Dr. Rodgers, of New York. In 1797 he was Moderator of the General Assembly of the Presbyterian Church. Dr. A. Alexander, who knew him personally, represents him as a man of great sweetness of temper and politeness of manner, and as distinguished for his hospitality. In his last hours he was blessed with an uninterrupted assurance of the favour of God.

James Watt studied theology, and in 1770 was ordained and installed pastor of the Presbyterian Church at Cape May, New Jersey, by the First Presbytery of Philadelphia. Mr. Watt died November 19, 1789. Upon his tombstone we read, "If disinterested kindness, integrity, justice and truth deserve the tributary tear, here it is claimed."

Simon Williams came to America from Ireland. Three years after his graduation, he was ordained pastor of the Congregational Church in Windham, New Hampshire. He died, September 10, 1793.

1764.

Thomas John Clagget was descended from an old English family who early settled in Calvert County, Maryland. He was born in Prince George County, Maryland, October 2, 1743. After graduating, he entered immediately upon the study of theology. Having completed his preparatory studies, he went to England for ordination, and in 1767 was admitted to the Order of Deacons; and the Priesthood by the Rev. Richard Terrick, Bishop of London. On his return to America, he became rector of All Saints' Parish, in Calvert County, Maryland. Here he continued until the opening of the Revolution, when he ceased to preach for two years.

In 1780, he was elected Rector of St. Paul's, Prince George County, Maryland. On May 31, 1792, he was unanimously elected Bishop of Maryland, and on September 13, was consecrated in Trinity Church, New York, by Bishop Prevost; Bishops Seabury, White and Madison assisting in the service—being the fifth Bishop then in the United States, and the first that was consecrated this side of the Atlantic.

In 1800, he acted as Chaplain to the Senate of the United States, the first Session held in Washington.

After presiding over the Episcopal Church in Maryland for twenty-five years, he died August 2, 1816, aged 73.

Bishop Clagget's publications consist of his Pastoral Letters, Addresses to the Convention, and a few occasional Sermons. He was a well-informed divine, and continued to the last devoted to the studies and the duties of his profession.

Bishop Clagget was a man of commanding person, voice

and manners, and of great dignity of character, yet exceedingly mild, affable, and easy of access. He was in the habit of wearing the mitre on special occasions, and Bishop Meade relates an amusing incident connected with the consecration of a church in Alexandria, at which Bishop Clagget officiated. Putting on his robes and his mitre at some distance from the church, he had to go along the street to reach it. This attracted the attention of a number of boys and others, who ran after and along side of him, admiring his peculiar dress and gigantic stature. His voice was as extraordinary for strength and ungovernableness as was his stature for size, and as he entered the door of the church where the people were in silence awaiting, and the first words of the service burst forth from his lips in his most peculiar manner, a young lady, turning around suddenly and seeing his huge form and uncommon appearance, was so convulsed that she was obliged to be taken out of the house.

William Foster, a native of Lancaster County, Pennsylvania, was licensed to preach by the Presbytery of New Castle, April 23, 1757, and ordained and installed pastor of Upper Octorora and Doe Run Presbyterian Churches, Pennsylvania, October 19, 1768.

In the Revolution, Mr. Foster engaged heartily in the cause of civil liberty, and encouraged all who heard him to do their utmost in defense of their rights, and on this account he became very obnoxious to the enemy, and more than once attempts were made to seize him.

On one occasion Mr. Foster was called to Lancaster to preach to the troops collected there previous to their joining the main army. The discourse was so acceptable, that it was printed and circulated, and did much to arouse the spirit of patriotism among the people. Mr. Foster was a man of very superior mind, and was much esteemed and respected by all who knew him for his solid sense and unaffected piety. He held a high place also among his brethren, as his name constantly occurs in connection with positions of trust and responsibility. He occasionally received theological students under his care. He died September 30, 1780. His deathbed was a scene of triumph.

Nathaniel Hazard, from the best information I can obtain, was a son of Nathaniel Hazard of New York, and a cousin of Ebenezer Hazard of the Class of 1762. He was admitted to a Master's degree at Yale in 1770. Mr. Hazard died in 1798.

Samuel Leake, a native of Virginia, was licensed by the Presbytery of Hanover, at Tinkling Spring, Virginia, April 18, 1766, and was ordained May 3, 1770, and settled as pastor of Rich Cove and North Garden Presbyterian Churches, Albemarle County, Virginia. Mr. Leake's pastorate was short, being brought to an end by his death, December 2, 1775. A large proportion of his very numerous descendants have been pious. The blessing of God has rested upon his house.

John McCrery studied theology and was licensed by the Presbytery of New Castle about 1767. He was ordained and installed as pastor of White Clay Creek Church, Delaware, in 1769. Mr. McCrery held this charge for thirty years. He died in 1800.

Alexander Miller received his license to preach from the Presbytery of New York in 1767, and was ordained in 1770. In 1771, he took charge of a Church gathered in Schenectady, New York, where he remained for eleven years, but during the distraction of the Revolutionary war, his congregation dispersed, and he was compelled to leave the field. Where Mr. Miller resided after leaving Schenectady, I have no means of determining. In 1785 he was elected a Trustee of the College; and resigned the post in 1795.

1764.

Joseph Smith, of Nottingham, Pennsylvania, was licensed by the Presbytery of New Castle, August 5, 1767, and was ordained and installed pastor of Lower Brandywine Church, Delaware, April 19, 1769. This charge he resigned in 1772, but in 1774, accepted a call from the second church in Wilmington, that Church having united with his old Brandywine Church. He laboured here until April, 1778, when he resigned on account of the distracted state of the country.

But now he was about to enter upon the great work of his life in Western Pennsylvania. Here he became prominent for piety and energy, and was one of the fathers of the Presbyterian Church in that region. The Revs. James Power and John McMillan, both graduates of Princeton, had already preceded him. His first charge was Buffalo and Cross Creek, where he was settled in 1780. A revival soon began in his church which never ceased till the day of his death, more than twelve years!

Mr. Smith was not a man of robust health. In person he was tall and slender, of fair complexion, and was somewhat disfigured by a cast in one of his eyes. His voice was remarkable alike for the terrific and the pathetic. Some one said of him, "I never knew a man who could so completely unbar the gates of hell, and make me look so far down into the dark, bottomless abyss, or like him, could so throw open the gates of heaven, and let me glance at the insufferable brightness of the great white Throne."

Mr. Smith died April 19, 1792.

Thomas Treadwell. For seven years, from 1776 to 1783, Mr. Treadwell was a member of the Assembly of New York from Suffolk County. From 1791 to 1795, he represented the State of New York in the House of Representatives of the United States. He died in 1826.

James Tuttle was ordained by the Presbytery of New York in 1765. He was the first settled pastor at

Rockaway and Parcipany, New Jersey. He died in April, 1771.

William Woodhull, probably a native of Long Island, was licensed by the Presbytery of Suffolk in 1768, and ordained by the Presbytery of New York in 1770. In 1783, on account of continued bodily infirmity, he ceased from preaching and devoted himself to secular pursuits. At his request the Presbytery dropped his name from their roll, but by order of the Synod it was restored.

It is an interesting fact that the commencement of this year was held in the "New Church," and Mr. Whitefield preached in the morning.

1765.

John Bacon was born in Canterbury, Connecticut. After leaving College, he studied theology, and was ordained a Congregational Minister, and preached for a time in Somerset County, Maryland. In 1771, he was settled with the Rev. John Hunt as a colleague pastor of the old South Church in Boston, as successor to the Rev. John Blair. His style of preaching was argumentative, and his manner approaching the severe. He left his church in 1775 on account of doctrinal difficulties which arose. He then removed to Stockbridge, Massachusetts, and became in turn, a magistrate, a representative in the Legislature, Associate Judge of the Court of Common Pleas, a member and President of the State Senate, and a Member of Congress. In his political views he accorded with the party of Mr. Jefferson.

Mr. Bacon was one of the original Trustees of Williams College. He died October 25, 1820.

He published, A Sermon, 1772; An Answer to Huntington on a Case of Discipline, 1781; A Speech on the Courts of the United States, 1802; Conjectures on the Prophecies, 1805.

Joel Benedict. The ancestors of Mr. Benedict were among the early settlers of New England. He was born in Salem, New York, January 8, 1745. After leaving Princeton, he taught school in the South, but the climate affecting his health, he returned to his father's house in Salem. He now determined to devote himself to the ministry, and pursued his studies under Dr. Bellamy. After his licensure he supplied destitute churches in Maine and Massachusetts until 1771, when he became pastor of a Congregational Church at Newent (now

Lisbon), Connecticut, where he laboured until 1781, when he resigned on account of his health, which had long been feeble. Recovering his health in 1784, he became pastor of the Church at Plainfield, Connecticut, where he preached with great acceptance until his death, February 13, 1816.

In 1808 the honorary degree of Doctor of Divinity was conferred upon him by Union College, and in 1814 by Dartmouth.

Dr. Benedict was a distinguished classical scholar, and Virgil was his favourite author through life. It is said that his reading of Latin poetry, even when he was in college, was so remarkable that the professors sometimes set him to reading Virgil merely for their own gratification. He was also profoundly versed in mathematics; and as a biblical scholar he had few superiors. The Hebrew language, which he was accustomed to call "the language of the angels," was his delight.

Dr. Benedict lived through the stirring scenes of the Revolution, and mingled in them with the spirit of a true patriot.

The only acknowledged publication of Dr. Benedict is a sermon preached at the funeral of Rev. Dr. Hart in 1811.

William Davies, the eldest son of President Davies, studied law, and settled at Norfolk, Virginia. In the Revolutionary War he attained the rank of Colonel in the American Army; was an officer of distinguished merit, and possessed, in an eminent degree, the esteem and confidence of the Commander-in-Chief. He was a man of powerful mind, highly cultivated and enriched by various knowledge. He died in Virginia before 1820.

Jonathan Edwards, a son of President Edwards, after leaving college, studied divinity with Dr. Bellamy, and was licensed by a Congregational Association at Litchfield, Connecticut, in 1766. In 1767 he was appointed tutor at Princeton, where he remained two years.

On the 5th of January, 1769, he was ordained and became pastor of a church at Colebrook, Connecticut, where he hoped to spend his life in retirement; but in June 1799, he was elected and inaugurated the President of Union College.

Dr. Edwards was a man of uncommon powers of mind. He has seldom been surpassed in acuteness and penetration. His manner in preaching was bold and animated, but he addressed the understanding and conscience rather than the passions of his audience. He died August 1, 1801.

The writings of Dr. Edwards are a book entitled, "The Salvation of all Men Strictly Examined," etc., in answer to Dr. Chauncy. A Dissertation on Liberty and Necessity. Observations on the Language of the Muhhekaneew or Stockbridge Indians, communicated to the Connecticut Society of Arts and Sciences, and republished in the Massachusetts Historical Collections, with Notes by J. Pickering. Brief Observations on the Doctrine of Universal Salvation. Three Sermons on the Atonement. Sermon at the Ordination of Timothy Dwight, Greenfield, 1785. Sermon at the Ordination of Daniel Bradley, Hamden, 1792. Sermon at the Ordination of William Brown, Glastenburg, 1792. Sermon at the Ordination of Edward Dorr Griffin, New Hartford, 1795. A Sermon on the Injustice and Impolicy of the Slave Trade, 1791. Human Depravity the Source of Infidelity: a Sermon published in the "American Preacher," vol. ii., Marriage of a Wife's Sister Considered, in the Anniversary Concio ad Clerum, in the Chapel of Yale College, 1792. A Sermon on the Death of Roger Sherman, 1793. An Election Sermon, 1794. A Sermon on a Future State of Existence and the Immortality of the Soul, printed in a volume entitled, " Sermons Collected, etc." A Farewell Sermon to the People of Colebrook. A number of pieces in the New York "Theological Magazine" under the signature of I. and O.

He also edited from the manuscripts of his father, The History of the Work of Redemption, two volumes of Sermons, and two volumes of Observations on Important Theological Subjects.

His whole works were edited and published by his grandson, Rev. Tryon Edwards, D. D.

Robert Halsted belonged to the Elizabethtown family of Halsteds. After graduating he studied medicine, and became quite eminent in his profession.

Richard Hutson was a son of the Rev. William

Hutson, one of the early Presbyterian ministers in South Carolina. He entered the profession of the law after leaving Princeton, and became one of the first Chancellors of South Carolina. He was an earnest patriot, and was a delegate to the Continental Congress from 1777 to 1779. In 1780 he was taken prisoner by the British, and confined for some time in St. Augustine, Florida.

Samuel Kirkland held a high rank as a scholar during his college course, and was esteemed a young man of marked ability. He left college eight months before his class graduated, but nevertheless received his degree. He immediately went on a missionary expedition to the Seneca tribe of Indians, the most warlike and distant tribe of the Six Nations. Sir William Johnson gave him every assistance in his mission. His adventures it is impossible here to relate. It was a scene of constant hardship, of unremitting labour, and often of imminent danger. After being a year absent, he returned to his home in Norwich, Connecticut, bringing one of the Seneca chiefs with him. He was now ordained, and returned to his mission, where he spent more than forty years. The influence which this mission had upon the interest of the country during the Revolution may be learned from an extract of a letter of Washington to Congress in 1775: "The Rev. Mr. Kirkland, the bearer of this, having been introduced to the Honourable Congress, can need no particular recommendation from me. But as he now wishes to have the affairs of his mission and public employ put upon some suitable footing, I cannot but intimate my sense of the importance of his station, and the great advantages which have and may result to the United Colonies from his situation being made respectable. All accounts agree that much of the favourable disposition shown by the Indians may be ascribed to his labour and influence."

The founding of Hamilton College is due to the far-seeing generosity of Mr. Kirkland. It was through his influence that Hamilton Oneida Academy was founded and incorporated in 1793. In the same year he conveyed to its Trustees several hundred acres of land. In 1812 this academy became Hamilton College under a new charter.

Mr. Kirkland was admitted to a Master's degree at Yale in 1768, and at Dartmouth in 1773. He died February 28, 1808.

Alexander Mitchel received his license from the First Presbytery of Philadelphia, in April, 1767, and was ordained and settled as pastor of the Deep Run Presbyterian Church, Bucks County, Pennsylvania, in November, 1768. In 1785, he received a call from the Upper Octorara and Doe Run Congregations, Pennsylvania, and was installed December 14, 1785. In 1795, a difficulty arose in the congregation of Octorara, on account of Mr. Mitchel's preaching against church members engaging in worldly amusements, and on this account, he resigned the charge in 1796. He still continued the pastor of Doe Run, where he remained until 1809, when, by reason of advancing years, he was unable to minister to them. He died December 6, 1812.

Robert Ogden, a son of Robert Ogden, of Elizabethtown, New Jersey, became a distinguished patriot and Christian. He, in connection with William Paterson, Luther Martin, Oliver Ellsworth and Tapping Reeve, were the founders of the Cliosophic Society. After graduating, he studied law with Richard Stockton, and was admitted to practice June 21, 1770. He opened his office in Elizabethtown, and soon acquired an extensive and lucrative practice.

Mr. Ogden was a warm and earnest patriot. He was also a fine scholar, and kept up his classical reading after entering upon his profession.

Jonathan Ogden also came from Elizabethtown, to

which place he returned after graduation. He never entered a profession.

Ebenezer Pemberton was probably born in Boston. He pronounced the Valedictory on Commencement day, on "Patriotism." He was appointed a tutor in the college in 1769. On one of the public occasions, while he was a tutor, he was addressed by Madison, then a student, in a Latin address, valedictory and complimentary, on the part of the class, to the teacher. His life was devoted to teaching, at one time in Phillips' Academy, and no teacher had a higher character for scholarship, manners, eloquence and piety. His last twenty years were years of infirmity. He was elegant and dignified in his appearance, and refined in his manners and utterance.

Mr. Pemberton was admitted to an *ad eundem* Master's degree at Harvard in 1787, at Yale in 1781, and at Dartmouth in 1782. In 1817, he received the honorary degree of Doctor of Laws from Allegheny College. He died June 25, 1835.

David Ramsay was a Pennsylvanian by birth. After leaving Princeton, he studied medicine, and settled in Charleston, South Carolina, where he rose to eminence. During the Revolution he was a determined Whig, and a leading member of the Legislature. He also acted as a Surgeon in the army. From 1782 to 1786, he was a Delegate to the Continental Congress, and was for a time President *pro tem.* His first wife was the daughter of President Witherspoon. He met his death by a pistol-shot, at the hands of an insane man, in 1815. Dr. Ramsay is chiefly celebrated for his historical works.

He published: A History of the Revolution in South Carolina, 2 vols., 8vo, 1785. History of the American Revolution, 2 vols., 8vo, 1789. Review of the Improvement, etc., of Medicine, 1800. The Life of Washington, 1807. Medical Register, 1802. Oration on the Acquisition of Louisiana, 1804. History of South Carolin 2 ls., 8vo, 1809. A Biographical Chart. Memoirs of Martha L. Ramsay, 1811. Eulogium on Dr. Rush, 1813. History of the United States, 3 vols., 1816–1817. Universal History Americanized, 8 vols. 1819.

Theodore Dirck Romeyn studied theology, and became a minister in the Reformed Dutch Church. He was first settled in Ulster County, New York, and afterwards at Hackensack, New Jersey. In November, 1784, he removed to Schenectady, New York, and in 1797 was appointed Professor of Theology of the Dutch Church. The establishment of Union College is principally ascribed to his efforts. He is represented to have been a "son of thunder" in the pulpit. Mr. Romeyn was born in New Barbadoes, New Jersey. He died April 16, 1804.

Jacob Rush was a brother of Dr. Benjamin Rush. On Commencement day he pronounced an oration on Liberty, and his class-mate, Pemberton, one on Patriotism, showing the tendency of the young American mind even at that early day. Mr. Rush entered the profession of the law, and rose to a distinguished position. He was for many years presiding Judge of the Court of Common Pleas for Philadelphia. He was afterwards Chief Justice of the State. He died in 1820.

Judge Rush published: Resolve in Committee Chamber, Philadelphia, 1774. Charges on Moral and Religious Subjects, 1803. Character of Christ, 1806. Christian Baptism, 1819.

John Staples was a native of Taunton, Massachusetts, and was a lineal descendant of Miles Standish. He entered the ministry of the Congregational Church, and was ordained April 17, 1772, and installed as pastor of the Church at Westminster, Connecticut. He remained in this charge until his death, which took place February 15, 1804. He was much beloved by his people, and was a faithful and successful preacher of the Gospel. A son of Mr. Staples was a lawyer of some note in New York City, and for many years an Elder in the University Place Presbyterian Church.

1765.

Alexander Thayer became pastor of the Congregational Church at Paxton, Massachusetts, November 28, 1770. During the Revolution he was suspected of favouring the British cause, and although these suspicions were groundless, yet for the sake of peace in his congregation, he resigned his charge August 14, 1782, and removed to Holliston, Massachusetts, where he ended his days.

Jacob Vanartsdalen, a native of Somerset County, New Jersey, was ordained by the Presbytery of New Brunswick, June 19, 1771; in which connection he remained until the latter part of 1774, when he was received by the Presbytery of New York and put in charge of the Church of Springfield, New Jersey. He continued in the orderly and faithful performance of the duties of the office, as far as his health permitted, for more than a quarter of a century. In the spring of 1797, and again three years later, he was by reason of long continued illness, disqualified for preaching. He was at length compelled to relinquish the pastoral office, and was dismissed from his charge, May 6, 1801. From 1793 to 1802 Mr. Vanarstdalen was a Trustee of the College. He died at Springfield, October 24, 1803.

Stephen Voorhees (or Van Voorhis) was licensed by the General Meeting and Elders of the Reformed Dutch Church in 1772, and was ordained and settled at Poughkeepsie, New York in 1773, where he remained until 1776. From 1776 to 1784 he was pastor of the Reformed Dutch Church at Rhinebeck Flats; and from 1785 to 1788 at Philipsburg (Tarrytown) and Cortlandtown, New York. In 1792 he joined the Presbytery of New Brunswick, and preached as a supply at Kingston and Assunpink, New Jersey. He died November 23, 1796.

Simeon Williams was a native of Easton, Massachusetts. After graduating, he studied theology, and was installed pastor of the Second Congregational Church at Weymouth, Massachusetts, October 27, 1768, where he remained until his death, which occurred May 22, 1819. Mr. Williams was admitted to a Master's degree at Harvard in 1769.

1766.

Waightstill Avery was a native of Norwich, Connecticut. After graduating, he removed to Maryland, and studied law with Littleton Dennis, Esq. Removing to North Carolina, he was admitted to the Bar of that State in 1769. Taking up his residence in Charlotte, he soon acquired friends and rapid promotion, and was from the beginning active in encouraging education and literature. The Minutes of the Council of Safety show his zeal in the cause of liberty; and the confidence of his countrymen in his talents is proved by the important duties he was engaged to perform. With Ephraim Brevard and Hezekiah James Balch, he was one of the leading spirits that sent forth the Mecklenberg Resolutions. He served many times in the Legislature of his State, and from 1775 to 1777 he was in the Provincial Congress of North Carolina. In 1777 he was appointed the first Attorney-General of the State. In 1781, by order of Cornwallis, his office, with all his books and papers, was destroyed by fire. He was an exemplary Christian, a pure patriot and an honest man, and at the time of his death the oldest member of the North Carolina Bar. He died in 1821.

Hezekiah Balch was born in Maryland, but removed, while a child, with his father's family to North Carolina. For some time after his graduation, he taught a school in Fauquier County, Virginia. Mr. Balch was licensed to preach by the Presbytery of New Castle, in 1768, and ordained in 1770. At first he performed missionary work in Virginia, and for one year, he preached in York, Pennsylvania. In 1784 he removed to Tennessee, then a vast wilderness, and, by reason of age and experience, took the lead in organizing churches. In his work in Tennessee he was closely associated with the Rev. Samuel Doak, another graduate of Princeton. About the year 1793 Mr. Balch conceived, matured, and communicated to some of his friends the plan of Greenville College, and obtained a charter for the same in 1794. The next year he visited New England to collect funds for the institution, which visit occasioned a theological controversy which gave a somewhat polemical character to his whole life. Mr. Balch's exertions in behalf of education gave an impulse to the cause through the whole south-western region. However imprudent he may have been in many things, he deserves the gratitude of the county for his labour in behalf of a higher education. The degree of Doctor of Divinity was conferred on him by Williams College in 1806.

Dr. Balch died full of labour, in April, 1810.

Hezekiah James Balch, a native of Deer Creek, Hartford County, Maryland, was licensed by the Presbytery of Donegal in 1768, soon after which he removed to North Carolina. He was one of the leaders in the Mecklenburg Convention, and one of the committee that prepared the Resolutions adopted by that Convention. Mr. Balch was the pastor of two churches, Rocky River and Poplar Tent. He saw the commencement of that war which ended with all the honour and independence to his country he ever desired; but before the strife of blood and plunder that followed the Declaration of Independence reached Carolina, he slept with those whose sleep shall not be awakened till the resurrection. He died in 1776.

Ebenezer Cowell was probably a brother of David Cowell, M.D., of the class of 1763. He was a lawyer in Trenton, New Jersey.

Samuel Edmiston, after leaving College, studied

Medicine and practiced at Fagg's Manor, Pennsylvania. Dr. Edmiston married a daughter of Rev. Samuel Blair, of Fagg's Manor. Four other graduates of Princeton married daughters of Dr. Blair: George Duffield, of the class of 1752; David Rice, of the class of 1761; John Carmichael, of the class of 1759, and William Foster, of the class of 1764; all of them distinguished clergymen.

Oliver Ellsworth was born in Windsor, Connecticut, April 29, 1745. Soon after his graduation he began teaching and the study of theology, but soon relinquished both for the law, and was admitted to the Bar in 1771. About 1775, he removed to Hartford, and soon after was appointed Attorney-General of the State. He was in the Legislature which assembled a few days after the battle of Lexington. In 1777 he was chosen a delegate to the Continental Congress, but did not take his seat until October, 1778. In 1780, he was a member of the Council of Connecticut, and continued a member of that body till 1784, when he was appointed a Judge of the Superior Court. In 1787 he was a member of the Convention which framed the Constitution of the United States. In an Assembly, illustrious for talent, erudition and patriotism, he held a distinguished place. In 1789 he was chosen a United States Senator, which place he filled till 1796, when he was appointed Chief Justice of the United States. Here he presided with great dignity and wisdom. In 1799, he was appointed by President Adams Envoy Extraordinary to France, one of his two colleagues, General Davie, being also a graduate of Princeton. With much reluctance he accepted this appointment. While abroad, his failing health induced him to resign his high office of Chief Justice.

Mr. Ellsworth was a model of a legislator and judge. His perceptions were unusually rapid, his reasoning clear and conclusive, and his eloquence powerful. He moved for more than thirty years in a most conspicuous sphere unassailed by the shafts of slander.

In private life he was the personification of social and personal virtue. He was always unassuming and humble. His dress, his equipage and mode of living were regulated by a principle of republican economy.

He was, above all, an exemplary Christian, having confessed Christ in his youth; and in every station he was not ashamed of his Gospel. His religion was practical and vital—always at the prayer meetings, and a life-long friend of Missions.

His speech in the Convention of Connecticut in favour of the Constitution, is preserved in the American Museum.

Mr. Ellsworth died November 26, 1807.

Joseph Hasbrouck, of Huguenot descent, was born in the village of Kingston, New York. He never studied a profession, but settled on the old homestead as a farmer. He was an ardent patriot and entered the Revolutionary army, in which he became a Colonel of Militia, and saw some service. He afterwards became a General in the State service.

He was a man of fine personal appearance, dignified and courteous in his manners, of acknowledged ability and great influence in the community in which he resided. He accumulated and left a large inheritance to his family, who enjoy a high social position. One of his nephews, the Hon. A. Bruyn Hasbrouck, LL. D., was for some time President of Rutgers College.

General Hasbrouck died February 26, 1808.

David Howell, a native of New Jersey, removed to Providence, Rhode Island, and was for three years a tutor in the College of Rhode Island, (Brown University,) being the first ever appointed in that institution; for nine years he was Professor of Natural Philosophy; for thirty-four years Professor of Law; for fifty-two years a member of the Board of Fellows; and for many years Secretary of the Corporation. Though abundantly competent to the task, he never delivered any lectures while he filled the chair of Professor of Law. Judge Howell practiced law in Providence for many years, and was among the most eminent members of the Rhode Island Bar. He represented Rhode Island in the Continental Congress from 1782 to 1785. In 1812, he was appointed United States Judge for the District of Rhode Island, and this office he sustained till his death. Judge Howell was endowed with extraordinary talents, and superadded to his endowments, extensive and accurate learning. As an able jurist he established for himself a solid reputation. He was, however, yet more distinguished as a keen and brilliant wit, and as a scholar, extensively acquainted not only with the ancient, but with several of the modern languages. As an effective and pungent political writer, he was almost unrivalled; and in conversation, whatever chanced to be the theme, whether politics or law—literature or theology—grammar or criticism—a Greek tragedy, or a difficult problem in mathematics, he was never found wanting. He died July 9, 1824.

Daniel Jones. All that I can learn of Mr. Jones is that he was licensed to preach by the Presbytery of New Castle in 1769, and ordained in 1781. His name soon disappears from the Records of the Synod.

Josiah Lewis was licensed by the Presbytery of New Castle in 1769, and ordained in 1771. In the autumn of 1771, he was preaching as a missionary in North and South Carolina, after which I can find no trace of him.

Peter Van Brugh Livingston was probably the fifth child of Philip Livingston, the signer of the Declaration of Independence. After graduating, he removed to Jamaica in the West Indies, and the family have no record of his death.

1766.

Daniel McCalla was born in Neshaminy, Pennsylvania. On leaving college he took charge of an academy in Philadelphia, and during his labours there, made himself familiar with the science of medicine, mastered several of the modern languages, and pursued a course of theological study. In 1774, he was ordained by the First Presbytery of Philadelphia, and installed as pastor of the churches at New Providence and Charleston, Pennsylvania. At the commencement of the war, he was appointed by Congress a Chaplain (the only one they ever appointed) of General Thompson's Corps, under orders for Canada. Soon after his arrival, he was taken prisoner, and confined for some months in a loathsome prison-ship, and subjected to brutal treatment. At length he was released on parole, and returned to his congregation in 1776. Soon after, he was charged with breaking his parole in praying for his country, and the danger becoming imminent, he escaped to Virginia, where he established an academy in Hanover County, and became pastor of the congregation made vacant by the removal of the Rev. Samuel Davies to Princeton. Mr. McCalla was eminently a social man, and perhaps not always discreet. Finding himself subject to censure, he left his position in Virginia in 1788, and removed to South Carolina, where he became pastor of an Independent Church at Wappetaw. He remained pastor of this church until the close of his life, a diligent student, and faithful pastor, a period of twenty-one years. The College of South Carolina conferred upon him the honorary degree of Doctor of Divinity. He died in May, 1809.

Dr. McCalla published, A Sermon at the Ordination of James Adams, 1799. In 1810 two volumes of his works were published, with notices of his life by Dr. Hollingshed; these volumes contain nine sermons on different subjects. He published also Twenty Numbers of Remarks on the "Age of Reason" over the signature of "Artemas." Remarks on Griesbach's Greek Testament. An Essay on the Excellency and Advantages of the Gospel. Remarks on the Theatre and Public Amusements, in thirteen numbers. Hints on Education, in fourteen numbers. The Sovereignty of the People, in twelve numbers. A Fair Statement and Appendix to the same, in eighteen numbers, containing an address to President Adams. Servility of Prejudice Displayed, in nine numbers. Federal Sedition and Anti-Democracy, in six numbers. A Vindication of Mr. Jefferson, in two numbers. The Retreat, a Poem.

John MacPherson was a native of Philadelphia, his father, John MacPherson, being a resident of that city, and greatly distinguished in privateering in the war of 1756. John MacPherson, the subject of this sketch, was an uncle of John MacPherson Berrien, of the class of 1796. After leaving Princeton he read law in Philadelphia with John Dickinson, author of the celebrated farmer's letter. When the war for independence began, he joined the army, and was an aid-de-camp of General Montgomery at the siege of Quebec, and fell at the same discharge of grape-shot by which his commander was killed, December 31, 1775. There is an interesting incident connected with his fall which deserves to be recorded. Major MacPherson had a brother William, who was an officer in the British service at this time, and who was as violent in favor of the English government, as his brother was enthusiastic in the cause of America. A few days before the attack, Major MacPherson accompanied General Montgomery to view the spot where Wolfe had fallen; on his return he found a letter from his brother, the English officer, full of the bitterest reproaches against him for having entered into the American service, and containing a pretty direct wish, if he would not abandon it, he might meet with the deserved fate of a rebel. Major MacPherson immediately returned him an answer, full of strong reasoning, in defence of his conduct, but by no means attempting to shake the opposite principles of his brother, and not only free from acrimony, but full of expressions of tenderness and affection; this letter he dated, "from the spot where Wolfe lost his life in fighting the cause of England, *in friendship with America*."

The letter had scarcely reached the officer at New York, before it was followed by the news of his brother's death. The effect was instantaneous; nature and perhaps reason prevailed. He instantly applied for permission to resign, unwilling to bear arms longer against his countrymen. This permission was granted on condition that he should not leave the British lines, within which he remained under the surveillance of a soldier; being indulged, however, with the liberty of going in pursuit of ducks on the East river, attended by his guard. Having one day advanced some distance from the city, he put his gun to the head of the attendant, and ordered him to pull over to the Long Island shore, where he was received by a party of Americans. The fact becoming known to Congress, he received from that body a Major's commission, and sought every occasion of distinguishing himself in the service of his country until the close of the war.

Luther Martin joined college from New Jersey. After his graduation he removed to Maryland, where he taught school until 1771, when he was admitted to the Bar. Removing to Virginia he practiced his profession in Accomac and Northampton Counties. He was soon regarded as one of the ablest lawyers at the Bar. He threw his whole strength on the side of American Independence, and by his bold speech and writings, animated the friends of the country. On the 11th of April, 1778, he was appointed Attorney-General of the State of Maryland. In this office he displayed remarkable firmness, professional knowledge, and uncompromising energy, and increased his reputation as an advocate and jurist. In 1804, he was employed in the defence of Judge Chase of the Supreme Court of the United States. In 1807 he was one of the counsel to defend Aaron Burr, who was his personal friend. In 1814 he was appointed Chief Judge of the Court of Oyer and Terminer for the City and County of Baltimore. In 1818 he was again appointed Attorney-General of Maryland. He died in New York, July 10, 1826.

As a lawyer, Judge Martin was learned, solid, and

second to no man among his contemporaries. He was not brilliant but solid. He was a man of warm heart and generous feelings, but in the discharge of his official duties he was vigorous and unyielding. In personal appearance he was about the medium size, but stout and muscular. He usually wore a brown or blue dress-coat, with ruffles around the wrists after the ancient fashion, and his hair tied behind, hanging below the collar of his coat. He often appeared walking in the street with his legal documents close to his eyes for perusal, wholly abstracted from the world, and absorbed in his profession.

Luther Martin was undoubtedly one of the ablest lawyers which our country has produced, and his name will descend to posterity among the brightest of those who have gained their reputation strictly at the bar.

Nathaniel Niles, a son of Samuel Niles, of Braintree, Massachusetts, was born in South Kingston, Rhode Island, April 3, 1741. In college he held a high rank in general scholarship, but excelled more particularly in the exact sciences, and in metaphysics. He was an able debater, and especially skilled in the Socratic method of arguing. It was doubtless this trait which acquired for him and his brother Samuel, while at college, the appellation said to have been given them—*Botheration Primus*, and *Botheration Secundus*.

After his graduation, he devoted some time to the study of medicine. He was also for a while a student of law; and was at one time a teacher in the city of New York. Among his pupils, to whom he taught the rudiments of English grammar, was Lindley Murray, afterwards the celebrated grammarian.

Resolving to enter the ministry, he commenced the study of theology, under Dr. Bellamy, and in due time was licensed to preach the gospel. He had many invitations to settle, but through want of health declined them all, and was never ordained.

He took up his residence in Norwich, Connecticut, and

while there displayed his mechanical talent in the invention of a method of making wire from bar iron by water power. This was the first invention of the kind in the United States. During his residence in Norwich he was several times a member of the Legislature of Connecticut.

After the close of the Revolutionary war he removed to Vermont, and in 1784 he was speaker of the House of Representatives; and for many years Judge of the Supreme Court. From 1791 to 1795 he represented Vermont in Congress. As a metaphysician and intellectual philosopher he had probably few superiors. When not absent on public business, he preached in his own house for twelve years. He was admitted to a Master's degree at Harvard in 1772, and at Dartmouth in 1791.

Mr. Niles was one of the most able and vigorous writers of his day. He wrote the "American Hero," a celebrated sapphic ode, which was set to music, and was the war song of the Revolution. He published four discourses on Secret Prayer in 1773; two on Confession and Forgiveness; two on the Perfection of God the Fountain of Good, 1777; a Sermon on Vain Amusements; and a letter on the power of sinners to make new hearts, 1809. He also wrote largely for newspapers and magazines. He maintained his studious habits through life, and in his latter days spent much time in reading the Septuagint Version of the Bible. He died in the utmost tranquillity, October 31, 1828.

James Power was born in Chester County, Pennsylvania, in 1746. He was one of the students who visited President Finley on his death-bed in Philadelphia; and the affecting scene left a powerful and enduring impression on his mind.

Mr. Power was licensed by the Presbytery of New Castle, June 24, 1772. The next year he travelled, and preached in Virginia. In 1774 he crossed the mountains and spent three months as a missionary in Western

Pennsylvania, after which he returned to the East and supplied a church in Maryland. In 1776 he was ordained, and removed permanently to Western Pennsylvania, and after supplying various churches, was installed pastor of Mount Pleasant and Sewickly churches in 1779. In 1787 his connection with the Sewickly church was dissolved; and from that time until April, 1817, he devoted himself to the Mount Pleasant Church, when, on account of age and infirmity, he gave up his charge. He received the degree of Doctor of Divinity from Jefferson College in 1808.

In person, Dr. Power was slender, erect, and of medium size. His manners were easy and graceful, and free from affectation. In his dress, he was always plain, and, at the same time, extremely neat; so that it was a matter of surprise that he could ride on horseback ten or fifteen miles in a rough country, over muddy roads, and yet appear in the pulpit, or rather on a preaching-stand in the woods, as neat and clean as if he had the minute before come from his toilet. He always rode a good horse, and it was believed he was a good judge of that animal, and that he selected one with such a movement as would not throw mud or dust on the rider. In his conversation and manners he was dignified and precise, seldom if ever indulging in anything like wit or levity. And yet he was sociable, and far from being morose or censorious. His voice was not loud, but remarkably clear and distinct. His enunciation was so perfect, that the whole volume of his voice was used in conveying to his hearers the words he uttered. He always preached without notes, but his discourses were clear, methodical and evangelical. During the Revolution, Dr. Power lived in the midst of Indian wars and alarms. The church in which he preached was of logs, upon which no plane, hammer, saw nor nail were used. The windows were small openings cut in adjacent logs, and *glazed* with paper or white linen oiled with hog's lard or bear's grease.

Such was one of our pioneer preachers in the West. To Dr. Power, with Thaddeus Dod and John McMillan, all graduates of Princeton, belongs the honour of firmly establishing the Presbyterian Church in the Western Wilderness. Dr. Power died at an advanced age in 1830.

Isaac Skillman, a native of New Jersey, after graduating, became a Baptist Minister, and in 1773 was chosen pastor of the Second Baptist Church in Boston. Here he remained until 1787, when he returned to New Jersey. In November 1790, he became pastor of the Baptist Church in Salem, New Jersey, where he remained until the close of his life, June 8, 1799. He received the degree of Doctor of Divinity from Rhode Island College in 1774.

Dr. Skillman was a man of learning and ability, but never very popular as a preacher.

Samuel Smith and **William Smith** were probably sons of Samuel Smith, of Burlington, New Jersey, who, in 1765, published his valuable History of New Jersey. I know nothing of them after their graduation.

Alpheus Spring was born in Massachusetts. He became a Congregational Minister, and settled at Eliot, Massachusetts, June 29, 1768. Mr. Spring died suddenly, June 14, 1791. He was much beloved by his people, and highly respected by his brethren in the ministry. Mr. Spring was admitted to a Master's degree at Dartmouth in 1785.

Benjamin Stelle was a son of the Rev. Isaac Stelle, pastor of a Baptist Church at Piscataway, New Jersey. Through the influence of President Manning, of Brown University, he went to Providence, Rhode Island, after leaving college, and established a Latin School. Here he met with encouraging success, giving great satisfaction to his patrons, and being highly esteemed throughout the community. In 1774 Mr. Stelle was admitted to a Master's degree at Rhode Island College.

Micah Townsend came to college from Vermont, to which State he returned after his graduation, and soon became active in public affairs. In 1781 he was appointed Secretary of State, and in 1785 was elected one of the Council of Censors. In 1786, he was again Secretary of State.

John Woodhull was born in Suffolk County, Long Island. He studied theology with the Rev. John Blair, and was licensed by the Presbytery of New Castle in 1768, and commenced his career with much more than ordinary popularity. On one occasion, while preaching as a licentiate, sixty persons were hopefully converted by hearing him preach in a private house. He had many calls, but chose to settle at Leacock, Lancaster County, Pennsylvania, where he was installed August 1, 1770. Mr. Woodhull was a strenuous Whig, and while in this charge advocated the cause so eloquently from the pulpit, that he succeeded in enlisting as soldiers every male member of his congregation capable of bearing arms, he going with them as chaplain. In 1779 he succeeded the Rev. William Tennent at Freehold, New Jersey. During many years of his ministry he conducted a grammar school, and superintended the studies of young men preparing for the ministry. He was a Trustee of the College for forty-four years. Mr. Woodhull received the degree of Doctor of Divinity from Yale in 1798.

Joseph Woodman became a Congregational Minister, and settled at Sanborn Town, New Hampshire, in 1771. He was released from his charge November 13, 1806, and died in Sanborn Town, April 28, 1807.

1767.

Francis Barber, a native of Princeton, New Jersey, after graduating, took charge of an Academy at Elizabethtown, New Jersey. The school soon became distinguished. Alexander Hamilton was prepared for college under Mr. Barber. At the commencement of the Revolution he offered his services to the country, and on the 9th of February, 1776, he was appointed, by the Legislature, Major of the Third Battalion, New Jersey troops, and on November 8th was promoted to the rank of Lieutenant-Colonel of the Third Regiment, and on January 1, 1777, he received his commission from Congress. Soon after this he was appointed Assistant Inspector-General under Baron Steuben.

Colonel Barber was in constant service during the whole war. Although a strict and rigid disciplinarian, always scrupulously performing his own duty, and requiring it from all under his command, yet so bland were his manners, and his whole conduct so tempered with justice and strict propriety, that he was the favourite of all the officers and men, and highly valued by Washington.

Colonel Barber was in many battles. He served in the Northern army under General Schuyler; was at the battles of Trenton, Princeton, Brandywine, Germantown and Monmouth, and in the latter was severely wounded. In 1779 he served as Adjutant-General with General Sullivan in his memorable expedition against the Indians, where he distinguished himself and was again wounded. In 1780 he was conspicuously engaged with the army in New Jersey, and was at the battle of Springfield. In 1781 he accompanied the Jersey line to Virginia, and was at the investment and capture of the British at Yorktown.

The day on which the Commander-in-Chief intended to communicate the joyful intelligence of Peace to the army, a number of the officers, with their families, were invited to dine with him, and among others, Colonel Barber and his wife. He was acting at the time as officer of the day in place of a friend. While on duty, and passing by the edge of a wood where some soldiers were cutting down a tree, it fell on him, and both rider and horse were instantly crushed to death.

Richard Devens. The parents of Mr. Devens resided in Charlestown, Massachusetts, where he was born October 23, 1749. His friends seeing signs of a remarkable intellect in the boy, prevailed upon his parents to give him an education, and he was sent to Princeton. At his graduation he stood at the head of his class. For three years he was engaged in teaching in various schools in New York and New Jersey. In 1770 he was appointed tutor in the College, where he remained until 1774, when in consequence of too close and intense application to his studies, he became insane. I do not discover that he ever recovered his reason. Previous to this he had written "A Paraphrase on some parts of the Book of Job," which gave evidence of a high poetical talent. From the appearance of the manuscript it seems to have been an unfinished work, and written probably for the author's private amusement. It was published by his friends in Boston in 1795, at which time Mr. Devens was still living.

Nathaniel Ramsay, a brother of David Ramsay, the Historian, after graduating, studied law and became eminent in his profession. When the war of the Revolution began, Mr. Ramsay, full of patriotic ardour, joined the Maryland line as a Major, and soon rose to the rank of Colonel. At the battle of Monmouth, when our army was pressed by the enemy advancing rapidly, General Washington asked for an officer; Colonel Ramsay presented himself; the General took him by the hand and said, "If you can stop the British ten minutes, till I can form, you will save my army." Colonel Ramsay answered, "I will stop them or fall." He advanced with his party, engaged and kept them in check for half an hour; nor did he retreat until the enemy and his troops were mingled, and at last, in the rear of his troops, fighting his way, sword in hand, fell pierced with many wounds in the sight of both armies.

From 1785 to 1787 Colonel Ramsay represented Maryland in the Continental Congress. He resumed and continued the practice of law in Baltimore until his death, which occurred, October 24, 1817.

William Schenck was a native of Allentown, New Jersey. He was licensed by the Presbytery of New Brunswick in 1771 and ordained in 1772. After preaching at various places in New York and New Jersey, he was finally settled, in 1780, at Pittsgrove and Cape May, where he remained until 1787, when he removed to Ballston, New York. Towards the close of 1793 he removed to Huntingdon, Long Island, and was installed pastor of the Presbyterian Church, December 27th of that year. In 1817 he left Huntingdon and removed to Franklin, Ohio, where he was pastor for several years, and died September 1, 1822. Mr. Schenck was the grandfather of the Hon. Robert C. Schenck, Minister to Great Britain. He was a dignified, excellent man, though not distinguished as a great or popular preacher. His labours were acceptable, and his church received large accessions under his ministry.

Samuel Whitham Stockton was a brother of the elder Richard Stockton. In 1774 he went to Europe as Secretary of the American Commission to the courts of Austria and Prussia. While abroad he negotiated a treaty with Holland. He returned to New Jersey in 1779, where he held various public offices. In 1794 he was Secretary of State of New Jersey. Mr. Stockton lost his life in being thrown from a carriage in the streets of Trenton, June 27, 1795.

Hugh Vance received his license to preach from Donegal Presbytery about 1771, and in 1772 was ordained and settled as pastor of Tuscarora and Back Creek Churches in Virginia. The only notice that I find of him after this, is in the journal of Rev. William Hill, kept while on a missionary tour soon after his licensure. He records under the date of September 17, 1791, "Visited Mr. Vance, who was upon the borders of the grave in the last stage of consumption." The next day he preached for Mr. Vance to a small audience, and records: "Mr. Vance rode out, and lay in one of the pews while I preached." He died December 31, 1791.

1768.

Robert Blackwell was the son of Jacob Francis Blackwell of Long Island, New York, and descended of an ancient family originally of England. The subject of this notice was born May 6, 1748. After his graduation he entered upon theological studies with a view of entering the ministry of the Church of England, and June 11, 1772, he was ordained a Deacon in the chapel of Fulham Palace, near London, by Bishop Richard Terrick; and subsequently to the order of the priesthood. Returning to the Provinces, he was stationed in the southern part of New Jersey as a missionary of the Society for the Propagation of the Gospel in Foreign Parts; in this capacity officiating at Gloucester and Waterford, and Greenwich. The war of the Revolution of course broke up the operations of the Propagation Society in the Provinces, and most of its missionaries returned to Great Britain. The family of Mr. Blackwell, who were considerable proprietors of land on Long Island, having espoused the cause of the colonies, he naturally did the same. A certificate of General Anthony Wayne, now before us, testifies that he was "Chaplain to the First Pennsylvania Brigade and surgeon to one of the regiments in the year 1778, and that he took and subscribed the oath as directed by Congress, at the Valley Forge, in common with other officers of the line."

In 1781, the Rev. Mr. Coombe, one of the Assistant Ministers of the United Churches of Christ Church and St. Peter's, Philadelphia, having retired to England in 1778, owing to the continuance of the Revolution, Mr. Blackwell was called to his place. He was accordingly, from 1781 till 1811, Senior Assistant Minister, and during the closing years of the War of Independence, one of the only two clergymen of the Church of England, whom the desolations of those times left in the extensive State of Pennsylvania. His friend and ministerial associate of thirty years, the Rev. William White, afterwards Bishop of the Diocese, being the other.

A cenotaph inscription designed for a tablet on the east exterior end of St. Peter's Church, Philadelphia, over the vault of William Bingham, in which Dr. Blackwell with his daughter and several of his descendants is buried, thus speaks of him: "In the Councils of the Church which he assisted to found in these United States, and in the earliest and most important of whose conventions, both General and Diocesan, he was a constant participator, he acquired general respect by his adherence to principle, his temperateness of conduct, and the practical wisdom of all his suggestions.

"In the sphere of Parochial Charge he was distinguished by propriety of life, and by the sincerity of feeling, the clearness of argument and soundness of scholarship, with which in the spirit of charity he inculcated the duties and doctrines of religion. Blessed in his private station with fortune above what is common to his profession, he gave a convincing proof of the effect on his own heart of those precepts which he urged upon others, in an unostentatious but constant and liberal charity towards the poor; from whom his face was never turned away, nor any petitions for relief addressed in vain. He was not more respectable in his public and sacred office, than amiable and engaging in social and domestic life. A fine person and benignant countenance, with a natural sweetness of temper and delicacy of feeling, united to manners refined by early associations, and made liberal by foreign travel, and intercourse with military life and character rendered him eminently agreeable to all."

Dr. Blackwell died February 12, 1831, in his eighty-third year.

1768.

Ephraim Brevard was of Huguenot extraction. After graduating, he returned to his home in North Carolina and studied medicine, and entered upon practice. He is especially distinguished for the part he took in the Mecklenburg Convention, where, beyond question, he was the leading spirit. The evidence is pretty clear that he drafted the Resolutions which have become so noted, as a copy was found in his handwriting among his papers. The papers which he drew up entitled "Instructions for the delegates of Mecklenburg County, proposed to the Consideration of the County," containing seventeen articles, will not suffer in comparison with any political paper of the age. Democratic republican principles are announced in their full extent—complete protection and extensive suffrage. The most remarkable articles are those which assert religious liberty. The merit of Ephraim Brevard is, not that he originated these principles, or was singular in adhering to them, but that he embodied them in so condensed a form, and expressed them so well.

When the British forces invaded the Southern States, Dr. Brevard entered the army as surgeon, and was taken prisoner at the surrender of Charleston, May 12, 1780. His sufferings and the sufferings of those taken prisoners at the same time, were extreme, and had it not been for the tender care of some patriotic women, among whom was the mother of Andrew Jackson, would have been unbearable. As it was multitudes perished, and Ephraim Brevard contracted a wasting fever which soon brought him to his end. He gave "life, fortune, and most sacred honour" in his country's service. The first was sacrificed; the last is imperishable. He died towards the close of 1780.

A British officer was once asked why he plundered the farm and burnt the house of widow Brevard, the mother of Ephraim; the answer was "She has seven sons in the rebel army."

1768.

Pierpont Edwards, a son of President Edwards, studied law, and was for many years distinguished at the Connecticut Bar. At one time he was Judge of the United States Court for the District of Connecticut. From 1787 to 1788 he was a member of the Continental Congress.

Judge Edwards died April 14, 1826.

William Churchill Houston was born in South Carolina. Before his graduation, he had charge of the grammar school of the college. In 1769 he was appointed tutor, and in 1771 he was elected Professor of Mathematics and Natural Philosophy in the college. In 1783 he resigned his Chair, having been previously admitted to the Bar.

Removing to Trenton, he soon acquired a large practice, notwithstanding his rigid adherence to the determination that he would never undertake a cause which he did not believe to be just. Mr. Houston was five times elected to the Continental Congress—the first time in 1779. He was one of the three delegates of New Jersey to the body of Commissioners which met at Annapolis in 1786, which resulted in suggesting the Convention which framed the Constitution of the United States. He was appointed to that Convention, but declining health prevented his attendance. He died at Frankfort, Pennsylvania, in 1788.

Adlai Osborne was a son of Alexander Osborne, a colonel in the Colonial Army. After graduating, Mr. Osborne returned to his home in North Carolina, and was soon appointed Clerk of Rowan County, under Royal rule, and held the same office after the war until 1809. He was a man of fine literary attainments, and an earnest advocate for education. During the Revolution, he served as a colonel in the American Army. Mr. Osborne was one of the original Trustees of the University of North Carolina. He died in 1815.

1768.

Thomas Reese was born in Pennsylvania in 1742. Removing to North Carolina with his parents, when quite young, he was prepared for college by Rev. Joseph Alexander. Returning to South Carolina after his graduation, he studied theology, and was licensed by Orange Presbytery in 1773, and was ordained and installed over Salem Church in the same year. During the years 1780 and 1781, all public worship was suspended, and most of the town and country churches were burned, or made depots for the stores of the enemy. Mr. Reese was thereupon compelled to abandon the field, while many of his congregation were cruelly murdered. After the peace, Mr. Reese pursued his duties with an ardour and diligence rarely exceeded. In 1792 he accepted a call to two churches in Pendleton District, hoping to benefit his health by the change. Mr. Reese received the degree of Doctor of Divinity from Princeton in 1794. Dr. Reese held a conspicuous place among learned and good men. He was an accomplished scholar. His appearance in the pulpit was graceful and dignified, his style flowing and elegant. He was in the habit of writing out his sermons with great care, and seldom, if ever, took the manuscript in the pulpit. His flowing tears and often suppressed voice told the feelings of the heart anxious only for the salvation of souls and the glory of God. As a teacher, he had a peculiar faculty of communicating knowledge, and the happy talent of commanding respect without severity. For a period of five or six years of his life, and that, too, past the meridian, exclusive of his performing the regular duties of a pastor, preaching on the Sabbaths, and lecturing to the coloured part of his congregation, he superintended a small farm, and attended to a large classical school. He died in 1796.

The publications of Dr. Reese are: An Essay on the Influence of Religion in Civil Society, which is preserved in the American Museum. A Sermon on The Death of Christians is Gain, in the "American Preacher," vol. i. A Sermon on the Character of Haman, in the "American Preacher," vol ii. A Farewell Sermon.

1768.

Thomas Smith was licensed by the Presbytery of New Castle about 1772, and ordained and settled as pastor of Middleton and Pecander Churches in Delaware in 1774. He died January 25, 1792.

Isaac Story became a Congregational Minister, and settled at Marblehead, Massachusetts, in 1771. After preaching thirty years, he left the ministry and engaged in secular pursuits. He died in 1816.

Dr. Allen, in his Biographical Dictionary, confounds Mr. Story with his son, Isaac Story, Esq., a young lawyer of Marblehead and a graduate of Harvard, and credits to the father "An Epistle from Yarico to Inkle," which was written by the son. Dr. Sprague perpetuates the error in a note in his invaluable annals.

The publications of Mr. Story are, according to Dr. Allibone: A Discourse, Salem, 1795, 8vo. A Thanksgiving Sermon, 1796, 8vo.

Elias Van Bunschooten received his license to preach in 1773, and settled over the Reformed Dutch Church at Schaghticoke, on the Hudson, where he laboured until 1785, when he resigned. On the 29th of August of the same year he was installed over three churches in Orange County, New York. His parochial charge extended fifty miles, through which the settler's axe had forced a few rough horse tracks. In 1792 he gathered an additional church at the Clove, now Port Jervis, where he resided until 1812, when, on account of the infirmities of age, he withdrew from active duties. He died January 10, 1815. Mr. Van Bunschooten left a large legacy to Rutgers College.

He was in person about six feet in height, erect and stately in his carriage, and was a man of great sternness of character. His manner in the pulpit was earnest and impressive, and his sermons highly evangelical. He preached both in Dutch and English.

1769.

John Beatty, a son of the Rev. Charles Beatty, after studying medicine with Dr. Rush, entered the army as a private soldier, reaching, by degrees, the rank of Lieutenant-Colonel. In 1776 he fell into the hands of the enemy at the capture of Fort Washington, and suffered a long and rigorous imprisonment. In 1779 he succeeded Elias Boudinot as Commissioner-General of prisoners. After the war he settled at Princeton, where he practiced medicine. He was at one time a member of the Legislature of New Jersey, and the Speaker of the Assembly. From 1795 to 1805 he was Secretary of State of New Jersey. In 1783 and 1784 he was a member of the Continental Congress. From May, 1815, until his death, he was President of the Trenton Banking Company. He was also an elder in the Presbyterian Church. Mr. Beatty was President of the Company which built the noble bridge that unites Trenton to his native county in Pennsylvania, and on May 24, 1804, he laid the foundation stone of its first pier. He died April 30, 1826, full of honour.

William Lawrence Blair was a son of the Rev. John Blair, who was at one time the Vice-President of the College, and acting President. He studied law after his graduation, and removed to Kentucky, where we lose sight of him.

Mathias Burnet studied theology with Dr. Witherspoon, and was ordained and installed pastor of the Presbyterian Church at Jamaica, Long Island, by the Presbytery of New York, April, 1775. Here he exercised his ministry during the whole of the Revolutionary war.

Unlike nearly all the Presbyterian clergy of the country, he never declared in favour of our Independence. It was generally understood that his sympathies were with the enemy. Hence, no doubt, it was that while Jamaica was occupied by the British army, he was permitted to exercise his ministerial functions without molestation. He left Jamaica in 1785, and was settled over a Congregational Church in Norwalk, Connecticut; in which year he received the degree of Doctor of Divinity from Yale. He continued in Norwalk until his death, which occurred June 30, 1806. Dr. Burnet was a native of Bottle Hill, New Jersey.

He published an Election Sermon. 1803. And two Sermons, one in the second and the other in the third volume of the "American Preacher." 1791.

William Channing became a distinguished lawyer at Newport, Rhode Island, and was at one time United States District-Attorney for Rhode Island. He was the father of William Ellery Channing the elder. He died in 1793.

John Davenport was the son of the Rev. James Davenport, of Southold, Long Island. He was ordained by the Presbytery of Suffolk, June 4, 1775, and served the Congregation in Southold, Long Island, for two years. On the 12th of August, 1795, he was settled at Deerfield, New Jersey, but resigned in 1805 on account of failing health. He died July 13, 1821.

John Rodgers Davies, a son of President Davies, studied law and practiced in Sussex County, Virginia, but never rose to any eminence. He died in 1836.

Peter Dewitt studied theology under Dr. Livingston, and was licensed by the General Meeting of Ministers and Elders of the Reformed Dutch Church in 1778. From 1787 to 1798, he was pastor of the Reformed Dutch Churches of Rhinebeck, Rhinebeck Flats, and upper Red

Hook, New York, and from 1799 to 1809, he was pastor of the churches of Ponds and Wyckoff, Bergen County, New Jersey. He died in 1809.

John Henry represented Maryland in the Continental Congress from 1778 to 1781, and again from 1784 to 1787. In 1789 he was elected to the first Senate of the United States under the Constitution. He had as fellow members two other graduates of Princeton—Oliver Ellsworth, of Connecticut, and William Paterson, of New Jersey. In 1797 Mr. Henry resigned his seat in the Senate, having been elected Governor of Maryland. He died in December, 1798.

James Linn represented the State of New Jersey in Congress from 1799 to 1801, when he was appointed, by Mr. Jefferson, Supervisor of the Revenue. Mr. Linn was also for many years, Secretary of State of New Jersey. He died December 28, 1820.

Thomas Melville was the son of Allan Melville, a merchant of Boston. Immediately after his graduation, he visited his relatives in Scotland, and during that visit he was presented with the freedom of the city of St. Andrews and of Renfrew. He returned to America in 1773, when he entered into mercantile life in Boston. In December of that year he was one of the famous "Tea Party." Mr. Melville took an active part in the Revolutionary war, and as Major in Craft's regiment of Massachusetts Artillery, was in the action in Rhode Island in 1776. Commissioned by Washington in 1789 as Naval Officer of the Port of Boston, he was continued by all the Presidents down to Jackson's time in 1829. To the time of his death he continued to wear the antiquated three-cornered hat, and from this habit was familiarly known in Boston, as the last of the Cocked Hats.

There is still preserved a small parcel of the veritable tea, in the attack upon which he took an active part.

This historic tea was found in his shoes the morning after he returned from his expedition, and was sealed up in a vial, and was at one time in possession of Chief Justice Shaw, of Massachusetts. Mr. Melville died in 1832.

Samuel Niles, a brother of Nathaniel Niles, of the class of 1766, was born at Braintree, Massachusetts, December 14, 1743. Mr. Niles studied theology with Dr. Bellamy, and was licensed to preach November 7, 1770. He first supplied a church at Abington, Massachusetts, then preached in Boston for a short time, and then returned to Abington, and was installed September 25, 1771. Mr. Niles continued to preach here until 1811, when he suffered a paralytic shock and was laid aside from work. He died January 16, 1814.

Mr. Niles was endowed with superior intellectual and reasoning powers. He had a clear and profound knowledge of the truth, connection, harmony, and consistency of the first principles and essential doctrines of Christianity, and on this account became a most powerful and instructive preacher. His grave and dignified appearance in the pulpit, in connection with his truly genuine eloquence, could hardly fail to strike his audience with awe and reverence, and to render him one of the most popular preachers of his day. He was intimately acquainted with human nature, and could render himself agreeable in common intercourse with all classes of people; but he was more especially entertaining in private circles, by the flashes of his wit, and his curious, amusing, striking and pertinent anecdotes.

The publications of Mr. Niles are, Remarks on a Sermon by John Reid. 1813. A Sermon on the Death of Washington. 1800. A Sermon before the Massachusetts Missionary Society. 1801.

Samuel Stanhope Smith, a son of Rev. Robert Smith, a distinguished clergyman of the Presbyterian Church, was born in Lancaster County, Pennsylvania, March 16, 1750. After leaving college, he returned to his father's house, assisting him in a school, and giving special attention to Belles-Lettres, and Moral and Intellectual Philosophy. In 1770, he was appointed tutor at Princeton, where he remained three years. In 1773, he was licensed by the Presbytery of New Castle. Feeling the need of a change of climate, he went as a missionary to Virginia, where he soon became a universal favourite; persons without distinction of sect or of rank flocked to hear him. Some of his most influential and wealthy friends resolved to retain him in Virginia and place him at the head of a literary institution. Accordingly funds were soon collected, and the buildings were erected in Prince Edward County, and a Charter obtained under the name of Hampden Sidney College. While all this was going on, Mr. Smith was laboriously engaged in his missionary work. After a little time, having married the daughter of Dr. Witherspoon, he took his place at the head of the college. In 1779, he was invited to the Chair of Moral Philosophy at Princeton, which he accepted. On arriving at Princeton, he found the affairs of the college in a deplorable condition, occasioned by the war, and the occupation of Dr. Witherspoon in the higher affairs of the nation. Mainly by the energy, wisdom and self-devotion of Mr. Smith, the college was speedily re-organized, and its usual exercises resumed. In 1782, his life was seriously threatened by hemorrhage from the lungs; but he gradually recovered his usual health. In 1783, he received the honorary degree of Doctor of Divinity from Yale, and in 1810, the degree of Doctor of Laws from Harvard.

In 1794, Dr. Witherspoon died, and Dr. Smith succeeded him in the Presidential Chair. Dr. A. Alexander who saw him about this time, said, "I have never seen his equal in elegance of person and manners. Dignity and winning grace were remarkably united in his expressive countenance. His large blue eyes had a penetration which commanded the respect of all beholders. Notwithstanding the want of health, his cheek had a bright rosy tint, and his smile lighted up the whole face. The tones of his elocution had a thrilling peculiarity, and this was more remarkable in his preaching, where it is well known that he imitated the elaborate polish and oratorical glow of the French school. Little of this impression can be derived from his published discourses, which disappoint those who do not know the charm of his delivery."

His reputation as a pulpit orator at this time was very great. Visitors from Philadelphia and New York were accustomed to go to Princeton to hear his Baccalaureate Discourses, which were always of the highest order. In 1802, when the institution was at the full-tide of its prosperity, the college edifice was destroyed by fire, with the libraries, furniture, etc. Dr. Smith assumed the labour of collecting money to rebuild ; and he was successful in raising during the year, about $100,000 from the Southern States, and much from other parts of the Union. This was his crowning achievement. In 1812, through repeated strokes of palsy, he became too much enfeebled to discharge the duties of his office, and at the Commencement he sent in to the Trustees his resignation.

He died August 21, 1819, in the utmost tranquillity, in the seventieth year of his age.

The publications of Dr. Smith are : An Essay on the Causes of the Variety of Complexion and Figure of the Human Species ; to which are added Strictures on Lord Kaime's Discourse on the Original Diversity of Mankind, 1 vol. 8vo, 1787. A Volume of Sermons, 8vo, 1799. Lectures on the Evidences of the Christian Religion, 12mo, 1809 Lectures on Moral and Political Philosophy, 12mo, 1812. A Comprehensive View of the Leading and Most Important Principles of Natural and Revealed Religion, 8vo, 1816. Sermons, to which is prefixed a Memoir of his Life and Writings, 2 vols. 8vo, 1821. A Funeral Sermon on the death of Richard Stockton, 1781. A Sermon on Slander, preached in Brattle Street Church, Boston, 1790. A Discourse on the Nature and Danger of Small Faults, delivered in the Old South Church, Boston, 1790. Oratio Inauguralis, 1794. A Discourse on the Nature and Reasonableness of Fasting, and on Existing Causes that call us to that duty, 1795. The Divine Goodness to the United States of America ; a discourse delivered on a day of general Thanksgiving and Prayer, 1795. A Discourse delivered on the death of Gilbert Tennent Snowden, 1797. An Oration upon the death of General George Washington, 1800. A Discourse upon the Nature, the Proper Subjects, and the Benefits of Baptism, with a brief Appendix on the Mode of Administering the Ordinance, 1808. The Resurrection of the Body; A Discourse delivered in the Presbyterian Church in Georgetown, D. C., 1809. On the Love of Praise; A Sermon delivered the Sunday preceding the Commencement, 1810.

Elihu Thayer was born in Massachusetts. After leaving college, he engaged for some time in teaching. Turning his attention to the ministry he was licensed, and supplied a church in Newburyport, Massachusetts, for some time. On the 18th of December, 1776, he was ordained as pastor over the Congregational Church in Kingston, New Hampshire.

In 1801, he was elected President of the New Hampshire Missionary Society. Mr. Thayer suffered all his life from ill-health. He was not only an excellent scholar in college, but he retained his relish for classical learning to the close of life. He received the degree of Doctor of Divinity from Dartmouth in 1807. He died April 3, 1812.

A volume of Dr. Thayer's Sermons was published in 1813.

David Zubley. It is probable that Mr. Zubley was a son of Rev. J. J. Zubley who was so conspicuous in Georgia at the opening of the Revolution, as I can find no traces of any other family of that name in the Colonies at that period.

In 1775, David Zubley was a lawyer in Georgia, and was a Representative in the Provincial Congress of that State. He was also a member of the Committee of Intelligence appointed by that body. On the 14th of July, 1775, he, as one of that Committee, signed a stirring petition to the King in favour of the rights of the people. As Mr. Zubley's name does not appear after 1776, it is probable that he sympathised with his father, and gave in his adherence to the king. He probably left the colonies.

1770.

Samuel Baldwin was a native of New Jersey. After graduating he emigrated to South Carolina, and opened a school in Charleston. But the Revolution coming on, he took up arms during the attack of the British upon that city. After its capture he was a prisoner in the hands of the enemy. Refusing to take the oath of allegiance, he was obliged to retire into the country. After the war, Mr. Baldwin returned to Newark, New Jersey, his native city, where he died at an advanced age in 1850.

Fredrick Frelinghuysen was a son of the Rev. John F. Frelinghuysen of New Jersey. He was sent as a delegate to the Continental Congress in 1775, from New Jersey when but twenty-two years of age. He resigned in 1777. He was a warm and active patriot. He entered the Revolutionary army as captain of a corps of artillery, and was at the battles of Trenton and Monmouth. He was afterwards engaged actively as a colonel of the militia of his native state. He also served in the Western Expedition as Major-General of the New Jersey and Pennsylvania troops. In 1793 he was elected to the Senate of the United States, and continued in that station until domestic bereavements, and the claims of his family, constrained him to resign in 1796. General Frelinghuysen stood also among the first at the Bar of New Jersey. He was the father of the Hon. Theodore Frelinghuysen. He died April 13, 1804, beloved and lamented by his country and friends, leaving for his children the rich legacy of a life unsullied by a stain, and that had abounded in benevolence and usefulness. General Frelinghuysen was a Trustee of the college from 1802 until his death.

Joshua Hart received ordination from the Presbytery of Suffolk, April 2, 1772; and was installed pastor of the Presbyterian Church at Smithtown, Long Island, April 13, 1774. In the time of the war, being an ardent patriot, he suffered much from imprisonment by the British in the City of New York. He was dismissed from his charge September 6, 1787. Mr. Hart was never again settled, but continued to labour as he had opportunity until his death, which occurred October 3, 1829, at the advanced age of 91.

Azariah Horton was the son of Rev. Azariah Horton, of South Hanover (Madison,) New Jersey. In his will his father gave to him his "whole library of books and pamphlets, except Flavel's works, Henry's and Dickinson's, and several hereinafter named. My two walking canes, and a silver spoon marked I. T. M;" "and my further wish is that my negro wench Phillis, and her two sons Pompey and Pizarro, be sold, the money arising from the sale to be equally divided between my wife and son Foster, and daughter Hannah." Azariah received no share of the sale of the negroes.

After graduating, Mr. Horton entered the American army, and is said to have been killed in battle.

Nathaniel Irwin a native of Chester County, Pennsylvania, was licensed by the Presbytery of New Castle in 1773, and preached awhile at Neshaminy, Pennsylvania. On November 3, 1774, he was ordained and installed as the pastor. Here he continued until his death. As a preacher he attained a high rank. He was clear, forcible, fluent, and often deeply pathetic. Mr. Irwin was accustomed to ride to church on his "mare Dobbin," and was in the habit of "letting her have her head," as he called it—that is, letting the rein lie loose upon her neck;

and she went slowly along while he prepared his sermon. Mr. Irwin was probably the most thoroughly scientific man of his day, in the county in which he lived; and he took pleasure in making his knowledge practical and useful. He was the first man who took John Fitch (of steamboat memory), by the hand, and encouraged him in his scientific investigations. Mr. Irwin was very tall, and had a voice, the sound of which, produced alarm on a first hearing. He seemed to utter everything with the greatest sound he could command. Mr. Irwin left in his will one share of the stock of the Bank of Pennsylvania, to the Trustees of the College, the interest to be devoted to the best orator belonging to the Whig Society. He died March 3, 1812.

Thomas McPherrin received license to preach from the Presbytery of Donegal in 1773, and was ordained and settled as pastor of two churches in Pennsylvania in 1775. He remained in this charge until his death, February 4, 1802.

John Cosins Ogden. For fifteen years after his graduation Mr. Ogden resided in New Haven. Having been ordained by Bishop Seabury, in 1786, he became Rector of an Episcopal Church in Portsmouth, New Hampshire, where he remained until 1793, when his mind becoming deranged he gave up his charge. He died in Chestertown, Maryland, in 1800. Mr. Ogden was a native of New Jersey.

Mr. Ogden published an Election Sermon, 1790. A Masonic Sermon. Letters. An Address. An Excursion into Bethlehem and Nazareth, Pennsylvania, in the year 1799, with a succinct History of the Society of United Brethren, commonly called Moravians, Philadelphia, 1800.

Nathan Perkins was born in Norwich, Connecticut, and was licensed to preach by the London Association, Connecticut. After preaching in various places, he was installed as pastor at West Hartford, October 14, 1772.

Here he laboured with great diligence and fidelity for sixty-six years. During his ministry he preached ten thousand sermons, and assisted more than one hundred and fifty students in their preparation for college. He had under his care, at different times, more than thirty theological students. In 1801 Princeton conferred upon him the degree of Doctor of Divinity.

Dr. Perkins was a man of highly respectable talents, good common sense, and uncommon prudence. He was kind, affectionate, and cheerful in his social and domestic relations, and a solemn, persuasive and affectionate preacher. He died January 18, 1838.

In 1795, he published Twenty-four Discourses on some of the important and interesting truths, duties, and institutions of the Gospel, and the general excellency of the Christian Religion ; calculated for the people of God of every communion, particularly for the benefit of pious families, and the instruction of all in the things which concern their salvation, 1 vol., 8vo. Three Sermons in the American Preacher, vol. iii., iv., 1793, 1794. Four Letters, showing the History and Origin of the Anabaptists, 1793. A Discourse at the ordination of Calvin Chapin, 1794. Two Discourses on the Grounds of the Christian Hope, 1800. A Sermon at the ordination of Elihu Mason, 1810. A Sermon at the interment of Rev. Timothy Pitkin, 1812. A Sermon on the State Fast, 1812. A Sermon at the interment of the Rev. Nathan Strong, D.D., 1816. A Half Century Sermon, 1822.

Caleb Russell after graduating studied law, and was admitted an Attorney of the Supreme Court of New Jersey, at the September Term, 1784. He died in 1805.

Isaac Smith studied theology, and settled as pastor of a Congregational Church at Gilmantown, New Hampshire, November 30, 1774. He died in 1817.

John Smith was a native of Plainfield, Connecticut. He became a Congregational minister, and on the 22d of April, 1772, was settled at Dighton, Massachusetts. In 1802, he became a Missionary in the neighbourhood of Canandaigua, New York. He gave a deed of six thousand acres of land to form a seminary of learning in Canandaigua. Afterwards, Mr. Smith removed to Lycoming

County, Pennsylvania, where he remained till 1812, when he removed to Nelson County, Kentucky, acting as a Missionary in both places. He died in Kentucky in 1820. Mr. Smith was the grandfather of Professor Henry B. Smith of the Union Theological Seminary, New York.

Stephen Tracy was a native of Norwich, Connecticut. He was ordained in April, 1773, and settled as pastor of the Congregational Church in Peru, Massachusetts, where he remained until October 8, 1815, when he was released from his charge. Mr. Tracy died May 14, 1825.

Caleb Wallace on leaving college studied theology, and was licensed by the Presbytery of New Brunswick, April 3, 1774, and was ordained by the Presbytery of Hanover, and installed pastor of Cub Creek and Falling River Churches, Virginia. In 1779, he resigned his charge, and in 1783 emigrated to Kentucky.

Abandoning the ministry, he entered the profession of the law, in which he was successful, and became Judge of the Supreme Court of Kentucky. Mr. Wallace was a native of Virginia.

Mathias Williamson was a native of Elizabethtown, New Jersey. After graduating, he studied law, and was admitted to the Bar in November, 1774; but the war commencing, he became an officer in the Commissary department. He died in Elizabethtown in 1836, aged 84.

James Wilson received his license to preach from the Presbytery of New Castle in 1771, and was ordained in 1773. Mr. Wilson probably died soon after, as his name disappears from the roll of Synod.

James Witherspoon, a son of President Witherspoon, was a young man of great promise. He joined the American army as aid to General Nash, and was killed at the battle of Germantown, October 4, 1777.

1771.

Gunning Bedford became a lawyer, and soon rose to eminence in Delaware, his native State. In 1785 and 1786 he was a member of the Continental Congress; and in 1787 was a member of the Convention which formed the Constitution of the United States.

While a student in college, Mr. Bedford married Miss Jane B. Parker, one of the most elegant and accomplished women of her times, who brought her first-born child to Princeton, leaving it in the care of Mrs. President Witherspoon, while she went to the church to hear her young husband's valedictory address at Commencement. Mr. Bedford was a personal friend of Washington, Franklin and other master spirits of the Revolution. In 1796, he was elected Governor of Delaware, and soon after was the first appointee of Washington to the United States District Court of Delaware, which position he held with distinguished honour until his death in March, 1812.

The house of Mr. Bedford was the resort of the wit, fashion and talent of the state and country. Distinguished jurists, statesmen, clergymen and civilians were guests at his fireside. Mr. Bedford was a consistent Christian, and for many years an Elder in the Presbyterian Church.

John Black, a South Carolinian by birth, was licensed by Donegal Presbytery, October 14, 1773, and was ordained and installed pastor of the Presbyterian Church of Upper Marsh Creek, York County, Pennsylvania, August 15, 1775. On the 10th of April, 1794, he was released from his charge, but continued to preach in various places without any regular settlement. Mr.

Black possessed a high order of talent, and was especially fond of philosophical disquisitions. He died August 6, 1802, in the exercise of a triumphant faith.

He published, A Discourse on Psalmody, in reply to Rev. Dr. John Anderson of the Associate Church.

Hugh Henry Brackenridge came to this country from Scotland when quite young. He supported himself while in the higher classes in college, by teaching the lower classes. In conjunction with his class-mate Philip Freneau, he wrote a poem in dialogue, between Acasto and Eugenio, on the Rising Glory of America, which he delivered at Commencement, and which was published the next year in Philadelphia. After graduation, he remained two years as a tutor, pursuing at the same time the study of theology. Mr. Brackenridge was licensed to preach by the Presbytery of Philadelphia in 1777, but resigned his license a few months afterwards. For several years after leaving the college, he taught school in Maryland, but in 1776 he went to Philadelphia, and supported himself by editing the United States Magazine. An anecdote of this time is related by his son. On several occasions the Magazine contained strictures on the celebrated General Lee, in regard to his conduct to Washington. On a certain day, Lee called at the office of Mr. Brackenridge with two of his aids, with the intention of assaulting the editor. Knocking at the door, Mr. Brackenridge from an upper window inquired what was wanting. "Come down," said Lee, "and I will give you as good a horse-whipping as any rascal ever received." "Excuse me, General," said the other, "I would not go down for two such favours."

Mr. Brackenridge was in the habit of making political harangues to the army, six of which were published at the time in a pamphlet, which had a large circulation.

In 1781, Mr. Brackenridge established himself at Pittsburg, from which city he was sent to the Legislature. He was closely associated with Albert Gallatin during the Whisky Insurrection, and when that affair was over, he published, "Incidents of the Insurrection in the Western parts of Pennsylvania, 1794."

In 1786, Mr. Brackenridge published "Modern Chivalry; or, The Adventures of Captain Farrago and Teague O'Reagan, his servant." After an interval of ten years he published the second part. The whole, with his last corrections, was published in Pittsburg in 1819. This political satire gave him great renown among the frontier men.

In 1789, Mr. Brackenridge was appointed Judge of the Supreme Court of Pennsylvania. A few years before his death, he removed to Carlisle, where he died June 25, 1816.

Few men have combined a greater variety of brilliant qualities. He was a man of decided talents, with a commanding person, an eagle eye, highly popular manners, and a mind richly stored with various learning. He had a profound knowledge of men, possessed great address, could reason clearly, and make the blood run cold by touches of genuine eloquence. His wit was rather delicate irony than broad humour, and always employed as the means of conveying some important truth, or correcting something wrong.

Besides the publications already noted, Judge Brackenridge wrote "A Eulogium on the Brave Men who fell in the Contest with Great Britain, 1779." "Gazette Publications Collected, 1806." "Laws of Miscellanies, containing instructions for the study of the law, 1814."

Donald Campbell joined the American army from New York, and rose to the rank of colonel in the regular Continental line. He served during the whole war.

Philip Freneau was born in the City of New York, on the second of January, 1752, being descended from a French Protestant family. He began to write verses very early, but it was while residing in New York in 1774 and 1775, that he published those poetical satires on the royalists and their cause, which have transmitted his name to posterity.

In 1776, he visited the Danish West Indies, where he wrote several of his best poems. Two years later he was at Bermuda; and in 1779 was in Philadelphia, superintending the publication of the United States Magazine. In 1780, he sailed in the "Aurora" for St. Eustatia, but was captured in sight of Cape Henlopen by the British frigate Iris, and carried to New York and confined in a prison-ship, from which he eventually escaped. He subsequently became a sea captain, and made many voyages between 1784 and 1789, and 1798 and 1809. In 1790, he was editor of the Daily Advertiser in New York; and in 1791 was appointed by Mr. Jefferson "interpreter of the French Language for the Department of State."

In 1795, he set up his own press at Mount Pleasant, Monmouth County, New Jersey, and commenced the publication of his "New Jersey Chronicle," which he continued about a year. In 1797, he started in New York "The Time-Piece and Literary Companion." It was published three times a week, in a neat folio form. In 1798, Freneau's name disappears from the paper.

Mr. Freneau's end was sad; he was found dead about two miles from his house in New Jersey, having perished in a snow-storm. His death occurred December 18, 1832, in the eightieth year of his age.

The first collection of Mr. Freneau's Poems was published in Philadelphia, in 1786. In 1795, a second edition appeared, and a third in 1809. A collection of poems connected with the war of 1812 and other subjects, in 2 vols., was published in New York.

Dr. Francis, of New York, in relating his reminiscences of Freneau, remarks, "His story of many of his occasional poems was quite romantic. I told him what I heard Jeffrey, the Scotch Reviewer, say of his writings—that the time would arrive when his poetry, like that of Hudibras, would command a commentator like Grey."

Charles McKnight, a son of the Rev. Charles McKnight, was born in Cranberry, New Jersey, October 10, 1750. After graduating, he studied medicine with

Dr. William Shippen, of Philadelphia, of the class of 1754, and entered the army as a surgeon, where his abilities soon attracted the attention of the Commander-in-Chief, and procured his appointment to the office of Senior Surgeon of the Flying Hospital of the Middle Department, in April, 1777. He was with the main army in all its movements, and the duties of his office he performed with signal ability. For some months in 1780 he acted as Surgeon-General; and from October 1, 1780 to January 1, 1782, as Surgeon-General of the Middle Department. His talent, his zeal, his devotion to duty and his ardent patriotism rendered him conspicuous among the heroes of the Revolution. At the close of the war he settled in New York city, and became Professor of Anatomy and Surgery in Columbia College, where he delivered lectures on these two branches of medical science, and where he enjoyed the reputation of being the most eminent surgeon of his day. Dr. McKnight died November 16, 1791.

James Madison, the son of James Madison, of Orange County, Virginia, was born March 5, 1751. Dr. Witherspoon remarked to Jefferson, in reference to Madison, that in his whole course in college, he had never known him do or say an indiscreet thing. While in college he was a laborious student, during a part of the course allowing himself but three hours out of the twenty-four for sleep. The state of opinion in the college in regard to the oppression of the colonies by Great Britain, may be learned from an extract of a letter from Madison to Thomas Martin, his former tutor, and himself a graduate of the class of 1762: "We have no public news but the base conduct of the merchants of New York in breaking through their spirited resolution not to import. Their letter to the merchants in Philadelphia, requesting their concurrence, was lately burned by the students of this place in the college yard, all of them appearing in their black gowns, and the bell tolling. . . . . There are about an hundred and fifteen in the college and in the grammar school, all of them in American cloth."

After graduating, Mr. Madison spent about a year at Princeton, studying Hebrew with Dr. Witherspoon. On his return to his home, he applied himself to the study of theology and kindred sciences, and few have gone through more laborious and extensive inquiries to arrive at the truth.

Mr. Madison entered upon public life in May, 1776, as a member of the Convention of Virginia which formed the first Constitution, and which instructed its delegates in Congress to prepare the Declaration of Independence. In October, 1776, he was elected to the Virginia House of Delegates. On December 14, 1779 he was appointed a member of the Continental Congress, in which, although the youngest member, he immediately took a prominent position. In 1784 he was a member of the House of Delegates of Virginia, and stood the peer of such men as Patrick Henry and Henry Lee, and was the author of the resolutions inviting the other States to meet in Convention to form the Constitution of the United States. Mr. Madison took a conspicuous and distinguished part in the deliberations of that body, and was the chief framer of what was called the Virginia Plan, which in its substantial features forms our present Constitution. After the adjournment of the Convention, he contributed by his pen to the adoption of the Constitution, and his articles in the *Federalist* place him among the foremost statesmen of the world. Mr. Madison was a member of the Federal Congress through the whole of Washington's administration. In 1799 he was again a member of the Virginia House of Delegates; and in 1801 was appointed by Mr. Jefferson Secretary of State, which position he held until 1809.

So successful had Mr. Madison been in the conduct of foreign affairs, that the eyes of the nation were turned to him as the next President, to which elevated position he was elected by an overwhelming vote. In 1817, having served two terms as President, he retired into private life. In 1826 he succeeded Mr. Jefferson as Rector of the University of Virginia, and in 1829 became a member of the Constitutional Convention of Virginia, his last public appearance.

Mr. Madison held a high and honourable and unstained character, and his memory is venerated. Shortly before his death he penned these sentences of advice to his countrymen: "The advice nearest to my heart and dearest to my convictions is, that the Union of the States be cherished and perpetuated. Let the avowed enemy to it be regarded as a Pandora with her box opened, and the disguised one as a serpent, creeping with deadly wiles into Paradise."

Mr. Madison died June 28, 1836, aged 85.

The publications of Mr. Madison consist of twenty-nine numbers of the Federalist, and other political papers. Notes on the Debates in the Convention to frame the Federal Constitution, published in 1840. A quarto volume of Correspondence, printed for private circulation.

There are enough of his unpublished manuscripts extant to fill twelve octavo volumes.

Samuel Spring was born in Massachusetts. One interesting fact is related of him while in college. He was called upon on a certain occasion to explain and defend the Copernican System in the presence of the class; when after proceeding awhile, he became overwhelmed with a sense of the Divine Majesty, and burst into tears; he was unable to proceed. In 1774 Mr. Spring was licensed to preach, and immediately joined the Continental army as a chaplain, and was in the severe campaign to Canada under Arnold. At the close of the year 1776, he left the army and began preaching at Newburyport, Massachusetts, where he was ordained and installed August 6, 1777. He remained at Newburyport until his death, March 4, 1819. The honorary degree of Doctor of Divinity was conferred upon him in 1806 by Princeton.

Dr. Spring was powerful in the pulpit, and in the fervency, and simplicity of his prayers excelled most ministers. As a preacher he was remarkable for a clear and forcible illustration of divine truth. His written sermons were prepared with care and labour, and were always weighty and instructive. But his extemporaneous preaching was far more striking and powerful. It was here that he showed his superior strength to the best advantage. Few ministers enjoy as fully as he did the confidence, the attachment, and the veneration of his people; and few exert so salutary and lasting an influence. Dr. Spring was the father of the Rev. Gardiner Spring, D.D., of New York.

The publications of Dr. Spring are, A Thanksgiving Sermon. 1777. A Sermon on the Importance of Sinners coming immediately to Christ. 1780. A Sermon on the Ordination of Benjamin Bell. 1784. A Thanksgiving Discourse. 1798. A Sermon on the Death of Washington. 1799. A Sermon before the Massachusetts Missionary Society. 1802. A Discourse in consequence of the late Duel. 1804. A Sermon at the Ordination of Charles Coffin, Jr. 1804. Two Discourses on Christ's Self-existence. 1805. A Sermon at the Ordination of Samuel Walker. 1805. An Address before the Merrimac Humane Society. 1807. A Sermon on the Death of Deacon Thomas Thompson. 1808. Two Sermons delivered on Fast Day. 1809. A Letter addressed to the Rev. Solomon Aikin, on the Subject of the Preceding Sermons. 1809. A Sermon at the Inauguration of the Rev. Dr. Grffin, as Professor at the Andover Theological Seminary. 1809. A Sermon at the Interment of the Rev. Samuel Noyes. 1810. A Sermon on the United Agency of God and Man in Salvation. 1817. A Sermon before the American Board of Commissioners for Foreign Missions. 1818. A Sermon before the Howard Benevolent Society. 1818.

1772.

Isaac Alexander, one of the Mechlenburg family of Alexanders, after graduating, returned to North Carolina and entered upon the study of medicine. In 1777 an Isaac Alexander was the President of Liberty Hall Academy in North Carolina. I am not certain that this is our graduate, although it is likely from the fact, that twelve out of the sixteen Trustees, were graduates of Princeton.

For many years he was an Elder in the Sugar Creek Presbyterian Church.

Moses Allen was born in Northampton, Massachusetts. He was licensed by the Presbytery of New Brunswick, February 1, 1774. On March 10, 1775, he was ordained near Charleston, South Carolina, and installed as pastor of an Independent Church at Wappetaw. In 1777 he resigned his charge and removed to Liberty County, Georgia, where he took charge of the Midway Presbyterian Church; but the next year his congregation was dispersed and his church burned. He therefore entered the army as chaplain, and at the capture of Savannah was taken prisoner, and being obnoxious to the enemy, on account of his patriotic exhortations from the pulpit and his animated exertions in the field, he was confined closely in a prison-ship. Wearied with his confinement for weeks in that loathsome place, he determined to escape by swimming, but was drowned in the attempt on the night of February 8, 1779. Mr. Allen, notwithstanding his clerical function, appeared among the foremost in the day of battle, and on all occasions sought the post of danger as the post of honour.

The friends of independence admired him for his popular talents, his courage and his many virtues. He was an eminently pious man.

Robert Archibald. Of the early life of Mr. Archibald, little is known. After leaving Princeton, he studied medicine and afterwards theology, and was licensed by the Presbytery of Orange in the autumn of 1775. He was ordained and installed pastor of Rocky River Presbyterian Church, North Carolina, October 7, 1778, and continued to hold this office till he was brought into difficulties for preaching erroneous doctrines, about the year 1792, for which, in 1794, he was suspended from the work of the ministry, and, in 1797, was solemnly deposed.

Mr. Archibald was a man of talent, of an amiable disposition, and considered a good classical scholar; but was careless in his manners and extremely negligent in his dress and general appearance. Some domestic afflictions, fancied or real, preyed upon his spirits, and were the occasion of indulgence, to an unwarrantable degree, in intoxicating drinks.

Mr. Archibald never returned to the communion of his church, nor retracted the errors for which he was deposed.

William Bradford, a grandson of William Bradford, the celebrated printer of Philadelphia, and son of Colonel William Bradford of the Revolutionary Army, was born in Philadelphia, September 14, 1755. He remained a year in Princeton after graduating, studying theology with Dr. Witherspoon. On returning to his home, he read law in the office of Edward Shippen; but the Revolution commencing, he joined the army, and rose to the rank of Colonel, but declining health induced him to resign his commission in April, 1779.

Returning to the study of the law, he was admitted to the Bar in the same year, and settled in Yorktown, Pennsylvania. His marked ability soon attracted attention, and in 1780, when but twenty-three years of age, he was appointed Attorney-General of the State. He held this position for eleven years, and on the 22d of August, 1791, was elevated to the Supreme Bench of Pennsylvania. This office he held until 1794, when he was appointed by Washington Attorney-General of the United States, in which office he remained until his death, which occurred August 23, 1795, at Rose Hill, near Philadelphia. Judge Bradford married a daughter of Elias Boudinot in 1782. His death was occasioned by a bilious fever contracted by exposure in the discharge of his duties.

He advanced with a rapid progress to an eminence of reputation which never was defaced by petty artifices of practice or ignoble associations of thought. His course was lofty, as his mind was pure; his eloquence was of the best kind; his language was uniformly classical. His style was modelled upon that of the best English writers. His splendid abilities, his great integrity, his clear judgment, his persuasive eloquence, his ardent patriotism, were crowned with the graces of the Christian character.

The publications of Mr. Bradford are: An Enquiry how far the Punishment of Death is necessary in Pennsylvania, with an Account of the Penitentiary House of Philadelphia, 1795. In the earlier periods of his life he was not unacquainted with the walks of poetry, and some of his poetical productions, in imitation of Shenstone, were published in the Philadelphia magazines.

Aaron Burr was the son of President Burr, and the grandson of President Edwards. In 1775 he joined the army at Cambridge, and accompanied Arnold in his expedition against Quebec. In 1779, with the rank of Lieutenant-Colonel, he retired from military life. In 1782 he commenced the practice of law at Albany, but soon removed to New York City. From 1791 to 1797 he was a member of the Senate of the United States. He and Jefferson had each seventy-three votes for President of the United States in 1800. On the thirty-sixth ballot in the House of Representatives, Jefferson was elected, and Burr became Vice-President. On the 12th of July, 1804, he mortally wounded Alexander Hamilton in a duel. In 1807 Mr. Burr was arrested for High Treason, and was tried in Richmond and acquitted. Luther Martin, of the class of 1766, a personal friend, was one of his counsel.

The remainder of Mr. Burr's life was passed in New York in obscurity and neglect. He died September 14, 1836, and was buried at Princeton, near the grave of his father.

John Debow received his license from the Presbytery of New Brunswick in 1773, and soon after removed to North Carolina, where he was ordained and installed pastor of a Presbyterian Church at Hawfields in 1776. Here he remained until his death, which occurred September 17, 1782. Mr. Debow was successful in his ministry, and a goodly number were added to the church.

Joseph Eckley was born in the city of London. He was licensed by the Presbytery of New York May 7, 1776. In 1779 he was ordained pastor of the Old South Church, Boston, where he remained until his death in April, 1811. His Alma Mater conferred upon him the degree of Doctor of Divinity about 1787. Dr. Eckley had a high standing in the community as a preacher, although he was inclined to abstraction. In person, he was about the medium stature and size. His countenance was a pleasing one, though his features were not remarkably delicate. His hair was turned back on his forehead, over the head to the neck, and arranged in "cannon curls" (the hair twisted around wire), according to the custom of the day.

Dr. Eckley published, Divine Glory brought to View in the Condemnation of the Ungodly; by a friend of the truth, 1782. A Sermon at the installation of the Rev. Israel Evans, at Concord, 1789. Artillery Election Sermon, 1792. A Discourse on the Annual Thanksgiving, 1798. A Sermon before the Boston Female Asylum, 1802. A Discourse before the Society for Propagating the Gospel, 1805. Dudleian Lecture at Harvard University, 1806. A Sermon at the installation of Rev. Horace Holley, Boston, 1809.

Israel Evans. The father and grandfather of Mr. Evans were settled ministers in this country, and his great-grandfather was a minister in Wales. Mr. Evans was ordained by the First Presbytery of Philadelphia in 1776, and immediately entered upon his duties as Chaplain in the American Army. From 1777 till the close of the war, he was Chaplain to the New Hampshire Brigade, and by means of this connection, he was introduced to the Church in Concord, New Hampshire, of which he became pastor July 1, 1789, his classmate, Joseph Eckley, preaching his installation sermon. He resigned this charge in July, 1797, but continued to reside in Concord, where he died March 9, 1807.

The publications of Mr. Evans are: Oration delivered at Hackensack, New Jersey, at the interment of Brigadier-General Enoc Poor, 1780. A Sermon delivered near York, Virginia, on the memorable occasion of the Surrender of the British Army, etc., 1781. A Sermon delivered in New York on the day set apart by Congress as a day of Public Thanksgiving for the blessings of Independence, Liberty and Peace, 1783. A Sermon to the Officers and Soldiers of the Western Army after their return from an expedition against the Five Nations. New Hampshire Election Sermon, 1791.

Ebenezer Finley, the eldest son of President Finley, studied medicine, and became a highly respectable physician in Charleston, South Carolina, and was distinguished for his piety and moral worth.

Philip Vicars Fithian was born in Cumberland County, New Jersey. In connection with his classmate, Andrew Hunter, and about forty other young patriots, he assisted in the destruction of a cargo of tea at Greenwich, New Jersey. This cargo had been brought over by the ship Grey Hound, which sailed up Cohausey Creek and deposited the tea in the cellar of a store-house which is still standing. In imitation of the proceedings of the Whigs of Boston in 1773, and animated by the same patriotic spirit, this company of young men, disguised as Indians, assembled on the evening of November 22, 1774, removed the chests of tea from the store-house, conveyed them to an adjoining field and then burned them. Mr. Fithian was licensed to preach by the Presbytery of Philadelphia in 1775. For some time he laboured as a missionary under direction of the Presbytery, and then entered the army as a chaplain. At the Battle of White Plains he fought in the ranks. He died in 1776 from disease contracted in camp. Mr. Fithian was never ordained.

James Grier, a native of Bucks County, Pennsylvania, graduated with the highest honours of his class, and acted as tutor for about one year. He was licensed by the First Presbytery of Philadelphia in 1775, and ordained and installed as pastor of Deep Run Presbyterian Church, Pennsylvania, in 1776, where he remained until his death, November 19, 1791.

Mr. Grier was amiable and conciliatory in his disposition and manners. Ordinarily using but little gesture, and that of the mildest kind, his manner was always earnest, and at times it became deeply impassioned. He had power over an audience to which few attain. To illustrate this—On a Communion Sabbath, he followed up the Sacramental Service with a sermon on the text, "And the door was shut." After reading the passage, he closed the Bible with an action somewhat energetic, and lifting up his hands, apparently in the deepest agony, exclaimed, "My God, and *is* the door shut." The impression on the whole congregation was perfectly overwhelming.

Andrew Hodge was the son of Andrew Hodge, a wealthy merchant of Philadelphia. After graduating, he commenced the study of law in the office of Governor

Reed. He was thus engaged at the opening of the Revolution, when his patriotism led him to join the First City Troop of Philadelphia, which was Washington's Body Guard, and was a participator in the battle of Trenton. Shortly before the close of the war he engaged in commercial business with his younger brother Hugh until 1783, when the firm was dissolved. He continued in business until about 1806, when the embargo and his impaired health caused him to retire from active life. He resided partly in Philadelphia and partly in Susquehanna County, Pennsylvania, until his death, which occurred in May, 1835.

Andrew Hunter, the son of a British officer, was born in Virginia. He was licensed to preach by the First Presbytery of Philadelphia about 1773, immediately after which he made a missionary tour through Pennsylvania and Virginia. In 1778 he was ordained, and was appointed a Brigade Chaplain in the American Army. In 1794 he was teaching a school at Woodbury, New Jersey, and in 1803, on account of ill health, was cultivating a farm on the Delaware River near Trenton. In 1788 he was elected a Trustee of the College of New Jersey, which position he held until 1804, when he was appointed Professor of Mathematics and Astronomy. In 1808 he resigned his professorship, and took charge of an academy at Bordentown, New Jersey, but was soon after appointed a Chaplain in the Navy, and was stationed at the Navy Yard at Washington until his death, which occurred at Burlington, New Jersey, February 24, 1823.

Mr. Hunter's second wife was a daughter of Richard Stockton, of the class of 1748.

Robert Keith, a native of Pennsylvania, studied theology after his graduation, and was licensed by the First Presbytery of Philadelphia about 1775, and for some time acted as a missionary in Pennsylvania and

Virginia. In 1779 he was ordained, and received the appointment of Chaplain in the Army, serving during the whole war. Mr. Keith was never permanently settled over a congregation. He died in 1784.

William Linn was born in Shippensburg, Pennsylvania, in 1752. Soon after being licensed, he entered the American army as a chaplain. In 1784, he was Rector of an academy in Somerset County, Maryland, where he acquired a high reputation as a teacher and scholar. In 1786, he removed to Elizabethtown, New Jersey, and became pastor of the Presbyterian Church in that place. He remained here but a few months, as in the November after his settlement, he received and accepted a call to the Reformed Dutch Church of the City of New York. In consequence of declining health, which it was supposed a change of air might benefit, he removed to Albany, where he died in January, 1808.

Mr. Linn received the honorary degree of Doctor of Divinity from King's College in 1789. He enjoyed a high reputation as a pulpit orator. His delivery was very emphatic, and his gesticulations often violent. He was in great demand on charitable and public occasions. In a series of sermons on the Signs of the Times, which were afterwards published, he excited interest and much opposition among a certain class, owing to the strong ground taken in them in favour of the French Revolution, a movement of which he was a warm partisan, until it became identified with infidelity and anarchy. In a sermon preached before the Tammany Society on the 4th of July, 1791, after claiming with Mr. Jefferson, that "making due allowance for our age and numbers, we have produced as many eminent men as fall to our share;" and invoking the patriotism of the country, he plunged into an attack on the foes of liberty, Edmund Burke in particular, and a glorification of the French Revolution. "May we not," he says, "indulge the pleasing thought, that the time is not far distant, when tyranny everywhere shall be destroyed; when mankind shall be the slaves of monsters and idiots no more, but recover the true dignity of their nature! The cause of liberty is continually gathering strength. The advocates of despotic rule must fail. The British orator, though he sublimely rave, he raves in vain. No force of genius, no brilliancy of fancy, and no ornament of language can support his wretched cause. He and his abettors only hasten its downfall. The Revolution in France is great, is astonishing, is glorious. It is, perhaps, not just to say, that the flame was kindled by us, but certainly we continue to blow and increase it, as France will in other nations, until blaze joining blaze, shall illumine the darkest and remotest corners of the earth."

The publications of Dr. Linn are: A Military Discourse, delivered in Carlisle, Pa., 1776. The Spiritual Death and Life of the Believer, and the Character and Misery of the Wicked; two Sermons in the American Preacher, Volume I. A Sermon on American Independence, 1791. A volume of Discourses entitled Sermons Historical and Characteristical, 1791. A Series of Sermons on the Signs of the Times, 1794. A Sermon at a Fast, 1798. A Funeral Eulogy on Washington, 1800.

William Smith Livingston, a son of Robert James Livingston, studied law and was admitted an attorney of the Supreme Court of New Jersey at the April Term, 1780. During the war he was an officer in the Revolutionary army. Afterwards he practised law in the City of New York.

George Luckey was a native of Faggs Manor, Pennsylvania. He was licensed by the Presbytery of New Castle in 1776, and was ordained and settled as pastor of Bethel and Centre Churches, Hartford County, Maryland, where he preached until 1799, when he resigned. Mr. Luckey was a fine classical scholar, an intelligent preacher, in his manners plain, in labours unwearied. Very few had an equal acquaintance with the Scriptures. He died at Bethel, probably in 1819, as his name disappears from the roll of Synod in that year.

1772.

Samuel Eusebius Maccorkle was born in Lancaster County, Pennsylvania, August 23, 1746. His parents removed to North Carolina when he was quite young, and he was prepared for college by Rev. David Caldwell of the Class of 1761. After graduating, he studied theology with his maternal uncle, the Rev. Joseph Montgomery, of the class of 1755, and was licensed by the Presbytery of New York in 1754. For two years he laboured as a missionary in Virginia, and in 1776 returned to North Carolina, and on the 2d of August, 1777, was installed pastor of the church at Thyatira, where he remained until his death.

He was an active friend of his country in its struggles for liberty, and was an earnest champion for the truth against the rising tide of French infidelity which threatened to sweep the land.

In 1785, Mr. Mccorkle commenced a classical school in his own house, to which he gave the name of *Zion Parnasus.* The first class that graduated at the State University, consisted of seven students, six of whom were from his school. Forty-five of his scholars afterwards became ministers. At the establishment of the University of North Carolina, the state of the funds did not permit them to appoint a President, but Mr. Maccorkle was elected the first Professor, having the Chair of Moral and Political Philosophy. He was a thorough scholar, and kept up his acquaintance, not only with the Latin and Greek classics, but with mathematics, philosophy, and every important branch of learning.

In person, Mr. Maccorkle was tall, about six feet one inch; finely formed; light hair and pale blue eyes; mild, grave and dignified in his appearance; cheerful in disposition; and of fine conversational powers. Firm in his opinions, and devotedly attached to the doctrines of the Presbyterian Church, he never unnecessarily attacked the opinions or forms of others. In appearance and gait, he is said to have very much resembled Mr. Jefferson. He died January 21, 1811. The honorary degree of Doctor of Divinity was conferred on him by Dartmouth in 1792.

His publications are: A Sermon on Sacrifices, 1792. A Charity Sermon delivered on several occasions, 1793. A National Thanksgiving Sermon, entitled, The Comparative Happiness and Duty of the United States of America contrasted with other Nations, particularly the Israelites, 1795. A Sermon preached at the Laying of the Corner Stone of the University of North Carolina. Four Discourses on the great first principles of Deism and Revelation contrasted, 1797. Three Discourses on Christian Communion. A National Fast Sermon, entitled, The Work of God for the French Republic; and then her Reformation or Ruin; or, The Novel and Useful Experiment of National Deism to us and all mankind. A Sermon entitled, The Angel's Seal set upon God's Faithful Servants, when Hurtful Winds are Blowing in the Church Militant.

John McMillan, a native of Chester County, Pennsylvania, became one of the most eminent founders of the Presbyterian Church in our Western country. He was licensed by the Presbytery of the New Castle, October 26, 1774. In 1775, he made a missionary tour through the Valley of Virginia, enduring much privation and meeting many difficulties. He made a second tour to the same region in 1776.

Crossing into Western Pennsylvania, he was ordained and settled as pastor of the Congregations of Chartiers and Pigeon Creek. Here he had to build his own house; had neither bedsteads nor tables, nor stools, chairs or buckets. Boxes served him for tables, and kegs for seats. Sometimes he had no bread for weeks; but his health was good, and he once remarked that he had not from his earliest recollection been confined half a day by sickness during his whole life. The revivals which occurred in his congregations are some of the most remarkable in the history of the Church.

Mr. McMillan very early turned his attention to the education of young men for the ministry. He started a school within a year after he removed his family to the West. In 1791, his school became merged with an academy at Cannonsburg, which in time became Jefferson College.

In personal appearance Mr. McMillan was far from attractive; he was about six feet high, and walked with his head and neck inclined forward. He was of a stout and clumsy form, his features coarse, his nose very prominent, and his general aspect somewhat forbidding. He wrote out his sermons in full, and learned them by heart. His voice was strong and coarse, and he poured out his words in such a torrent that it often offended delicate ears.

He received the honorary degree of Doctor of Divinity from Jefferson College in 1805. Dr. McMillan's influence in preaching the Gospel himself, and training others for the same work, it is not easy to estimate. He died November 5, 1833.

Oliver Reese was licensed by the Presbytery of New Brunswick in 1774, and in 1775 was ordained and settled as pastor of Wilton Presbyterian Church in South Carolina. Among the accounts of the Church still extant, is a bill of one Christian Mote against the Trustees, for a dinner furnished for "fifty persons and fifteen boys at the ordination of the Rev. Oliver Reese." The bill amounted to £77. There is also a bill against "the estate of Rev. Oliver Reese," of a tailor named Long, for "two suits of cloaths," at a cost of £20. It is probable that he was a young man of promise. The congregation seem to have rejoiced in securing him as their pastor in these troublous times. But his connexion with them, and his work on earth were alike brief. He died either in the same year or the succeeding one.

James Templeton received his license from the Presbytery of Hanover, October 26, 1775, soon after which he removed to North Carolina. In 1794, he became stated supply of Nazareth Church in South Carolina, and continued so for nearly eight years. He is spoken of as being far from an animated preacher, but as taking a great interest in the general business of the church. In 1797, Mr. Templeton was at the head of the "Philanthropic Society," organized with the view of advancing and perpetuating an academy of high order. This Society was incorporated by the Legislature of South Carolina in 1797.

1773.

James Francis Armstrong was a native of Maryland. He was licensed by the Presbytery of New Castle in January, 1777, and ordained in January, 1778. He was appointed Chaplain in Sullivan's Brigade, and accompanied the troops on the Southern campaign. He remained in the army until the surrender of Yorktown. In 1782, Mr. Armstrong returned to New Jersey, and supplied the church in Elizabethtown lately made vacant by the murder of Rev. James Caldwell. In 1783, he suspended his labours on account of ill health; but in 1786 he resumed them again, and became pastor of the Presbyterian Church in Trenton, New Jersey. In 1815, Mr. Armstrong performed his last public service. He was in personal appearance noble and striking. He had a princely, generous spirit, which always answered to the claims of human wretchedness. The interest of letters and religion were more than anything else impressive and absorbing with him. He was an acceptable preacher, and had his health remained firm, would have been an eloquent and attractive one, beyond most of his contemporaries. From 1790 to 1816 he was a Trustee of the college. He died January 19, 1816.

David Bard received his license to preach from the Presbytery of Donegal, about 1777. In 1778 he was ordained and installed by the same Presbytery, pastor of the Church in Bedford, Pennsylvania. He was afterwards settled at Frankstown in the same State. Mr. Bard was a representative in Congress from Pennsylvania from 1795 to 1799; and again from 1803 to 1813. He died in 1813.

1773.

Ebenezer Bradford was born in Canterbury, Connecticut. After leaving college he studied theology, and from April, 1777, to November, 1779, was stated supply of the First Congregational Church in Danbury, Connecticut. On August 4, 1782, he was installed pastor of the Church at Rowley, Massachusetts, where he continued to labour until his death in 1801.

Mr. Bradford was admitted to a Master's degree at Dartmouth in 1785, and at Brown University in 1800.

Mr. Bradford published, A Sermon at the Ordination of Nathaniel Howe, Hopkinton, Massachusetts, 1791. Strictures on Dr. Langdon's Remarks on Hopkins's System. 1794. A Fast Sermon. 1795. A Sermon at the Installation of Rev. John H. Stevens. 1795.

Archibald Craig. From the best information I can obtain, Mr. Craig was a native of Monmouth County, New Jersey. He studied medicine and removed to Albany, New York, where he practiced his profession for many years; dying at an advanced age.

Thaddeus Dod was born near Newark, New Jersey. He became one of the founders of the Presbyterian Church in the West. He was licensed by the Presbytery of New York in 1775. In 1777, getting up from a bed of sickness, he made a missionary tour through Maryland and Virginia. In the autumn of that year the Indians had made a formidable attack upon Fort Henry at the mouth of Wheeling Creek. This was one of the most memorable events in the Border warfare. For weeks after the whole county was anticipating another attack. While in this state of apprehension and anxiety, there arrived a young man of slender form, black hair, and keen penetrating dark eyes, not unknown to some of the inhabitants; and his arrival gave them no ordinary joy. It was the Rev. Thaddeus Dod. He had been ordained by the Presbytery of New York to go out to the frontier, and he entered at once on his work. His colabourers in those bloody times were, Smith, McMillan and Power, all graduates of Princeton. Mr. Dod was a remarkable scholar, especially in mathematics. An interesting anecdote is related of him by a relative: Before the death of Chief-Justice Kirkpatrick, who was a Trustee of the college, Albert B. Dod was nominated for the Mathematical chair, and the Chief-Justice remarked, that he was not acquainted with the candidate, and did not know his reputation as a mathematician; nevertheless he would vote for him most cheerfully; he liked the name; that he never knew a Dod that was not born a mathematician; that there was one Thaddeus Dod in college when he was a student who seemed to understand mathematics by instinct; that all the students applied to him for aid when anything difficult occurred in their mathematical studies. He presumed the candidate was of the same stock, and he would vote for him. Professor Dod was the grand nephew of Thaddeus Dod. Mr. Dod was not only a fine mathematician, but was as eminent as a classical scholar, and had an exquisite taste for music. He laboured faithfully in building up the Church and the cause of higher education till his death.

When we consider a man of such mathematical talent, classical taste, and poetic imagination, we cannot but admire the orderings of Providence, that assigned to such a man such a perilous and self-denying charge. Often were he and his family driven to the neighbouring fort by the savages, and they were in constant danger and alarm.

Mr. Dod had not been long at his post before he started a classical school under the very walls of the fort, his neighbours turning out and erecting a building for him. On the 20th of January, 1789, he was appointed the first Principal of Washington Academy, at Washington, Pennsylvania, which had been incorporated in 1787. This academy, under a new charter, became Washington College. Mr. Dod died in 1793.

James Dunlap is a fit companion to his classmate

Dod. He was born in Chester County, Pennsylvania, and after graduating, acted as tutor for two years. He was licensed by the Presbytery of Donegal, sometime between 1776 and 1781, and ordained by the Presbytery of New Castle, August 21, 1781. Shortly after his ordination he removed to Western Pennsylvania and settled first at Little Redstone and Dunlap Creek; afterwards he became pastor of Laurel Hill Church, where he remained until 1803, when he was elected President of Jefferson College. This post he held until 1811. He is represented to have been a very pious man and a remarkable scholar. He was especially distinguished for his accurate attainments in classical literature. He seemed to have the classics completely in his memory; for he could hear long recitations in Virgil, Homer, etc., without a book in his hand, and then thoroughly drill the reciting class; asking all the words and sentences while walking to and fro with his hands behind his back—his usual position on such occasions. He received the degree of Doctor of Divinity from Jefferson College in 1806. Dr. Dunlap died in 1818.

William Graham stood pre-eminent in college, and during the course anticipated a whole year. He was licensed by the Presbytery of Hanover on the 26th of October, 1775. He immediately took charge of a classical school which had been started at Mount Pleasant, in the Valley of Virginia. After a short time the school was removed to Timber Ridge, and Mr. Graham became pastor of the church as well as rector of the school. On account of the troubles occasioned by the war, the buildings at Timber Ridge were abandoned; Mr. Graham removing to a farm, but still attempting to keep up the school at Timber Ridge. This becoming inconvenient, he opened a school at his own house. In course of time a building for the school was erected, when in 1782 it received an act of incorporation, and the name of Liberty Hall; which name it retained until it was endowed by

General Washington, when his name was substituted for that which it had before borne. Before this donation was received, Mr. Graham had resigned his office of President.

Mr. Graham possessed a mind formed for accurate and profound investigation. He had studied the Latin and Greek classics with great care, and relished the beauties of these exquisite compositions. He was a lover of natural science. But the science which engaged his attention more than all others, except Theology, was the Philosophy of the Mind. From the time of his ordination, in 1775, he became a teacher of Theology. He was not much given to writing nor the reading of many books; but he was a nervous and independent thinker. Kaimes and Butler were his favourite authors. He was distinguished for the depth and boldness of his investigations, and loved to examine every subject for himself. He confessed that the chief advantage he derived from books, was from the table of contents, which suggested to his mind matter for thought. As a preacher he was at once argumentative and impressive; but it was as a teacher that his excellence was most apparent. His lectures were fascinating, from their originality and ingenuity; while his penetrating eye and the power of sarcasm kept the most unruly in awe.

It may truly be said that the patriotic fire burned in no bosom with a warmer flame than in that of Mr. Graham. On a certain occasion it was resolved, by order of the Governor, to raise a volunteer company of riflemen to go into active service; but there appeared to be a backwardness in the men to come forward. Mr. Graham, who was present, stepped out and had his own name enrolled, which produced such an effect that the company was immediately filled, of which he was unanimously elected Captain; but they were not called into service.

Mr. Graham died June 8, 1799.

Hugh Hodge, a younger brother of Andrew Hodge

of the previous class, after graduating, studied medicine with Dr. John Cadwalader, of Philadelphia; and when the Revolution broke out he offered his services to his country. He was appointed Surgeon of the First Battalion, Cadwalader Brigade. He served a short time, and was captured by the British at Fort Washington, New York. He was released on parole through the exertions of Robert Morris. While upon parole, he engaged in mercantile pursuits with his brother Andrew; but owing to captures at sea and other causes, they were not very successful. He resumed the practice of his profession about 1788 or 1789, and rose to eminence in connection with Drs. Rush and Wistar. He was the father of Dr. Charles Hodge, of Princeton. He died in Philadelphia.

Andrew King was born in North Carolina. He was probably licensed by the Presbytery of New York in 1775. On the 11th of June, 1777, he was ordained and installed pastor of the Presbyterian Church at Wallkill, New York. He continued in this relation until his death, November 16, 1815. Mr. King was neither learned nor eloquent, but was greatly prospered during his ministry. He was known as a "peace-maker," and in various instances was called on by the Presbytery to settle differences in congregations.

Henry Lee was a son of Henry Lee, of Prince William County, Virginia. He is commonly known as "Light Horse Harry." In 1774 he was appointed a Captain of Cavalry under Colonel Bland. His skill in discipline, and his gallant bearing, soon attracted the notice of Washington, and he was promoted to the rank of Major, and then advanced to that of Lieutenant-Colonel. From 1780 to the close of the war, he served under General Green. The services of Lee's Legion in various actions were very important; he especially distinguished himself at the Battle of Guilford; afterwards he succeeded in capturing Fort Cornwallis and other forts; he was also conspicuous at Ninety Six and at the Eutaw Springs. In 1786 he was appointed to Congress from Virginia, in which position he remained until the Constitution was adopted. In 1791 he became Governor of Virginia, and remained in office for three years. By appointment of Washington he commanded the forces sent to suppress the Whisky Insurrection in Pennsylvania. In 1799 he was again in Congress, and was selected to pronounce a funeral oration on Washington, in which occurred the memorable words, "First in war, first in peace, and first in the hearts of his countrymen." After the accession of Mr. Jefferson in 1801, he retired to private life. He was an uncle of the late General Robert E. Lee. He died March 25, 1818.

General Lee published, An Oration on the Death of Washington, 1800. Memoirs of the War in the South, 2 vols. 8vo, 1812.

Morgan Lewis, a son of one of the Signers of the Declaration of Independence, was born in the city of New York. After graduating, he entered the army, and at the surrender of General Burgoyne, was a Colonel of one of the Continental regiments. In 1791 he was appointed Attorney-General of New York, succeeding Aaron Burr; and in 1801 he was appointed to the Bench of the Supreme Court of the State, the next year being made Chief-Justice. Brockholst Livingston and Smith Thompson, two graduates of Princeton, were appointed Judges of the Supreme Court at the same time. In 1804 he was elected Governor of the State—his opponent being Aaron Burr.

Mr. Lewis was a kind parent, a benevolent man, a good citizen and an able lawyer. He died in New York, April 7, 1844, at the advanced age of 90.

John Linn, a native of Pennsylvania, was born in the year 1749. He was licensed to preach by the Presbytery of Donegal in December, 1776. Shortly after, he was ordained and became pastor of Sherman Valley

Churches in Pennsylvania. He remained here till the close of his life.

Mr. Linn was of medium height, portly and symmetrical in his form, and muscular and active in his bodily movements. He was accustomed to write out his sermons in full and deliver them from memory. He had a remarkably clear voice, and spoke with great solemnity and impressiveness. He was distinguished for sobriety of mind rather than versatility—reflection rather than imagination. In his family, and indeed in all his relations, he was a fine example of Christian dignity, tenderness and fidelity.

He died in 1820.

James Macconnell received license and was ordained by Hanover Presbytery, and was installed as pastor of the Presbyterian Church at High Bridge, Virginia, June 18, 1778. By indiscretion and want of family economy, he became involved in difficulties, and ceased to serve the congregation. In 1787 he removed beyond the Alleghanies.

John McKnight was born near Carlisle, Pennsylvania, October 1, 1754. He was licensed by the Presbytery of Donegal about 1774, and ordained in 1775. The same year he removed to Virginia, and became pastor of a congregation at Elk Branch. He remained in this charge till 1783, when he removed to Adams County, Pennsylvania, and became pastor of Lower Marsh Creek Presbyterian Church.

An amusing incident is related in connection with his pastorate at this place. He had just ordained three ruling elders; and one of them was appointed to attend the meeting of Presbytery to be held the next week. He came to the pastor on the evening of the day of his ordination, under a good deal of agitation, to inquire what were the duties that would be expected of him. Perceiving the state of his mind, Mr. McKnight assumed a serious air, and replied—"You are to see that my horse is fed and saddled in time to start; to go before and have breakfast and dinner prepared for us; to pay the bills, and in Presbytery to vote as I do." This playfulness relieved the anxious elder, whose countenance changed from its solemn gravity to a smile,—when opportunity was given to inform him what his real duties would be as a member of the body.

In 1789 Mr. McKnight became colleague pastor with Dr. Rodgers in New York City. In 1791 Yale conferred upon him the honorary degree of Doctor of Divinity. Dr. McKnight remained in New York in the faithful discharge of his duties for twenty years. In 1809 he resigned his charge, and removed to the neighbourhood of Chambersburg, Pennsylvania. In 1815 he was elected President of Dickinson College, but resigned the Chair in little more than a year, returning to his farm near Chambersburg, where he died October 21, 1823.

Dr. McKnight was a man of slender person, and rather above the medium height. His manner was graceful and dignified. As a preacher he was calm and dispassionate.

Dr. McKnight published, Six Sermons on Faith, 1790. A Sermon before the New York Missionary Society, 1799. A Sermon on the present state of the political and religious world, 1802. A Sermon on the death of the Rev. Dr. John King, 1811.

Aaron Ogden belonged to a distinguished family of Elizabethtown, New Jersey. After leaving college he became an assistant teacher in the school of Francis Barber of the class of 1767. In the winter of 1775-1776, he was one of a party of young men who boarded and captured a vessel lying off Sandy Hook, and carried her safely into Elizabethport. In the spring of 1777, the school of Mr. Barber was broken up; and principal and assistant both entered the army, the one as a major, the other as a captain. Mr. Ogden remained in the service till the close of the war. He was at the Battle of Brandywine in 1777; and was in the advanced corps of General

Lee at the Battle of Monmouth, and served as aid-de-camp to Lord Stirling on that memorable day. In 1779, he attended Sullivan in his expedition against the Indians, and was at the Battle of Springfield in 1780, where he had a horse shot under him, and highly distinguished himself. The same year he was chosen from the whole army by General Washington to go upon a most delicate and interesting mission to the British lines, the purpose of which was to effect, if possible, an exchange of Arnold for Andre, which duty he performed with the utmost skill and address.

At the siege of Yorktown, the company which he commanded, stormed the left redoubt of the enemy, for which he was honoured with the peculiar approbation of Washington.

At the close of the war Mr. Ogden devoted himself to the study and practice of the law, and for many years occupied a conspicuous place in the foremost rank at the New Jersey Bar. From 1801 to 1803, he served as a Senator in the Congress of the United States, and in 1812, was elected Governor of his native state.

To learning and industry, Mr. Ogden united great ingenuity and fertility of resources, quickness and accuracy of discrimination, and an eloquence which at times, when he was deeply moved or strongly excited, was of a very high order. His manner was gracious and imposing; his voice, though not musical, was strong and varied; his countenance had great power and diversity of expression; but, more than all this, he understood well the springs of human action.

He died April 19, 1839.

Richard Platt was a gallant soldier of the Revolution, a major in the New York line. He was at Quebec with Montgomery, and at the surrender of Cornwallis at Yorktown. He died in New York, March 4th, 1830.

Belcher Peartree Smith was a son of the eminent

William Peartree Smith of Elizabethtown, one of the original Trustees of the college. He studied law after graduation, and practiced in Elizabethtown. He died in 1787.

John Blair Smith was a son of the Rev. Robert Smith of Pequea, Pennsylvania, and was born June 12, 1756. He received license from Hanover Presbytery, June 18, 1777. He was ordained by the same body October 26, 1779. At the same meeting of Presbytery his brother, Samuel Stanhope Smith, asked leave to resign the Presidency of Hampden Sidney College; his request was granted, and John Blair Smith was immediately appointed to succeed him.

During the revival which swept through Virginia in 1786 and 1787, Mr. Smith entered into the work with such glowing zeal, and his preaching was so eloquent and powerful, that his services were in constant demand at places remote from his residence. In 1789, he resigned his office in order to give himself up wholly to preaching. In 1791, he became pastor of the Pine Street Church in Philadelphia, and in 1795 he was elected the first President of Union College, New York; but after presiding over that infant institution for three years, he returned to his former charge in Philadelphia, and was installed in 1799. He died of yellow fever in Philadelphia, August, 22, 1799. In 1793, the degree of Doctor of Divinity was conferred upon him by Hampden-Sidney and Union Colleges.

The natural disposition of Dr. Smith was full of vivacity, his temper quiet, and his actions rapid. At first his preaching was less impressive than his brother's; but at the commencement of the great revival, he underwent a great change in his own feelings and in the fervency of his preaching, so that he became one of the most powerful preachers of the day.

In person he was about the middle size. His hair was uncommonly black, and was divided on the top and fell down on each side of his face. A large blue eye of open expression, was so piercing, that it was common to say Dr. Smith looked you through.

Dr. Smith's only acknowledged publication was A Sermon entitled, "The Enlargement of Christ's Kingdom, the Object of a Christian's Prayers and Exertions," delivered in the Dutch Church, Albany, before the Northern Missionary Society of N. Y., 1797.

William R. Smith, a brother of President Samuel Stanhope Smith, was licensed by the Presbytery of New Castle in 1776; was settled as pastor of the Second Church in Wilmington, Delaware, about 1786; resigned his charge in 1796, and became pastor of the Reformed Dutch Church of Harlingen and Shannock, New Jersey, in which relation he died about the year 1820. Mr. Smith was plain in his manners, a judicious and instructive preacher, without much power of elocution, a faithful pastor, and amiable and exemplary in his spirit and deportment.

Samuel Waugh was a native of Pennsylvania. He was licensed by Donegal Presbytery in 1777, and was settled as the pastor of the United Churches of Pennsborough and Monaghan, Pennsylvania, in 1782; in which relation he continued till his death, which took place in January, 1807. He was a sound divine, a very acceptable preacher, and highly esteemed by his people.

Lewis Feuilleteau Wilson came from the Island of St. Christopher. A circumstance occurred in connexion with his graduation that was illustrative equally of his fine scholarship, and his noble spirit. When the honours were distributed in his class by the Trustees of the college, five were appointed to deliver orations, and the second oration fell to him. When the announcement was made by the President, he rose and made a most respectful and grateful acknowledgment of the honour that had been conferred upon him, but begged to decline it, and expressed a wish that it might be given to another. He was accordingly excused, and a person to whom he knew the appointment would be acceptable, was substituted in his place.

After graduation, he visited London, intending to take orders in the Church of England; but, changing his mind, he returned to Princeton, and commenced the study of Divinity with Dr. Witherspoon. Being interrupted in his studies by the war, he studied medicine and acted as surgeon in the Continental army for several years. After the war, he again visited England, and on his return, settled as a physician in Princeton.

In 1786, through the influence of one of his college friends, he removed to North Carolina, but his old desire to preach the Gospel returned, and he abandoned medicine, and was licensed to preach in 1791; and in 1793, he was ordained and installed as pastor of Fourth Creek and Concord Churches in North Carolina. Mr. Wilson was intimately connected with the great revivals in the West and South near the end of the last century. In 1803, he resigned his charge, and died in perfect peace December 11, 1804.

John Witherspoon, a son of President Witherspoon, studied medicine, and was settled for several years as a practitioner at St. Stephens Parish, South Carolina, and is believed to have died at sea between New York and Charleston in the summer of 1795.

1774.

Stephen Bloomer Balch was born in Maryland, but removed while a boy to North Carolina.. After leaving college, he took charge of a school in Calvert County, Maryland, to which he had been recommended by Dr. Witherspoon. Here he remained four years. He was licensed by the Presbytery of Donegal, June 17, 1779, and returned to North Carolina. Here engaging in missionary work he endured many privations. On one occasion night overtook him, and he entered a strange dwelling and asked for a night's lodging. The master of the house was absent, but his wife received him hospitably. Being much fatigued he soon fell asleep, but was aroused by the arrival of the owner of the house, who proved to be General Williams of North Carolina; entering the room where Mr. Balch was sleeping, he said, "I will allow no one who is not a Whig to sleep under my roof;" Mr. Balch replied, "Let me rest in peace, then, for I was educated under Dr. Witherspoon, one of the signers of the Declaration of Independence."

In 1780, Mr. Balch removed to Georgetown, (D. C.,) and established a Presbyterian Church. Here he remained until his death, which took place September 7, 1833.

In person Mr. Balch was tall and rather commanding. His eyes were small and keen. His gait was slow and cautious, indicating that he was absent-minded. He had an exuberance of good humour, which continued with him till the last. His preaching was generally doctrinal and characterized by great fearlessness and energy.

William Bradford was born in Canterbury, Connecticut, and after graduating was licensed by the Litchfield South Association in 1775. The last years of Mr. Bradford's life were spent as pastor of the North Congregational Church in Canterbury. He died in 1808.

Daniel Breck, a native of Boston, became a Congregational minister, and entered the army as a chaplain, and accompanied Porter's regiment to Canada and shared in the hardships and perils of that campaign. He was present in the attack upon Quebec. After the war he visited the Northwest Territory, and delivered the first sermon ever preached on the spot where Marietta, Ohio, now stands. He was a man of high Christian character. Mr. Breck was the father of Judge Breck, of Kentucky. He died in Vermont in 1845, aged ninety-seven years.

John Ewing Calhoun entered college from North Carolina. After graduating he studied law, in which profession he became distinguished. For many years he was a member of the South Carolina Legislature, and in 1801 represented that State in the United States Senate. He was a man of independent thought and resolution. He dared while in the Senate to secede alone from his party, and to oppose singly a popular measure, because it appeared to him to be unconstitutional and perilous in its consequences. Mr. Calhoun was on a select committee to whom was referred a modification of the Judiciary System of the United States. He died in 1802.

John Noble Cumming early espoused the cause of his country, and rose to the rank of a General. He participated in a number of the battles of the Revolution. Mr. Cumming was a man of integrity and honour, a patron of civil order and a supporter of religious institutions. He died in Newark, July 6, 1821.

Peter Fish was descended from an old family of Long Island. He was licensed to preach by the Presbytery of

New York in 1779. On the 20th of October, 1785, he was appointed by the Presbytery stated supply of the Presbyterian Church at Newtown, Long Island. He remained here until November, 1788, when he removed to Connecticut Farms, New Jersey, where he was ordained and installed, March 25, 1789. He remained in this charge for ten years, when he removed to Holland Patent, New York, where he laboured for a time; but being in poor health, he purchased a place in Newtown, and removed there in the spring of 1807, with the intention of seeking repose from the arduous duties of the ministry; but the church becoming vacant, he consented to supply them for a time, but his labours were suddenly terminated by his death, on November 12, 1810. He possessed through life a delicacy of constitution that greatly restricted his usefulness. In person he was tall and spare.

James Hall was born at Carlisle, Pennsylvania, August 22, 1744, but removed to North Carolina while a boy. He had a high reputation while in college, especially in the exact sciences; insomuch that, soon after his graduation, Dr. Witherspoon expressed a desire that he should be retained in the college as a teacher of mathematics. The proposal he declined, saying that he had devoted his life to the sacred ministry. He was licensed by the Presbytery of Orange about 1776. He was installed pastor of the United Congregations of Fourth Creek, Concord, and Bethany, North Carolina, April 8, 1778. When the Revolutionary war opened, he entered with all his heart into the conflict; gathering the people together and setting forth to them their obligations as patriots, he made most effective appeals in favour of the cause of liberty. When the forces of Cornwallis were desolating South Carolina, Mr. Hall assembled his flock and addressed them with great fervour and pathos. A select company of cavalry was immediately organized, and by general consent he was demanded for their leader, which post he accepted. One of his contemporaries writes: "When a boy at school at Charlotte, I saw James Hall pass through the town with a three-cornered hat and long sword, the Captain at the head of a company, and Chaplain of the regiment." Mr. Hall accompanied an expedition into Georgia against the Indians, preaching as he had opportunity. After the skirmish at Cowan's Ford, on the Catawba, between the forces of Cornwallis and the North Carolina Militia, he was selected by General Green as a suitable person to succeed General Davidson, who had fallen, and a commission was actually tendered to him. This he declined, on the ground that others could fill the post, at least with as much advantage as himself, while he had solemnly pledged his life to the defence of the Gospel.

A full account of the actions of Mr. Hall during the Revolutionary war, would fill a volume. His active, enterprising spirit would not let him be neuter; his principles, drawn from the word of God and the doctrines of his Church, and cultivated by Dr. Witherspoon, carried him with all his heart to the defence of his country. To that he gave his powers of mind, body and estate.

After the war Mr. Hall set himself to repair the waste places of Zion; and he was the instrument in bringing about an extensive revival of religion. From 1793 to 1801 he made missionary excursions through the south-western States, an account of which was published in the newspapers of the day.

He was a warm friend of education. Soon after entering upon his work, he became connected with a literary institution in the neighbourhood of his churches; and afterwards he opened an "Academy of Sciences" at his own house, of which he was himself the sole Professor. He died on the 25th of July, 1826.

Dr. Hall published, A Sermon on Proverbs xiv. 34, preached at the opening of a Court House in South Carolina. A Sermon preached at the Ordination of Mr. Samuel C. Caldwell, as pastor of Sugar Creek Church. 1792. A Narrative of a most extraordinary work of Religion in North Carolina. 1802. A Report of a Missionary Tour through Mississippi and the South-western Country.

Hugh Hodge, a native of Philadelphia, and a cousin of Hugh Hodge of the class of 1773, became a merchant in Philadelphia, and was lost at sea going or returning from Europe.

Samuel Leake was born in New Jersey. After graduating, he received from Dr. Witherspoon a written certificate of his qualifications to teach Latin, Greek and Mathematics, to which was appended the following: "I must also add that he gave particular attention to the English language while here, and is probably better acquainted with its structure, propriety and force, than most of his years and standing in this country." Mr. Leake, however, did not engage in teaching, but entered upon the study of the law, and was admitted to practice in 1776. He began the practice in Salem, New Jersey, but in October, 1785, removed to Trenton, where he pursued his profession so successfully as to be able to retire before he was enfeebled by age. He paid unusual attention to the students in his office, regularly devoting one hour every day to their examination.

Mr. Leake died March 8, 1820. The epitaph on his tomb describes his character: "Educated to the Bar, he attained the highest degree of eminence. Distinguished for candour, integrity, zeal for his clients, and profound knowledge of jurisprudence, he fulfilled the duties of his station with singular usefulness, 'without fear and without reproach.' Deeply versed in human literature, and devoutly studious of the words of sacred truth, he lived the life of a Christian and died the death of the righteous."

Henry Brockholst Livingston was the son of Governor William Livingston, of New Jersey. In 1776 he entered the military family of General Schuyler, commander of the Northern army, and was afterwards attached to the suit of Arnold at the time of the capture of Burgoyne. In 1779, when Mr. Jay, who had married his sister, repaired to the Court of Spain, Mr. Livingston accompanied him as his private secretary. After three years' absence he returned and studied law, and was admitted to the Bar in 1783. On the 8th of June, 1802, he was appointed Judge of the Supreme Court of New York. In November, 1806, he was appointed Associate Justice of the Supreme Court of the United States. He died in Washington during a session of the court, March 18, 1823. His mind was acute and powerful, and he was distinguished as a scholar and a jurist.

Thomas Harris Maccaule. Nothing is known of the parentage of Mr. Maccaule. He was ordained and settled as pastor of Centre Presbyterian Church in North Carolina in 1776. He entered warmly into the Revolutionary struggle, and in the time of the invasion went with his flock to the field, and was beside General Davidson when he fell. Such was his reputation in civil life, that he was nominated for Governor, but lost his election by a few votes.

In 1784 he was appointed President of Mount Zion College, South Carolina. The accommodations of the college at first were of the most primitive kind. Mr. Maccaule commenced his instructions in an old log-cabin about twenty-five feet by twenty, a story and a half high, with a single chimney. Upon taking charge he proposed enlarging the institution, on the plan of his *Alma Mater* at Princeton. His plan was adopted, and the institution was incorporated March 19, 1785. In 1786 there were from sixty to eighty students in the college. Besides his duties in the college, Mr. Maccaule had charge of Jackson Creek and Mount Olivet Presbyterian Churches, to whom he preached until September, 1792, when he resigned.

In person, Mr. Maccaule was scarcely of a medium height, but of a stout frame and full body; of dark, piercing eyes, a pleasant countenance and winning manners. He had a fine voice, and was popular both as a preacher and a man. He died about 1796.

Jonathan Mason was a Senator of the United States from Massachusetts from 1800 to 1803, and in the House of Representatives from 1817 to 1820.

Lewis Morris entered the Continental Army from New York as a Major, and served during the whole war.

William Stevens Smith, after graduating, commenced the study of the law in New York City, and was about finishing his studies when the American Army assembled there after the unfortunate affair of Long Island. He immediately resolved to take arms in defence of his country, but his parents disapproving of this step, he enlisted as a common soldier, without making himself known, or pretending to any superior rank. Being one day on duty at the door of a general officer, he was discovered by a friend of the family, who spoke of him, to that general officer. He was immediately invited to dinner; but he answered that he could not quit his duty; his corporal was sent for to relieve him, and he returned to his post after dinner. A few days only elapsed before that general officer, charmed with his zeal, made him his aid-de-camp. In 1780 he commanded a battalion of light infantry under Lafayette, and the year following was made aid-de-camp to General Washington, with whom he remained until the peace. In 1783 Lieutenant-Colonel Smith was appointed, with two others, to superintend the embarkation of the British troops at the evacuation of New York. His correspondence with General Washington while engaged in this duty is preserved in "New York in the Revolution," printed privately in 1861. In this correspondence, there is a list of books ordered by General Washington through Colonel Smith, which gives us an insight into the character of the reading which the Commander-in-Chief followed at this time.

At the close of the war, when John Adams was appointed Minister-Plenipotentiary to the Court of Great Britain, Lieutenant-Colonel Smith became his Secretary of Legation. It was during his residence in that capacity at London that Mr. Smith became the son-in-law of Mr. Adams by marriage with his only daughter.

That Mr. Smith enjoyed the esteem of General Washington, is apparent from the fact that, when, in the year 1798, Washington was created by Congress Lieutenant-General and Commander-in-Chief of the United States Armies, the name of William S. Smith was immediately proposed by him to the Secretary of War as a brigadier-general, or, failing that, as an adjutant-general. He did not obtain either of these appointments, but was made colonel, and afterwards, surveyor and inspector of the port of New York. He was engaged in the expedition under General Miranda, upon the failure of which he retired to the interior of New York State, from whence he was sent as representative to Congress in 1813. He died in 1816.

Nicholas Bayard Van Cortlandt was a son of John and Hester Bayard Van Cortlandt, of New York, and a grandson of Stephen Van Cortlandt, of Second River, New Jersey. He was born March 19, 1756, and died at Parsipany, New Jersey, May 1, 1782.

John Warford received his license to preach from the Presbytery of New Brunswick in 1776, and was ordained in 1777. In July, 1789, he was installed pastor of the Presbyterian Church at Salem, New York, where he preached for fourteen years. His heart was enlisted in the cause of Christian philanthropy and missionary enterprise.

Samuel Whitwell studied medicine and entered the Continental Army as a surgeon. He died in 1791.

1774.

David Witherspoon was a son of President Witherspoon. After graduating, he studied law, and emigrated to North Carolina, where, for several years, he was a successful practitioner at Newbern.

1775.

Charles Clinton Beatty soon ended his course. He was the second son of the Rev. Charles Beatty, that bright light in the early Presbyterian Church of this country. Instead of entering the ministry as he intended, he entered the army, and was accidentally shot by a brother officer in October, 1776.

John Durburrow Blair was the son of the Rev. John Blair, at one time Vice-President of the college. On the recommendation of Dr. Witherspoon, he was appointed in 1780, Principal of Washington Henry Academy in Virginia, where he remained for a number of years.

On the 28th of October, 1784, he was licensed to preach by the Presbytery of Hanover, and installed as pastor of a church in Hanover County, Virginia, where Samuel Davies formerly preached with success. About 1792, Mr. Blair was induced to remove to Richmond and open a classical school. At the same time he began to gather a church, holding his services in the capitol. In due course of time a building was erected for his congregation. But increasing infirmities soon brought his career to a close. He died January 10, 1823.

Mr. Blair was highly esteemed in the community, and became intimate with the most enlightened men of Richmond, among whom were Judge Marshall and Judge Washington. Mr. Blair was a man of polished manners and fitted to adorn any company. He was of a medium height and of a slender figure, but had a great delicacy of person, and an uncommonly intellectual expression of countenance. As a preacher he was solid and orthodox.

His style was graceful and polished, and his manner of delivery was in perfect keeping with his style. His voice was soft and pleasant and fell like music on the ear of his audience.

Mr. Blair published a few occasional sermons during his life, and after his death a volume of his sermons was published under the direction of his successor the Rev. J. B. Hoge.

Ichabod Burnet, the second son of Dr. William Burnet of the class of 1749, joined the American army from New Jersey. In 1780, he was an aid to General Greene, with the rank of Major, and was stationed at West Point. He was one of the two officers designated by General Greene to communicate to Andre the sentence of the court, and to attend him to the place of execution. He died in 1783.

Thomas B. Craighead was a son of the Rev. Alexander Craighead of Sugar Creek, North Carolina. He was ordained by the Presbytery of Orange in 1780. For a few months he preached at Sugar Creek, his native place, and then removed to Tennessee. Here he was brought to trial before the Presbytery for holding certain Pelagian views; and the controversy which arose, lasted for many years.

Mr. Craighead was one of the founders of Davidson Academy, which afterwards became Nashville University. It originated in his little congregation, six miles east of Nashville, and Mr. Craighead became the first President, which position he held for two years and three months.

Mr. Craighead was of a tall but spare figure, not less than six feet in height; homely and hard features, with sandy hair and a large clear blue eye. His health was delicate and his voice was weak; his manner grave and his actions natural, but not vehement. He excelled as an extemporaneous orator, but not as a writer. His eloquence was of that fervid kind which captivates and carries away the hearer even in spite of himself. He died in 1825.

Mr. Craighead published: A Sermon on Regeneration, with an Address and an Appendix. Letters to Rev. J. P. Campbell, occasioned by his Letters to the Author, containing some original Disquisitions, Philosophical, Moral and Religious, Nashville, 1811. These were connected with his controversy and trial.

The Philosophy of the Human Mind, in respect to Religion, 1833. Essays and Dialogues on the Powers and Susceptibilities of the Human Mind for Religion, 12mo, 1834. A Defence of the Elkhorn Association in sixteen letters to Elder Toler, 1822.

Edward Crawford received his license to preach from the Presbytery of Hanover in 1777. On the 27th of October in the same year, he was settled as pastor of the Sinking Spring and Spreading Spring Congregations, Virginia. Some time after 1786, he removed to Tennessee, and took charge of Glade Spring and Rocky Spring Churches, where he remained until 1803. Mr. Crawford was one of the original Trustees of Washington College, Tennessee.

Samuel Doak, a son of Samuel Doak and Jane Mitchell, was born in Augusta County, Virginia, in August, 1749. After graduating, he assisted the Rev. Dr. Smith in his school at Pequea, Pennsylvania. Shortly after this, he became tutor in Hampden Sidney College, and pursued his theological studies under Dr. J. B. Smith, the President, and afterwards with Rev. William Graham at Timber Ridge. He was licensed to preach by the Presbytery of Hanover, October 31, 1777, soon after which he removed to Holston, in what is now a part of East Tennessee. Here he was in the midst of danger from the savages. On one occasion his wife was apprised by the barking of the dogs that the Indians were near. Taking her infant in her arms, she stealthily fled to the woods, and from her hiding place she saw the house and all that it contained burned by the Indians. After residing in Holston a year or two, Mr. Doak removed to

Washington County, and purchased a farm, and put up a small church edifice and a building of logs for a school. The literary institution which he here started, was the first ever established in the Valley of the Mississippi. In 1785, it was incorporated, with the name of Martin Academy, and in 1795 it became Washington College. From its incorporation as an Academy until 1818, Mr. Doak continued to preside over it, and the elders of his congregation formed a part of its Board of Trustees.

While Mr. Doak was attending a meeting of the General Assemby in Philadelphia, he received a donation of books for his college, which he carried in a sack upon a pack horse five hundred miles through forests and over mountains, and this constituted the nucleus of the library of Washington College.

In 1818, he resigned the Presidency, and removed to Bethel in the same State, and opened a private school which he called Tusculum, which has since under his son, grown into Tusculum College.

Mr. Doak was also successful in his ministry. Several powerful revivals occurred in connection with it; and many churches were founded by him. He was distinguished for his talents and his usefulness, and may be considered the Apostle of Presbyterianism in Tennessee. His style of preaching was original, bold, pungent, and sometimes pathetic. He died October 6, 1820.

John Joline was ordained by the Presbytery of New York and installed as pastor of the Church at Mendham, New Jersey, in May, 1778. About 1796 he resigned his charge, and on the 13th of June, 1797, was installed as pastor of the Churches at Florida and Warwick, Orange County, New York. Mr. Joline was regularly dismissed from this charge, but he probably died soon after, as his grave is at Florida, but without a monumental stone to record the date of his death.

Isaac Stockton Keith, a native of Pennslyvania, was

engaged for a short time after graduating in teaching at Elizabethtown, New Jersey. In 1778, he was licensed by the Presbytery of Philadelphia, and in 1780, became pastor of the Presbyterian Church at Alexandria, Virginia. In 1788, he removed to Charleston, South Carolina, and was installed as pastor of an Independent Church in that city. For twenty-five years he laboured here, revered and beloved by all.

Dr. Keith was large in stature, dignified in manner, grave in aspect and in speech, and you felt that you were in the presence of no ordinary man. He held a high rank as a preacher; his discourses were well elaborated and his applications direct and pungent. Mr. Keith received the honorary degree of Doctor of Divinity from Philadelphia College in 1791. He died December 13, 1813.

Dr. Keith published about half-a-dozen sermons during his life. These, with two or three others, together also with the sermon occasioned by his death, a brief biographical notice of him, and a somewhat extended selection from his correspondence, were published in a volume in the year, 1816.

Andrew Kirkpatrick was descended from Scotch ancestors. His grandfather came to this country in 1736. The subject of our sketch was born at Mine Brook, New Jersey, February 17, 1756. There being no railroads nor steamboats in those days, to carry young men to college, young Kirkpatrick was accustomed to walk to and fro between his home and Princeton, carrying his little knapsack with him. Soon after graduating he commenced the study of theology, but at the end of a few months he relinquished it for the law, as being more agreeable to his tastes. This step he took, knowing that by it he would forfeit his father's favour, and all pecuniary aid from him. His resolution was deliberately taken, and he entered upon his favorite pursuit relying for subsistence upon his own extraordinary and unaided exertions. Completing his legal studies in the office of Judge Paterson, he was admitted to the Bar in 1785, and commenced practice in Morristown, New Jersey. While living here, by a fire in 1787, he lost all of his law books, a very serious loss to one of his limited means. Returning to New Brunswick, he was successful in obtaining a considerable practice, and was soon enabled to replace the volumes which had been destroyed.

Mr. Kirkpatrick's remarkable success in his profession was the result, after a high order of intellect, of the energy of his character and the most persevering industry. In 1797, he was elected a member of the House of Assembly. He sat with this body during the first session, but on the 17th of January he resigned his seat, having accepted the position of a judge of the Supreme Court; six years later he was advanced to the office of Chief-Justice. He was twice re-elected, holding the high position for twenty-one years.

No one could enter the court in which he sat without being struck by his extraordinary personal presence. His snow-white hair, his clear, florid complexion, his dark lustrous eye, his strong but delicately chiselled features, the expression of gravity and firmness, blended with a placid sweetness in his countenance, his imposing form, and the graceful dignity with which he discharged his judicial duties, arrested the attention of all.

Chief-Justice Kirkpatrick was a learned, and in regard to real estate, a profoundly learned lawyer. He stood without a superior among American jurists. His mind was not rapid, but it was uncommonly exact; and the want of quickness was carefully supplied by unwearying application to the object of investigation. He passed the last few years of his life retired from public employment.

Judge Kirkpatrick was one of the original trustees of the Theological Seminary at Princeton, and was the first President of the Board, holding that office until his death. He was a trustee of the college from 1807 to the time of his decease, and was one of the vice-presidents of the

Alumni Association founded in 1826, James Madison being president.

In 1813 Daniel Webster, at that time on a visit to Richard Stockton, at the table of Samuel Bayard, Esq., who had invited him to meet his kinsman Kirkpatrick, and Ashbel Green, pronounced the Chief-Justice and the college President to be two of the most remarkable men he had ever met.

It would be a delightful task, if space permitted, to relate the charming traits of this great man in his social relations and his grand and comprehensive views of the Christian system, as uttered in his declining years.

He died in the parlour of his own house, in New Brunswick, on the 7th of January, 1831, and was buried in the grave-yard of the first Presbyterian Church, of which he was for many years a Trustee, and where, for half a century, he had listened to the Word of God.

Charles Lee was a brother of Henry Lee of the class of 1773. He became an eminent lawyer, and in 1795 was appointed Attorney-General of the United States, to succeed William Bradford. Mr. Lee died June 24, 1815.

Spruce Macay came to college from North Carolina. After graduating, he returned to his home in Rowan County, and entered upon the practice of law. In 1790 he was appointed Judge of the Superior Court of Law and Equity. He was for some years in the State Legislature.

Mr. Macay died in 1808.

James McRee was born in North Carolina, May 10, 1752. He spent the first year after graduating as tutor in a private family in Virginia. He then studied theology, and was licensed by Concord Presbytery in April, 1778, and was immediately settled as pastor of Steel Creek Congregation in North Carolina, where he remained about twenty years. In 1798 he left Steel Creek and settled as pastor of Centre Church, and continued its pastor about thirty years. On account of the infirmities of age, he was at last compelled to cease preaching. Mr. McRee received the degree of Doctor of Divinity from the University of North Carolina in 1810.

In person Dr. McRee was of middling stature, handsomely proportioned. He was agreeable in his manners, winning in conversation, neat in dress, dignified in the pulpit, fluent in his delivery, and was a most popular preacher. He retained his influence long after he ceased active work. He was always a friend of education, and in the latter part of his life became increasingly anxious for the prosperity of academies, colleges and theological seminaries, being deeply convinced that the welfare of the country depended upon intelligence, morality and religion.

Dr. McRee died March 28, 1840.

John Montgomery was born in Augusta County, Virginia. He was licensed by the Presbytery of Hanover, October 28, 1778, and was for a time tutor in Liberty Hall, Virginia. He was ordained April 26, 1780, and settled as pastor of Cedar Creek and Opecquon Churches in Virginia. After spending a few years with these congregations, in 1789 he removed to Augusta County. Here he passed the remainder of his life. Mr. Montgomery was a very popular preacher, a good scholar and an amiable man. In the latter part of his life his ministry was interrupted by bodily infirmities.

John Richardson Bayard Rodgers was a son of the distinguished clergyman, Rev. John Rodgers, of New York. He received his degree of Doctor of Medicine in Edinburgh, and became a practitioner of medicine in New York city, and was for many years the leading physician in the city and a professor in Columbia College. He was distinguished for his benevolence and high Christian character. He was an Elder in the First Presbyterian Church for a long time. Dr. Rodgers was the father of the late eminent surgeon, J. Kearny Rodgers, of New York, and of the Rev. Ravaud K. Rodgers, D.D., of New Jersey. He died in 1833.

Archibald Scott was a lonely emigrant from Scotland to Pennsylvania, and in early life followed the plough for a livelihood. He received his early education at the school of Mr., afterwards President, Finley. After leaving college he studied theology with William Graham, supporting himself in the meantime by teaching. He was licensed by the Presbytery of Hanover, October 31, 1777. For about a year he supplied various churches in the Valley of Virginia, and in December, 1778, was ordained and installed pastor of North Mountain and Brown's meeting-house, afterwards called Bethel. He remained here for more than twenty years.

During the Revolution Mr. Scott and his congregation were warm patriots. Captain Tate and his company were from this congregation. On the eve of their departure to the field, which proved to be the battle of the Cowpens, Dr. Waddel addressed them, and exhorted them to patriotism and courage and prompt obedience to the military rules, under which they now came. The day after the battle of Guilford, news was brought that Tarlton with his force was approaching. Mr. Scott was at the time hearing a class in the catechism. This he hastily dismissed, and went home to spread the alarm. Mr. Scott was sound in doctrine and very tender in his preaching. His usefulness was increasing and his hold on his people growing stronger and stronger till the day of his death. He died March 4, 1799.

John Anderson Scudder, after graduating, studied medicine. He served for a number of years in the Legislature of New Jersey, and in 1810 was appointed to Congress to fill an unexpired term.

1775.

John Springer. In a letter which Mr. Springer wrote, while a sophomore in college, to a merchant in London who had taken an interest in him, he gives an account of his religious experience, and a brief account of the college, and concludes, "May the same hand that has reared and supported this institution, continue to bless it to the latest ages, and to make it a continual fountain from whence streams may issue to make glad the city of God."

Mr. Springer was a native of Delaware. After graduating, he acted as tutor in the college; and in the early part of the Revolution was a tutor in Hampden Sidney College, Virginia. When Virginia became the seat of war, he removed to North Carolina and opened an academy, and from thence to South Carolina, where he taught with distinguished success at White Hall and Cambridge. On the 18th of October, 1788, he was licensed by Orange Presbytery, and supplied various churches until July 21, 1790, when he was ordained by the Presbytery of South Carolina, and installed pastor of a Presbyterian Church at Washington, Georgia; the services taking place under the shade of a tall tree, there being no church edifice. Mr. Springer was the first Presbyterian minister ordained south of the Savannah river, and the first minister in the upper part of Georgia. Besides the charge of his church, he taught an academy, at which John Forsyth, of the class of 1799, was fitted for college. Mr. Springer was an attractive preacher, and delivered his discourses, which were unwritten, with uncommon ease and elegance. The Lecture and Sermon which were parts of trial before Presbytery, were published in Augusta, Georgia, in 1805, with a short Life prefixed. He died September 30, 1798.

Isaac Tichenor became a lawyer, and soon rose to eminence in Vermont. In 1791 he was appointed a Judge of the Supreme Court of the State, which position he held until 1797, being at that time the Chief-Justice. In October of that year, he was elected Governor of the State, which office he held with fidelity for eleven years. Mr. Tichenor was elected to the Senate of the United States in 1796, and held the same position from 1815 to 1821. He received the honorary degree of Doctor of Laws from Dartmouth in 1789. He died in December, 1838.

1776.

Nathaniel Alexander was born in North Carolina. On his return to his native State, he studied medicine, but the war coming on, he relinquished his studies and entered the army. At the close of the war he returned to his profession. In 1805 he represented the State in the United States House of Representatives; and in 1806 was elected Governor of North Carolina. In all his public stations he discharged his duty with ability and firmness. He died March 8, 1808.

William Richardson Davie came from England when quite young. He joined the American Army while a student in college, but returned and graduated with his class. On rejoining the army, he became an officer in Pulaski's Legion of Cavalry, where, by his talents and zeal, he soon rose to the rank of Colonel. At the battle of Stono he was severely wounded. After the defeat of General Gates, he asked the Legislature of North Carolina to raise a troop of cavalry, but they professing themselves to be too poor, he, with a patriotism worthy of lasting record, disposed of every cent of an estate bequeathed to him by an uncle, and equipped the troop with the proceeds. Taking command of the regiment, he was in all the battles that followed in the Southern campaign. He stood high in the esteem of General Greene, who appointed him a Commissary General.

After the war General Davie devoted himself to the practice of the law; and if his career in arms had been brilliant, his success at the Bar more than eclipsed his military fame. He was a member of the Convention that framed the Constitution of the United States, though his absence prevented his name being affixed to it. In 1791 he was a member of the Legislature of North Carolina. In 1799 he was elected Governor of North Carolina, but was soon after appointed Envoy to France with Ellsworth and Murray. His efforts in the Legislature in behalf of education deserve to be preserved. "I was present," says Judge Murphy, "in the House of Commons when Davie addressed that body, asking for a loan of money to erect the buildings of the University of North Carolina; and although more than thirty years have elapsed, I have the most vivid recollection of the greatness of his manner and the power of his eloquence upon that occasion. His eloquence was irresistible."

In 1798 he was appointed Brigadier-General in the North Carolina Militia, and prepared a System of Cavalry Tactics, which was printed by order of the State. The University of North Carolina conferred upon him the degree of Doctor of Laws in 1811. General Davie died in South Carolina, November 8, 1820.

Jonathan Dayton was a son of General Elias Dayton, of New Jersey. In 1778 he entered the American Army as Paymaster; in 1779 accompanied General Sullivan on his Western Expedition, and in 1780 was a Captain in his father's regiment. After the Peace, he was chosen to the Legislature of New Jersey, of which he was Speaker in 1790. He represented his native State in the Convention, 1787, for the formation of the Federal Constitution, and in 1791 was elected to Congress. Thrice he was re-elected, serving four terms in the House, of which he was Speaker from 1795 to 1799. In 1799 he was chosen Senator of the United States, and served until 1805. He was appointed by President Adams a Brigadier-General, with the privilege of retaining his seat in the Senate.

General Dayton became largely interested with Symmes and others in the purchase and settlement of Western military lands, the town of Dayton, in Ohio, being named in compliment to him. His early intimacy in boyhood with Aaron Burr, and his later association with him in the Senate of the United States, led him to look with more favour than prudence would have dictated upon the schemes of that aspiring and crafty politician; so that, by advancing money to aid Burr in his adventures, he became compromised with him in the charge of treason. The indictment, however, was not tried, and Mr. Dayton's bail was released. This unhappy affair, and the breaking up of the Federal party, of which he was a leader, put an end to Mr. Dayton's political aspirations. He was subsequently elected repeatedly to the Upper House of the New Jersey Legislature, and held several important offices in his native town. He received in 1798, from his *Alma Mater*, the honorary degree of Doctor of Laws. His later days were passed at home in the enjoyment of a comfortable competence, respected and venerated by all who knew him. He died October 9, 1824.

Benjamin Erwin was ordained by the Presbytery of Hanover, June 20, 1780, and settled as pastor of Mossy Creek and Cooks Creek Presbyterian Churches, Virginia. He remained in this charge until an advanced age, when he resigned.

George Faitoute acted as a tutor in the college for a short time after graduating. He received his license from the Presbytery of New Brunswick about 1778, and was ordained and settled at Greenwich, New Jersey, in 1782. In 1789 he removed to Long Island, and became pastor of the Presbyterian Church at Jamaica, where he died suddenly on Sabbath, August 21, 1815, having preached with his usual vigor in the morning. Mr. Faitoute was an amiable, pious man.

John Evans Finley, a nephew of President Finley, was licensed to preach by New Castle Presbytery about

1780, and was settled at Faggs Manor, Pennsylvania. About the year 1795 he removed to Kentucky, and became pastor of the Presbyterian Church at Bracken, Mason County, where he exercised his ministry during the great revival in the West.

Joseph Washington Henderson was licensed by the Presbytery of Donegal sometime between 1778 and 1781, and became pastor of the Presbyterian Church of Great Connewago, Pennsylvania, where he remained until 1797. From 1799 to 1824 he was pastor of the Churches of Bethlehem and Ebenezer in Western Pennsylvania.

John Wilkes Kittera lived and practiced law in Lancaster, Pennsylvania. He represented Pennsylvania in Congress from 1791 to 1801, when he was appointed United States District Attorney for the Eastern District of Pennsylvania.

Henry Philip Livingston was the youngest son of Philip Livingston, the signer of the Declaration of Independence, and a brother of Philip Phills Livingston of the class of 1758. Immediately after graduating, he entered the American Army, and became an officer in the celebrated Body Guard of General Washington. An estimate of his character may be formed by an extract from a letter written to his brother-in-law announcing the death of his father. The letter is dated Yorkville, June 14, 1778, and was written when he was but eighteen years old: "I sincerely lament," he writes, "that Providence has made it necessary to address my friends on so mournful an occasion as the present. Oh! for words to soften their distress and lessen the bitter pangs of grief! I feel myself unequal to the duty, and utterly at a loss what to say. My dear friend! have you received my letter of the 11th? written with intent to prepare the minds of the family for the melancholy subject of this, and to prevent, in some measure, the effects of a too sudden impression. Unhappily, my apprehensions were not ill founded, for the disorder was too malignant and obstinate to struggle with.

"Must I tell you! my dear father expired early on the morning of the 12th, and was buried the same evening. . . . . My dear mother and sister! grieve not immoderately, even at the loss of an excellent husband and parent! Consider that worth and excellence cannot exempt one from the lot of human nature, for no sooner do we enter the world than we begin to leave it. It is not only natural, but commendable to regret the loss of so tender a connection, but what can an excess of sorrow avail?"

Cyrus Pierson, a son of Deacon John Pierson, of South Orange, New Jersey, after leaving college studied medicine, and became a highly respectable practitioner in Newark, where he died, October, 1804. Dr. McWhorter's old book of funerals and marriages testifies, that at the funeral of Dr. Pierson he "received a scarf but no gloves."

John Pintard entered upon the study of the law, but never practiced. During the Revolution he joined a company commanded by a professor of the college, and afterwards acted for three years as clerk to his uncle, Lewis Pintard, commissioner for American prisoners in New York City. For a short time he was editor of the New York *Commercial Advertiser*, and afterwards became eminent as a merchant. Mr. Pintard was the chief founder of the New York Historical Society, and was the zealous promoter of other useful institutions. He was an intelligent antiquary, and author of a number of papers in periodicals of the day.

He died in 1844.

Among the best known of his productions, are an Account of the City of New Orleans, published in New York in the Medical Repository; and a Notice of Philip Freneau in the New York Mirror for June 12, 1833.

Joseph Rue, a native of New Jersey, was ordained by the Presbytery of New Brunswick in 1784, and was settled as pastor of the Presbyterian Church at Pennington, New Jersey. Here he remained a faithful pastor for forty-one years. He died in 1826.

John Rutherford was born in New York City, and was a nephew of William Alexander, Earl of Stirling. He became a lawyer. From 1791 to 1798 he represented New York in the United States Senate, and was the last survivor of the senators during the administration of Washington. He early retired from public life, and resided upon his large landed estate in New Jersey until his death, which occurred February 23, 1840.

Nathaniel Welshard Sample came to Princeton from Pennsylvania. He was licensed by the New Castle Presbytery in 1799. Having supplied a church at St. Georges, Delaware, for six months, and declining their call to settle, he accepted a call to Leacock, Lancaster, and Middle Octorara Churches in Pennsylvania. His relation to these churches continued forty years. He was released from his charge September 26, 1821, and died August 26, 1834.

Samuel Shannon received his license to preach from the Presbytery of Hanover, October 25, 1781, and in 1784 was ordained and settled as pastor of Windy Cove and Blue Spring Congregations in Virginia. About 1788 he removed to Kentucky, and became pastor of Bethel and Sinking Spring Presbyterian Churches, where he preached four years. He then took charge of Woodford Church, of which he continued pastor until 1806.

In the war of 1812, Mr. Shannon volunteered to accompany the Northern Army as a chaplain. He was a man of great physical strength. His fist was like a sledge-hammer, and he is said to have lopped off a stout bough at a single stroke of his sword when charging through the woods. Notwithstanding his strength, he was one of the best-natured men in the world, and nothing could provoke or ruffle him. To a rough, awkward, slovenly appearance, was added a slow and stammering utterance. He laboured indefatigably, but had no animation. The latter years of his life were employed in missionary labours, chiefly in the destitute regions of Indiana. He died in the summer of 1822.

Benjamin Parker Snowden, the first of five brothers who graduated at Princeton, was the son of Isaac Snowden, of Philadelphia, for a number of years a Trustee of the College. The son, after leaving college, studied medicine, and was lost at sea.

Nehemiah Wade was admitted as an Attorney of the Supreme Court of New Jersey at the September Term, 1784. He lived and died in Elizabethtown, New Jersey.

1777.

James Ashton Bayard was the eldest son of that distinguished friend of his country, Colonel John Bayard, of Philadelphia. He was born in 1760, and therefore graduated at the early age of seventeen. Mr. Bayard married a daughter of the Rev. John Rodgers, of New York. There is an interesting incident related of him by his sister. Owing to the progress of the war, the College at Princeton was vacated. Dr. Witherspoon was in Congress, and the other officers and students were dispersed. Mr. Bayard, among the others, had to return home. He procured a horse, and took, what he supposed, the safest road to avoid the enemy. Unfortunately he fell in with a party of marauders, who seized him, and inquired his name. When he told them, they immediately pronounced him a rebel. They then pinioned his arms and carried him to Philadelphia, and committed him to prison, where a fearful doom awaited him. His mother hearing the sad news, obtained a safe conduct, and made application to the commanding officer, and was successful in securing the release of her son. Several years after he pointed out to his sister the place where he stood when the order for his release came; it was a gate by the roadside; the halter was round his neck, and he was awaiting the moment of execution. Mr. Bayard died in 1788.

James Crawford graduated in perilous times, and, on account of the proximity of the British army, failed to get his degree at the proper time, but received it afterwards. A curious trait of the times is seen in the certificate of church membership which his pastor, the Rev.

John Craighead, gave him the year of his graduation; to the usual certificate was added these words: "And also he appears well affected to the cause of American liberty!" When we bear in mind the probability, from the date, that this was furnished as a part of the credentials necessary for his reception by the Presbytery as a candidate, it gives us insight into the political preferences of the Presbyterian clergy. Warm patriots themselves, it doubtless constituted a strong recommendation for a candidate to entertain similar sentiments. In 1779 Mr. Crawford was licensed by Hanover Presbytery, and in 1784 he removed to Kentucky, where he settled at Walnut Hill, and gathered and organized a flourishing church. He remained here until his death, which took place in 1803. Mr. Crawford was a plain-looking man of very grave demeanour; not a popular preacher, but highly useful and instructive.

John Young Noel read law in the office of the Hon. William Paterson, of the class of 1763, and was admitted as an Attorney of the Supreme Court of New Jersey, at the April Term, 1783; and as a Counsellor at the May term, 1786. Mr. Noel removed soon after to the State of Georgia, and became one of the most eminent lawyers in the South. Many of the most distinguished men in Georgia studied law in his office, among whom were Governor Troup and Governor Forsyth, both graduates of Princeton. Mr. Noel died in Augusta, Georgia.

1778.

William Boyd was a native of Franklin County, Pennsylvania. On leaving college he engaged for a few years in teaching, first an academy in Annapolis, Maryland, and then a school near Baltimore. In 1783 he was licensed by the Presbytery of Donegal. In 1784 he became pastor of the Presbyterian Church at Lamington, New Jersey, where he remained till the close of life. In 1800 he was elected a Trustee of the College of New Jersey, which office he held while he lived. Mr. Boyd was a man of great dignity and gravity. His mind was cast in a superior mould. He had a vein of keen wit, which he brought into exercise on suitable occasions, but never in a way to disparage his ministerial character. He was distinguished for uncommon knowledge of the Scriptures. He never used notes in the pulpit, but his thoughts were always well matured. His manner was animated and earnest, and well fitted to secure attention. He died May 17, 1807.

Jacob Morton studied law and was admitted an Attorney of the Supreme Court of New Jersey, at the September term, 1782. He removed soon after to the city of New York, where he became prominent at the Bar. In 1797 he was appointed, by Governor Jay, Justice of the Peace in a new court just established by the Legislature. The governor selected several of the most promising young lawyers for these positions. John Wells, of the class of 1788, was an associate of Mr. Morton on the Bench. From 1807 to 1808 he was Comptroller of the City of New York. During the war of 1812 Mr. Morton was quite prominent, and became a general of militia.

He never returned to the active pursuit of his profession, but was for twenty years the Clerk of the Common Council of New York City. Mr. Morton died in 1837.

Joseph Scudder was the son of Nathaniel Scudder, of the class of 1751, and the father of the distinguished missionary, Rev. Dr. John Scudder. He was admitted to the Bar by the Supreme Court of New Jersey, in November, 1786, and practiced law in New Brunswick and in Freehold, New Jersey. For a number of years he was the Clerk of Monmouth County.

Peter Wilson was ordained by the Presbytery of New Brunswick about 1785, and was settled as pastor of Hackettstown and Mansfield Presbyterian Churches, New Jersey, where he remained until his death, July 24, 1799.

Matthew Woods was ordained by the Presbytery of Donegal about 1783, and died September 13, 1784. Whether Mr. Woods was a pastor during the few months that intervened between his ordination and his death, I have not discovered.

1779.

Andrew Bayard was a son of Colonel John Bayard, and a brother of James Ashton Bayard of the class of 1777. He became a merchant in Philadelphia, and was for many years the President of the Commercial Bank in that city. In 1808 Mr. Bayard was elected a Trustee of the College, and served in that position until 1823. He died in 1832.

Matthew McCallister, although a native of Pennsylvania, entered the profession of the law and began the practice in the State of Georgia about 1783. He soon became distinguished for the fidelity with which he discharged the many public and private duties which devolved upon him. From May 25, 1801, to May 26, 1802, he was Judge of the Superior Courts of the Eastern District of Georgia. He died May 9, 1823, deeply regretted by all who knew him.

George Merchant, after graduating, became an eminent classical teacher.

James Riddle, a native of Pennsylvania, served as a tutor in college for two years after graduating. He became a lawyer, and attained some eminence. He was for a long time Judge of the High Court of Errors and Appeals of Pennsylvania. Judge Riddle was a man of learning and worth. He died February 5, 1837.

Richard Stockton was a son of Richard Stockton of the class of 1748. He was admitted to the Bar at the age of twenty, and soon became distinguished for his legal ability. From 1796 to 1799 he represented New Jersey in the United States Senate, and from 1813 to 1815 was in the House of Representatives. He was eminently distinguished for his talents; was an eloquent and profound lawyer, and during more than a quarter of a century was at the head of the New Jersey Bar. He received the honorary degree of Doctor of Laws from Columbia College in 1815, and from Union College in 1816. He was for thirty-seven years a Trustee of the College. He died in Princeton, New Jersey, March 7, 1828. Mr. Stockton was the father of the late Commodore Robert F. Stockton, and the grandfather of the Hon. John P. Stockton of the United States Senate.

Aaron Dickinson Woodruff, the eldest son of Elias and Mary J. Woodruff, was born at Elizabethtown, New Jersey, September 12, 1762. He was the Valedictorian of his class. Mr. Woodruff was admitted to the Bar in 1784. In 1793 he was elected Attorney-General of the State, and was annually re-elected, except in 1811, until his death. He also served in the Legislature. He was for many years a trustee in the Presbyterian Church in Trenton. The epitaph upon Mr. Woodruff's tomb describes well his character: "For twenty-four years he filled the important station of Attorney-General with incorruptible integrity. Adverse to legal subtleties, his professional knowledge was exerted in the cause of truth and justice. The native benevolence of his heart made him a patron of the poor, a defender of the fatherless; it exulted in the joys, or participated in the sorrows, of his friends."

1780.

Ebenezer Stockton, a native of New Jersey, studied medicine and entered the army as a surgeon. After the war he practiced for many years in Princeton. He was a man of professional skill, and was highly esteemed by the whole community during a long life. Towards the close of his life, he gave up the practice of his profession on account of bodily infirmity. Dr. Stockton died in 1837.

Samuel W. Venable fought bravely in the Revolutionary war. After leaving college he expected to study law, but was led by some circumstances to engage in merchandise, which he carried on largely in Prince Edward County, Virginia.

Mr. Venable was a man of clear head and sound judgment, and had made observations on the characters of men as they passed before him; and these observations he reduced to maxims. He was one of the main founders of Hampden Sidney College. Dr. Archibald Alexander was accustomed to speak of him as the most remarkable instance of wisdom matured by experience and observation, that he had ever known; in which respect he was fond of comparing him to Franklin.

When about fifty years of age, Mr. Venable relinquished active business, hoping to spend the rest of his life in a course of reading and study; but he soon fell into a hypochondriac state, fancying that his lungs were seriously affected, and the opinions of his friends and physicians could not convince him of his error. Colonel Venable died suddenly at the Virginia Springs in 1825.

1780.

Abraham B. Venable, a brother of the preceding, also became distinguished for his patriotic ardour on the field of battle. He represented Virginia in Congress from 1791 to 1799; and from 1803 to 1804 he was in the Senate of the United States. He perished in the burning of the Richmond theatre, December 26, 1811.

1781.

Joseph Clark was from Elizabethtown, New Jersey. When the British entered the State, he left college and joined the American Army. He continued several years in the service of his country, rendered important aid in the Revolutionary contest, and received attentions from distinguished military characters, very flattering to a youth of his age. On leaving the army he returned to Princeton and received his degree.

On the 23d of April, 1783, he was licensed by the Presbytery of New Brunswick, and commenced preaching at Allentown, New Jersey, but was not installed as pastor until June, 1788.

In 1796, he removed to New Brunswick as pastor of the Presbyterian Church, where he remained until his death. In 1802, he was elected a Trustee of the College, and remained in office till his death. In 1809, he received the degree of Doctor of Divinity from Jefferson College.

Dr. Clark's health was always feeble, but notwithstanding, he was one of the most active ministers of the day. He possessed a mind of a high order, enlarged and cultivated by much study. In the pulpit he was solemn and dignified; his discourses solid and judicious. He possessed extraordinary colloquial powers and a strong relish for cultivated society. In details of business, few men probably have surpassed him. In person, he was of full medium stature, but slender; his eyes sharp and blue; his hair light and not very abundant. His memory well deserves to be honoured and embalmed. He died October 19, 1813.

Dr. Clark's only publications were: A Sermon occasioned by the death of the Hon. William Paterson, 1806. Two Discourses in the New Jersey Preacher, 1813.

William Crawford served in the House of Representatives of the United States, from Pennsylvania, from 1809 to 1817. He died in 1823.

William Branch Giles entered Congress from Virginia as early as 1796, where he remained for many years. In 1811, he was elected to the United States Senate, but resigned his seat in 1815. In 1826, he was elected Governor of Virginia, and continued in office three years. He died December 8, 1830.

Governor Giles published: A Speech on the Embargo Laws, 1808. Political Letters to the people of Virginia, 1813. A Series of Letters, signed "A Constituent," in the *Richmond Enquirer*, January, 1818, against the plan for general education. And a number of Letters on Public Affairs.

Edward Livingston was a brother of Robert R. Livingston, the Chancellor of New York, and was related to the family of Governor Livingston of New Jersey. He was born at Claremont, Livingston Manor, New York, in 1764. After graduating, he studied law with his brother the Chancellor, and was admitted to the Bar in 1785. He pursued his profession in New York City until 1794, when he was elected to Congress, and held the seat until 1802. Returning to New York, he was appointed by Jefferson United States District Attorney, being at the same time Mayor of the city. In 1804, Mr. Livingston removed to New Orleans, where he immediately became conspicuous at that Bar. At the invasion of Louisiana, he acted as aid to General Jackson. In 1823, he was elected a member of the House of Representatives, and in 1829 was transferred to the United States Senate. In 1831, he was appointed Secretary of State, and in 1833, Minister to France.

Mr. Livingston was employed, with others, by the Legislature of Louisiana, to prepare a system of Jurisprudence, and also of Municipal law, and performed the service with great industry and deep research. His Penal Code, his own unaided work, is a monument of his profound learning, and his desire to promote the welfare of mankind. Mr. Livingston died in 1836.

The publications of Mr. Livingston are: Judicial Opinions delivered in the Mayor's Court in the City of New York, 1802. The Batture Case at New Orleans, 8vo, 1808. The Batture Case; in answer to President Jefferson's pamphlet of 1812–1814. Reports made to the General Assembly of the State of Louisiana, of the Plan of the Penal Code of said State, 8vo, 1822. (This was reprinted in London and Paris.) A System of Penal Law for the State of Louisiana, 1826.

1782.

Conrad Elmendorf was a member of the House of Representatives from New York from 1797 to 1803; and a member of the New York Assembly during 1804, 1805; and a State Senator from 1814 to 1817.

John A. Hanna came to college from Pennsylvania. After his graduation he resided at Harrisburg, and from 1792 to 1805 he was a member of the House of Representatives of the United States. Mr. Hanna died in 1805.

William Mahon received a license to preach from the Presbytery of Hanover about 1790. He presided at the meeting of Presbytery at which Dr. Archibald Alexander was ordained in 1794. In 1796 he removed to Kentucky, and became pastor of New Providence Church in Transylvania Presbytery, but was brought before Presbytery on various charges, and admonished to maintain a stricter guard over his temper. The people being dissatisfied with him, the connection was dissolved by Presbytery, October 5, of the same year. Mr. Mahon was finally deposed for drunkenness in 1804. He applied in 1812 to be restored; but the Presbytery, not being satisfied of his reformation, refused his request.

Robert Pearson studied law after his graduation, and was admitted an Attorney of the Supreme Court of New Jersey at the April Term, 1789; and as a Counsellor at the May Term, 1794. He practiced in Gloucester County, New Jersey.

1782.

Richard N. Venable, a brother of Abraham B. and Samuel W. Venable of the class of 1780, studied law, and practiced in Prince Edward County, Virginia, where he died in 1805.

Samuel Wilson received a license to preach from the Presbytery of New Castle, and became pastor of Big Spring Presbyterian Church, Pennsylvania, about 1788. He remained in this charge until his death in 1799.

1783.

Timothy Ford was the eldest son of Colonel Jacob Ford, Jr., of Morris County, New Jersey, and brother of Gabriel Ford of the class of 1784, and Jacob Ford of the class of 1792. His father died in 1777, and he was reared by his mother, at whose house Washington had his headquarters, while the army was at Morristown.

Ashbel Green was born at Hanover, New Jersey, July 6, 1762. He was the son of the Rev. Jacob Green, who was for forty-five years pastor of the Presbyterian Church at Hanover. When only sixteen years old, Mr. Green entered the army as a private, and rose to be sergeant of his company. On one occasion, after a rencontre with a party of British troops, his captain said to his company, "I think you might get a shot at those men in the boats! Who of you will try?" "I will," was Green's immediate answer; and although only one other man would accompany him, he was as good as his word. He was also present with the American troops who pursued the British after they had burned the village of Connecticut Farms, and murdered the wife of the Rev. James Caldwell. At this time Mr. Green was the teacher of a classical school; and on both the above occasions he dismissed his school to rally with others around the standard of his country.

The Commencement at which Mr. Green graduated, was a memorable one. Congress had been driven by a disorderly corps of soldiers from Philadelphia, and had adjourned to Princeton. They held their sessions in the library of the college. Dr. Boudinot, a trustee of the college, was then President of Congress, and General Washington was in attendance, in the latter part of the summer and beginning of autumn, for the final disbanding of the army.

On the arrival of the Commencement, Congress, as a compliment to the college, and their own president, as well as to the president of the college, who had recently been one of their own members, determined to adjourn and attend the exercises of the day. A large stage was erected, on which were seated all the members of Congress, two foreign ministers and General Washington. At the close of the valedictory oration, which had been assigned to Mr. Green, he had an address of some length to the General. Let me give the words of Dr. Green: "The General colored as I addressed him, but his modesty was among the qualities which so highly distinguished him. The next day, as he was going to attend a Committee of Congress, he met me in one of the long entries of the college edifice, stopped, and took me by the hand, and complimented me on my address in language which I should lack his modesty if I repeated it even to you."

Mr. Green held the office of tutor in the college for two years, and was then appointed to the Chair of Mathematics and Natural Philosophy, which he retained for a year and a half. In February, 1786, he was licensed to preach by the Presbytery of New Brunswick. In May, 1787, he was settled as colleague of Rev. Dr. Sproat, in Philadelphia; and the same year was elected a member of the American Philosophical Society. In 1792 the University of Pennslyvania conferred upon him the degree of Doctor of Divinity; and the same year he was elected Chaplain to Congress, and was re-elected by every successive Congress till the removal to Washington. Dr. Green was one of the chief instruments in founding the Theological Seminary at Princeton. In August, 1812, he was elected President of the College; and in the same year received the degree of Doctor of Laws from the University of North Carolina. Dr. Green occupied the Presidential Chair until 1822, when, on account of increasing infirmity, he resigned. He immediately took up his residence in Philadelphia, and became the editor of the *Christian Advocate*, a monthly religious magazine. The work was continued through twelve volumes, in which the editor displayed the fertility of his active, well-disciplined mind, the extent of his learning, the acuteness of his critical powers, and his devotion to the interests of the kingdom of Christ.

The last regular sermon preached by this venerable man was in the African Church at Princeton, July 16, 1843, in his eighty-second year. He died on the 14th of May, 1848.

Dr. Green in person was of a medium height, but portly, having features well formed; a florid complexion, enlivened with dark brilliant eyes. He was in his youth handsome. His intellectual powers were of a high order. He was characterized by much firmness and decision. He rejoiced to preach the Gospel, and his discourses were uniformly written. Dr. Carnahan, his immediate successor, said of him: "He was by his talents fitted to fill any station; and by his eloquence to adorn the walls of our National Legislature." Dr. Green's publications are numerous.

He superintended an edition of Witherspoon's works, 1802, and left in manuscript a biography of that eminent man.

In 1822, he published a History of the College of New Jersey, in connexion with a Series of Baccalaureate Discourses. A History of Presbyterian Missions. A Sermon at the funeral of the Rev. George Duffield, D.D., 1790. The Address and Petition of a number of the Clergy of Philadelphia, to the Senate and House of Representatives of the State of Pennsylvania, relative to Theatrical Amusements, 1793. A Sermon occasioned by the death of the Rev. Dr. Sproat, 1793. Obedience to the Laws of God; a Fast Sermon, 1798. An Address of the Trustees of the College of New Jersey, 1802. A Discourse at the opening for Public Worship of the Presbyterian Church in the Northern Liberties of Philadelphia, 1805. An Address of the Bible Society of Philadelphia, 1809. An Address to the Students and Faculty of the College of New Jersey, 1802. Report of a Committee of the General Assembly exhibiting the Plan of a Theological Seminary, 1810. Life and Death of the Righteous; an Address at the funeral of the Rev. William M. Tennent, D. D., 1810. Advice and Exhortation addressed to the People of the Second Presbyterian Church in Philadelphia, on resigning the pastoral charge of that congregation, 1812. A Report to the Trustees of the College of New Jersey relative to a Revival of Religion among the students of said college, in the winter and spring of 1815. Doing good in imitation of Christ; a Discourse delivered in the College of New Jersey the Sabbath preceding the annual Commencement, 1822. Christ Crucified the Characteristic of Apostolic preaching; a Sermon delivered at the opening of the General Assembly of the Presbyterian Church, 1825. The Christian Duty of Christian Women; a Discourse delivered at Princeton before a Female Society, for the support of a Female School in India, 1825. A Sermon (National Preacher, No. 9), delivered at the opening of the Synod of Philadelphia, 1826. An Address at the interment of Robert Ralston, 1836. A Sermon at the Whitefield Chapel, 1836. Lectures on the Shorter Catechism, 2 vols. 12mo, originally published in the *Christian Advocate*.

James Hunt was probably the son of Rev. James Hunt of Montgomery County, Maryland, of the class of 1759, and a brother of William Pitt Hunt of the class of 1786. He probably assisted and succeeded his father in his admirable classical school so long a blessing to Maryland.

Nathaniel Lawrence belonged to an influential family of Long Island. He was a son of Captain John Lawrence, a naval officer in the old French war. Immediately upon his graduation, he joined the North Carolina line of the regular American army as a lieutenant, and was made prisoner by the enemy after behaving with great gallantry. In 1788, he was chosen from Queens County, New York, to the Convention which ratified the Constitution of the United States. He also held the office of Attorney General of the State from December 24, 1792, to November 30, 1795, and represented Queens County in the Legislature for four years. His daughter married the Rev. Philip Lindsley, D.D., formerly professor in the college. He died at Hempstead, Long Island, July 5, 1797.

Jacob Radcliff was a son of William Radcliff of Dutchess County, New York, a Brigadier-General during the Revolution. After graduating, he read law, and commenced practice at Poughkeepsie, which he followed with distinguished success, and at an early age was raised to the Bench of the Supreme Court of New York. Removing to New York City, he soon after resigned his judicial office, returning to the practice of his profession. In 1810, he was elected Mayor of the City of New York, and was again elected in 1811, 1812 and 1813.

Mr. Radcliff continued his professional pursuits for many years, dying at a venerable age in 1823.

Gilbert Tennent Snowden, a brother of Benjamin Parker Snowden of the class of 1776, was licensed to preach by the Presbytery of Philadelphia. On the 24th of November, 1790, he was transferred to the Presbytery of New Brunswick, and ordained and installed pastor of the Presbyterian Church at Cranberry, New Jersey.

Before entering the ministry, Mr. Snowden had applied himself intensely to the study of law. But on one occasion, attending the funeral of an eminent member of the Bar, he was so deeply impressed with the vanity of the fame, wealth, and honours of the world, that he resolved to renounce his former purpose and devote himself to the Gospel ministry. His ministry was a short one, but filled with labour and crowned with fruit. He died February 20, 1797. President Samuel Stanhope Smith preached his funeral sermon, in which he says: "The best eulogy of Gilbert Tennent Snowden, would be a faithful history of himself."

Edward Taylor studied medicine after graduating, and received his degree under Dr. Rush in Philadelphia in 1786. Dr. Taylor was a native of Upper Freehold, Monmouth County, New Jersey. He began the practice of medicine and surgery at Pemberton, New Jersey, but shortly after removed to his native place, where he was assiduously engaged during a long life of remarkable activity and usefulness in the arduous labours and responsibilities of a large county practice—often extending from the Delaware river to the sea coast, and usually traveling in the saddle, and not unfrequently during whole nights, regardless of weather. Notwithstanding such a life of intense physical and mental toil, his temperate habits in eating, with abstinence from intoxicating drinks, preserved his well-formed, compact, medium-sized frame, in an unusually healthful condition to the close of his life.

In the latter part of his life, from a conviction of duty, (having joined the Society of Friends,) he removed to and superintended the "Friends' Asylum for the Insane" at Frankfort, Pennsylvania, which responsible duty he fulfilled for nine years; when he returned to his home in New Jersey, about three years prior to his decease.

Few men, perhaps, have occupied a higher position in the estimation of all who knew them, than did the subject of this notice, for strict integrity to his high standard of morality, and justice to all. In life and conversation he adorned the "doctrine of Christ" our Saviour, and this was the great object of his life, and made him honoured and beloved in his own religious society, and out of it—and he left a large unbroken family of children to mourn his loss. He died May 2, 1835.

Joseph Venable, a native of Virginia, studied law, and removed to Kentucky soon after his admission to the Bar, when we lose sight of him.

George Whitefield Woodruff, a brother of A. D. Woodruff of the class of 1779, was born at Elizabethtown, New Jersey, March 16, 1765. After graduating, he studied law, and was admitted to practice as an Attorney at the April term of the Supreme Court, in 1788. He removed then to the State of Georgia, and acquired a position of much respectability at the Bar of that State; so that he was appointed, by President John Adams, United States District Attorney. Having acquired an ample fortune, he returned to New Jersey and took up his residence near Trenton. Here he lived in much companionship with books, withdrawn from active business, but not from constant amiable intercourse with men, until his death, which occurred in 1846, at the age of eighty-two. At the time of his death Mr. Woodruff was the oldest member of the New Jersey Bar. It is said that his most intimate friends never knew him to be betrayed into an angry deed or word. Possessed of fortune, and a well-cultivated and well-stored mind, he exercised, notwithstanding his retiring manners, the influence which wealth and intelligence confer.

A son of Mr. Woodruff graduated in the class of 1836.

1784.

John Baldwin, a son of Jonathan Baldwin of the class of 1755, after graduating, studied law and practiced for a number of years in New York City.

James Ashton Bayard, a son of James A. Bayard, M.D., and a nephew of Colonel John Bayard, was born in Philadelphia in 1767. After leaving college, he studied law in Philadelphia and commenced practice in Delaware. In 1796 he was elected to the House of Representatives of the United States. He was in the House that elected Mr. Jefferson President, and was very influential in the result. In 1804 he was chosen to the United States Senate. He remained in this position until he was selected by Mr. Madison, as a Commissioner, with Mr. Gallatin, to negotiate a peace with Great Britain, and sailed on his mission, May 9, 1813. In 1814, while in Europe, he was appointed Envoy to the Court of Russia, but he declined the appointment, stating "that he had no wish to serve the administration, except when his services were necessary for the good of his country." Soon after this he was seized with violent illness, and was obliged to return home. He arrived in June, and died at Wilmington, August 6, 1815.

Mr. Bayard was a keen and able debater, and eloquent beyond most of his contemporaries. His fine countenance and manly person recommended his eloquent words.

Mr. Bayard's Speech on the Foreign Intercourse Bill was published in 1798, and his Speech on the Repeal of the Judiciary, in a volume of the speeches delivered in this controversy, in 1802.

1784.

Samuel Bayard was a son of Colonel John Bayard, of Philadelphia. He resided the greater part of his life in Princeton, and was a man of sterling worth and high Christian character. He was for some years a Judge of the Court of Common Pleas. Mr. Bayard corresponded with W. Pitt, Lord Erskine, Lord Lansdowne, Sir John Sinclair and Wilberforce. Dr. James W. Alexander writes of him, in 1839, "Our old friend Bayard, now in his seventy-third year, is one of the most pleasing specimens of religious serenity and hope that I have seen. He is tottering over the grave, but his inward man is renewed day by day."

Judge Bayard was for several years a Trustee of the College. He died May 12, 1840.

Mr. Bayard published, Letters on the Sacrament of the Lord's Supper.

Joseph Clay was born in Savannah, Georgia, August 16, 1764. He was a son of the Hon. Joseph Clay, a soldier, patriot and Judge, of the Revolution. Returning to his home in Savannah, Mr. Clay entered upon the study of the law, and having been admitted to the Bar, soon rose to the highest eminence in his profession. He was particularly distinguished as an advocate in criminal cases. He was a leading member of the Convention which formed the Constitution of Georgia. In 1796 he was appointed District Judge of the United States for the District of Georgia, where he presided with distinguished ability and universal approbation. He resigned the office in 1801.

In 1803 Mr. Clay became a member of the Baptist Church, and was ordained the next year as pastor of a church in Savannah. In 1807 he visited New England, and was induced to take charge of a Baptist Church in Boston; but in a year or two he resigned on account of ill health. A lawyer in Providence once hearing him preach, remarked to a friend, "See what a lawyer can do." The reply was, "See what the grace of God can do with a lawyer." Mr. Clay died in Savannah, December, 1804. He published his Installation Sermon in 1807.

Ira Condict, after leaving college, taught a school in Freehold, New Jersey, and studied theology with the Rev. John Woodhull. In April, 1786, he was licensed by the Presbytery of New Brunswick; and in 1787 he was installed pastor of the Presbyterian Churches of Newton and Shappenac, New Jersey. In 1793 he became pastor of the Reformed Dutch Church in New Brunswick. At the revival of Queens College (afterwards Rutgers) in 1808, in effecting which he had an important agency, he was chosen Vice-President. Dr. Livingston was the President, but the office was a nominal one, as he confined himself to his theological professorship, and Mr. Condict was virtually the President until his death in 1811.

Mr. Condict had a strong athletic frame, and was considerably above the medium height; had dark eyes and hair, with an expression of countenance which indicated a vigorous masculine intellect. He was a man of great reserve and remarkable gravity. He was a Trustee of the College for six years.

Gabriel H. Ford was a brother of Timothy Ford of the class of 1783. He was admitted to the Bar in 1789, and practiced in Morristown, New Jersey, his native place. On the 15th of November, 1820, he was elevated to the Bench of the Supreme Court of New Jersey, and held the position for twenty-one years. Judge Ford was considered an efficient and eloquent lawyer, and an upright and conscientious judge. He died at Morristown, August 27, 1849.

James Hopkins, a native of Pennsylvania, was admitted to the Bar in Philadelphia, and soon after removed to Lancaster, where he was enrolled as a member of that Bar in 1787. Mr. Hopkins soon secured a most extensive practice and a distinguished standing at the Bar. President Buchanan read law in his office, although afterwards they were usually opposing advocates. While engaged as leading counsel in an important ejectment suit, in September, 1834, in which Mr. Buchanan was the leading counsel upon the opposite side, and while in the act of citing an authority, with the words of the sentence half finished, Mr. Hopkins was struck with apoplexy, and never spoke again. It is rather a singular coincidence, that this was also the last instance in which Mr. Buchanan was engaged in the trial of a case in a court of law, having been very soon thereafter called to positions of official trust. Mr. Hopkins died September 14, 1834, in the seventy-second year of his age.

Mr. Hopkins's son, George Washington, graduated at Princeton in 1817, and afterwards had a short but brilliant career at the Lancaster Bar. He was so much prostrated while defending a man who was accused of the crime of murder, that he never rallied from the effects of the prostration, dying a few months before his father.

Alexander Cumming McWhorter was the son of the Rev. Alexander McWhorter, D. D., of the class of 1757. Mr. McWhorter studied law, and was admitted to the Bar in September, 1788, and became a highly respectable practitioner in Newark, New Jersey. He died in 1808.

Isaac Ogden became a lawyer in Delaware County, New York, and was for many years a prominent member of the Legislature of New York. He was a man of strong and vigorous intellect, and of great decision of character.

William Radcliff was a brother of Jacob Radcliff of the class of 1783. He removed to South America, and was for some time United States Consul at the City of Lima. He afterwards returned to the United States, and died in Brooklyn in 1847.

1784.

John E. Spencer was a son of the Rev. Elihu Spencer, D.D., so long a Trustee and friend of the college. He studied law, and was admitted an Attorney of the Supreme Court of New Jersey, at the April Term, 1789, and as Counsellor at the April Term, 1798. Mr. Spencer resided and practiced at Elizabethtown, New Jersey.

Abner Woodruff was a brother of George W. Woodruff of the preceding class. He was the son of Elias Woodruff of Elizabethtown, New Jersey, and was born December 28, 1767. In 1772, his father removed to Princeton. In February, 1779, Abner Woodruff joined the grammar school in Nassau Hall, and, as he says, "commenced the rudiments of education." In 1780, he entered the Freshman Class. Soon after graduating he took up his residence in Sussex County, New Jersey, where he engaged in mercantile operations until 1787, when he returned to Princeton in September of that year, and was admitted to the degree of Master of Arts. In September, 1794, having resumed business in Sussex County, he, with his partner, who both belonged to a volunteer troop of horse, joined the expedition to quell the Whiskey Insurrection in Western Pennsylvania. Mr. Woodruff became a Paymaster of the Second Regiment of New Jersey Cavalry. In December of the same year, he returned to New Jersey. In 1798, he received an appointment as Midshipman in the Navy, and continued in the service until 1803, when he resigned his commission and removed to Georgia, where he resided for a number of years. Returning from Georgia, he took up his residence at Perth Amboy, New Jersey, where he died January 11, 1842.

1785.

Mathias Cazier became pastor of a Congregational Church in Pelham, Massachusetts, in the same year that he graduated. In August, 1799, he removed to Connecticut, and was installed pastor of a church in South Britain, where he laboured until January, 1804. In May of that year, he supplied Salem Church in the town of Waterbury, but for how long a period I do not find. Mr. Cazier died in 1837.

Robert Goodloe Harper was born in Virginia in 1765. When a youth he served in a troop of horse, under General Greene, in the Southern campaign. While in college he acted as tutor to one or two of the lower classes. Soon after graduating he went to Charleston, South Carolina, and found himself among strangers with but a dollar or two in his pocket. While standing on the wharf after landing, a by-stander asked him whether he had not taught school in Princeton. This proved to be a gentleman whose son he had taught while in college. He offered him assistance and his friendship, and introduced him to a lawyer, in whose office he studied for a year, when he was admitted to the Bar. He then entered into professional life in the interior of the State, and soon became known by a series of articles published in a newspaper, on a proposed change in the Constitution of the State. He was soon elected to the Legislature, and then to Congress, where he became distinguished. After the election of Mr. Jefferson as President, Mr. Harper retired from Congress, and having married the daughter of Charles Carroll, of Carrollton, he entered upon the practice of the law at Baltimore. He was employed in the defence of Judge Chase of the Supreme Court at the time of his impeachment. In course of time he was elected to the United States Senate from Maryland. In 1819 and 1820, Mr. Harper visited Europe, and on his return became an active member of the American Colonization Society, a scheme in which he took the deepest interest. He died January 15, 1825.

Mr. Harper published: A Speech in behalf of the American Colonization Society. An Address on the British Treaty, 1796. Observations on the Dispute between the United States and France, 1797. Letter on the Proceedings of Congress. Letters to his Constituents, 1801. Correspondence with Robert Walsh respecting Germany, 1813. Address on the Russian Victories, 1813. Select Works, 1814.

John Vernon Henry studied law and entered upon its practice in Albany, New York. In 1800, he was appointed Comptroller of the State; but owing to the change of parties, he was removed the next year. Deeply disgusted at the transaction, he resolved never again to accept any office, but to devote himself to his profession. This resolution he kept, and by his assiduous application he attained the highest eminence at the Bar. His distinguished talents, and high and deserved character for integrity and honour, were everywhere acknowledged. The great superiority of Mr. Henry as an advocate consisted in his skill in condensing his argument—in saying everything which could be said in favour of the position he wished to establish, with the fewest possible number of words. These words were selected in the best possible manner. He never used a single word but such as was the very best to express precisely the idea he desired to impress on the mind of his hearer. Of course he was neither florid nor brilliant, but luminous and strictly logical, and at times powerfully eloquent.

He received the degree of Doctor of Laws in 1823. A son of Mr. Henry graduated in the class of 1815. He died in 1829.

James Wilkin studied law and entered upon the

practice in Goshen, New York, his native place. In 1800, he was elected a member of the Legislature. He also represented his State in Congress, and held almost every station in the gift of his immediate fellow citizens, having been through life greatly beloved and respected. He died in Goshen in 1805. A son of Mr. Wilkin graduated in the class of 1812, and a grandson in 1843.

1786.

Henry Clymer was born in Philadelphia, July 31, 1767. He was the third son (the first and second having died in infancy) of George Clymer who signed the Declaration of Independence. His mother was a daughter of Reese Meredith, of the Society of Friends, born in Wales, but afterwards a prosperous and respected merchant in Philadelphia. Henry Clymer, after graduating, entered the office of James Wilson, the leading lawyer in Philadelphia, and a signer of the Declaration of Independence. In 1794 he married the third daughter of Thomas Willing, who, for thirty-nine years, was partner of Robert Morris. Mr. Clymer's taste inclining him to agriculture, led him in the summer of 1799 into the country, where he resided on a farm near Morrisville, Pennsylvania, opposite Trenton, New Jersey. There he continued to live until his father's death, at the son's residence, in 1813, when the large landed interests of his father's estate carried him to Northumberland and then to Wilkesbarre. In these two places on the Susquehanna, he resided till the winter of 1819, when he moved to Trenton, and afterwards to a country seat on the opposite bank of the Delaware, in Pennsylvania, where he died April 17, 1830.

Mr. Clymer was a great friend of education, connecting himself with what was useful wherever he happened to live. Three of his sons graduated at Princeton in 1821, 1822 and 1823, respectively.

William Gordon Forman was a native of Monmouth County, New Jersey. He studied law, and was admitted an Attornev by the Supreme Court, at the September Term, 1791. Soon after his admission to the Bar, he removed to Natchez, Mississippi. In 1806, Mr. Forman married a daughter of Dr. John Woodhull, of the class of 1766. He died in Lexington, Kentucky, October 3, 1812.

Edward Graham joined the college from North Carolina, to which State he returned after graduating, and entered upon the practice of the law.

Thomas Grant was ordained by the Presbytery of New Brunswick in 1791, and was settled as pastor of the Churches of Amwell and Flemington, New Jersey. Mr. Grant died in 1811, being succeeded in his churches by Rev. Jacob Kirkpatrick, D. D.

William King Hugg studied law, and was admitted an Attorney of the Supreme Court of New Jersey, September, 1790.

Ralph P. Hunt studied law, and was admitted an Attorney of the Supreme Court of New Jersey at the September Term, 1791, and practiced in Hunterdon County, New Jersey. He is said to have died young.

William Pitt Hunt was a son of the Rev. James Hunt, of the class of 1759. After leaving college, he studied law, and practiced at his home in Montgomery County, Maryland. William Wirt, afterwards so eminent as a lawyer, commenced the study of law in Mr. Hunt's office. Mr. Hunt afterwards removed to Virginia, the place of his father's birth. He died about 1800. His widow married the Rev. Moses Hoge, D. D.

James Henderson Imlay acted as tutor in the college for one year after graduating. He was admitted an Attorney of the Supreme Court of New Jersey at the April Term, 1790, and a Counsellor at the April Term,

1796. From 1797 to 1801, Mr. Imlay was in the House of Representatives of the United States. He lived and died in Allentown, New Jersey.

Maturin Livingston, a brother of William Smith Livingston of the class of 1772, studied law, and was admitted to the Bar in New York City, where he practiced for many years. On the 10th of November, 1804, he was appointed Recorder of the City. Mr. Livingston was a brother-in-law of Governor Morgan Lewis, of the class of 1773.

Peter William Livingston was a son of Peter Robert Livingston of the class of 1758. I can find nothing of him after his graduation.

Amos Marsh entered college from New England. After graduating, he took up his residence in Vermont, and probably pursued the profession of law. In 1789, he was admitted to a Master's degree at Dartmouth. From 1799 to 1801, Mr. Marsh was Speaker of the General Assembly of Vermont. He died in 1811.

Thomas Pollock was a native of North Carolina. His mother was Eunice, the fourth daughter of President Edwards. After graduating, he studied law, but never practiced his profession, but living the uneventful life of a planter. He died in Italy, September, 1803.

Henry Smalley was from New Jersey. In 1788, he was licensed to preach by the Piscataway Baptist Church. In 1790, he became pastor of the Cohansey Baptist Church in Cumberland County, New Jersey. In this charge he remained forty-nine years.

Mr. Smalley was a laborious and successful minister. He died February 11, 1839.

Charles Smith was born near Princeton, New Jersey. He studied medicine, and after receiving his diploma, was appointed a surgeon in the army raised in New Jersey, which, under Governor Howell of that State, took part in suppressing the "Whiskey Insurrection." At the close of the war he began the practice of medicine in New Brunswick, in partnership with Dr. Moses Scott. After the death of Dr. Scott, he practiced many years in New Brunswick, where he was highly esteemed as a man and physician. He was for a long time a Trustee of Rutgers College, and also President of the State Bank at New Brunswick. He died in 1845.

Samuel Finley Snowden, a brother of Gilbert T. Snowden of the class of 1783, was licensed to preach by the Presbytery of New Brunswick, April 24, 1794, and ordained and installed pastor of the Presbyterian Church at Princeton on the 25th of November following. This charge Mr. Snowden resigned April 29, 1801, on account of ill health. He was afterwards settled successively at Whitesboro, New Hartford, and Sackett's Harbour in the State of New York. He died suddenly in May, 1845.

Samuel Robert Stewart read law with Samuel Leake, of Trenton, of the class of 1774, and was admitted to the Bar, September, 1790. He settled and practiced at Flemington, New Jersey. Mr. Stewart was the father of the Rev. Charles S. Stewart, of the class of 1815, the Missionary, and afterwards Chaplain in the Navy. Mr. Stewart died in 1802, at the early age of 36.

John W. Vancleve was a son of Benjamin Vancleve of Lawrence Township, Hunterdon County (now in Mercer) New Jersey, for many years a member of the Legislature. From 1787 to 1791, Mr. Vancleve served as a tutor in the college. He was admitted to the Bar in September, 1791, and practiced in Trenton, New Jersey. He died of yellow fever in Philadelphia in 1802.

1787.

John Nelson Abeel served as tutor in the college for two years after his graduation. He then commenced the study of the law under Judge Paterson of New Jersey; but relinquishing the purpose of becoming a lawyer, he entered upon the study of theology under Dr. Livingston, and was licensed to preach in April, 1793. He first became pastor of a Presbyterian Church in Philadelphia, but in 1795, was installed as pastor of the Reformed Dutch Church in the City of New York. With a discriminating mind, and a sweet and melodious voice, and his soul inflamed with pious zeal, he was pre-eminent among extemporaneous orators. In performing his pastoral duties he was indefatigable. Mr. Abeel was a man of unassuming manners, and a truly eloquent preacher. He received the honorary degree of Doctor of Divinity from Harvard in 1804. Dr. Abeel died January 20, 1812.

Evan Alexander was from North Carolina. He was a member of the House of Commons of that State from 1797 to 1803, and was in Congress from 1805 to 1809. He died October 28, 1809.

Meredith Clymer was the son of George Clymer, a signer of the Declaration of Independence, and a brother of Henry Clymer of the class of 1786. After graduating, he pursued a course of reading and study under his father, and in the office of Mr. Milligan, and was admitted to the Bar at the age of twenty-one, with a career of promise before him. But as a member of the First City Troop of Philadelphia, he was soon called to assist in quelling the "Whiskey Insurrection" in Western Pennsylvania. From exposure in the camp he took a cold which terminated his life November 18, 1794, about thirty miles above Pittsburg. His death was noticed with respect by his brethren of the Troop, and by Dr. Rush in the newspapers of the day. Dr. Rush, in his notice of Mr. Clymer, says: "Few young men have ever died richer in the love of their friends. He had been strictly educated in Republican principles and habits, and hence arose the zeal with which he joined the standard of Liberty in the form of law in the expedition to the western counties of Pennsylvania. His genius was of the first order, his knowledge extensive, accurate and useful; there was a commanding poignancy of ideas in his conversation; above all, his morals were pure, and his temper kind and benevolent."

George Clymer, the father, resided near Princeton for two years, superintending the education of his sons. The house he occupied was on the Lawrenceville road, adjoining "Morven." On leaving Princeton, he placed his sons in the family of Colonel George Morgan, whose home was at "Prospect," where now stands the handsome residence of Mrs. Potter.

Robert Finley graduated before he was sixteen years old. He was the son of an old friend of Dr. Witherspoon, who followed him from Scotland, and resided in Princeton. By the advice of Dr. Witherspoon, our graduate was appointed teacher of the grammar school connected with the college. After remaining in this situation some time, he took charge of an Academy at Allentown, New Jersey. In 1791 he removed to Charleston, South Carolina, and became Principal of an Academy in that city, where he gained a high reputation as a gentleman, a Christian, and a teacher.

Having determined to devote himself to the ministry, he returned to Princeton, and again conducted the grammar school, but was soon appointed tutor in the college, and served in that capacity from 1793 to 1795.

On the 16th of September, 1794, he was licensed to preach by the Presbytery of New Brunswick, and on the 16th of June was ordained and installed pastor of the Presbyterian Church at Baskingridge, New Jersey. While here, he was induced to take a few boys into his family for the purpose of fitting them for college. This soon grew to be one of the largest and most popular schools of the day.

About this time Mr. Finley conceived the idea of African Colonization, and he may be considered as the founder of the American Colonization Society. In 1817 he was elected to the Presidency of the University of Georgia, but he had hardly entered upon the duties of his new position, when disease seized him, and he died October 3, 1817.

Dr. Finley had a large well-proportioned frame, and a countenance marked by decision and energy; his perceptions were uncommonly vivid, and his feelings proportionately strong. He sustained a high rank as a preacher. Dr. Finley was for ten years a Trustee of the College.

The publications of Dr. Finley are: A Sermon on the Baptism of John, showing it to be a peculiar dispensation, and no example for Christians. 1807. A Sermon at the Funeral of the Rev. William Boyd, of Lamington, New Jersey. 1807. A Sermon on the Nature and Design, the Benefits and Proper Subjects, of Baptism. 1808. Two Sermons in the New Jersey Preacher. 1813. Thoughts on Colonization. 1816.

James Gibson was born in Pennsylvania, September 13, 1769. After graduating, he was admitted to the Bar, after the usual study, and became a lawyer of high standing in Philadelphia. Mr. Gibson died July 8, 1856.

Charles Dickinson Green was an uncle of Chief-Justice Green, and John C. Green, Esq., the munificent friend of the college. Mr. Green studied theology, and was licensed and ordained by the Presbytery of New Brunswick, but never entered upon his profession. He was a fine scholar and a man of considerable ability. He died in 1857.

George Pollock, a brother of Thomas Pollock of the class of 1786, was a grandson of President Edwards. Like his brother, he was bred to the law, but never practiced. He followed planting as a business. He died in April, 1839, in Halifax County, North Carolina.

Elijah D. Rattoone was ordained Deacon by Bishop Provost, January 10, 1790. Shortly after, he took charge of St. Anne's Church, Brooklyn. In 1792 he was elected Professor of the Latin and Greek languages, and in 1794 Professor of Grecian and Roman Antiquities, in Columbia College. He resigned these positions in 1797, and the same year became Rector of Grace Church, Jamaica, Long Island, where he continued till April, 1802, when he accepted a call to the Associate Rectorship of St. Paul's Church, Baltimore. Some peculiar circumstances induced him to resign this charge after a number of years, upon which Trinity Church, in the same city, was at once built for him, where he ministered with his usual popularity till the autumn of 1809. At that time he left Baltimore for Charleston, South Carolina, having been elected President of Charleston College; and there he died of yellow fever in 1810. He received the degree of Doctor of Divinity from Charleston College in 1804.

Dr. Rattoone was a highly accomplished scholar and an eloquent preacher.

John Read was from Delaware, and was the son of George Read, a signer of the Declaration of Independence, and was the father of John M. Read, of Philadelphia. In 1817 he was a member of the Legislature of Pennsylvania. He died in 1854.

Mr. Read published, Arguments on the British Debt. 1798.

John R. Smith was a native of Pennsylvania. After

graduating, he studied law and practiced in Philadelphia until his death. Mr. Smith was a brother of the first editor of the *National Intelligencer* of Washington City.

Nathaniel Randolph Snowden, a brother of Samuel F. Snowden of the class of 1786, was licensed by the Presbytery of Carlisle, in 1794, and was settled over the Presbyterian Churches of Harrisburg, Paxton and Derry, Pennsylvania. These charges he resigned in about three years, and afterwards supplied many congregations, but making no permanent settlement. He died November 3, 1850.

Lucius Horatio Stockton was a son of Richard Stockton of the class of 1748. He studied law and settled in Trenton, New Jersey. Mr. Stockton was for some time District Attorney of New Jersey. A few weeks before the close of the administration of President Adams, he was nominated as Secretary of War, which gave great umbrage to Mr. Jefferson, just coming into office.

Mr. Stockton was eccentric, and a very earnest politician, but did not deserve to be called "a crazy, fanatical young man," as Wolcott wrote in Gibbs's "Federal Administration."

Mr. Stockton wrote a long series of articles in the Trenton *Federalist,* in 1803, defending himself and his uncle Samuel Witham Stockton from attacks in the *Democratic True American.* He died May 26, 1835.

Daniel Thew, a native of Newark, New Jersey, after graduating, studied law, and was admitted to the Bar in the City of New York, where he practiced for many years. Mr. Thew married a daughter of Dr. William Burnet of the class of 1749. He died in 1814.

1788.

Thomas A. Bellach was a native of Kent County, Delaware. After graduating, he studied law and was admitted to the Bar.

George Clarkson, a son of Gerardus Clarkson, M.D., of Philadelphia, was born February 27, 1772. He graduated in his seventeenth year, with the highest honours of his class. He died April 3, 1804.

Aaron Condict was a native of Orange, New Jersey. He was licensed by the Presbytery of New York in 1790. Shortly after, he became pastor of the Presbyterian Church at Stillwater, New York, where he remained for about three years. On the 13th of December, 1796, he was installed pastor of the Church at Hanover, New Jersey, which he served for thirty-five years, when he resigned on account of ill health. His ministry was eminently successful. He was distinguished for his wisdom, humility, benevolence, hospitality and a deep interest in the affairs of the Church. He died in April, 1852.

Richard Eppes was born near Petersburg, Virginia. He came to New York, on his way to college, in a schooner, and was three weeks on the passage. Mr. Eppes remained seven years in Princeton without once returning home.

It is probable that after graduation he studied law in Princeton. After his return home he was admitted to the Bar.

Mr. Eppes died unmarried in 1801.

1788.

Thomas R. Harris, after leaving college, studied medicine, and in 1790, received the degree of Bachelor of Medicine from the University of Pennsylvania, which was an inferior honour to that of Doctor of Medicine. I can trace him no further.

Nathaniel W. Howell resided, after graduation, in Ontario County, New York, and was a lawyer of high standing. He was a Judge of the Supreme Court of the State, and a Representative in Congress from 1813 to 1815. He died October 16, 1851.

William Kirkpatrick, a son of William Kirkpatrick of the class of 1757, was born at Amwell, New Jersey, November 7, 1769. After leaving college, he studied medicine with Dr. Benjamin Rush, of Philadelphia, and in 1795, commenced practice in Whitestown, New York. The professional education of Dr. Kirkpatrick was of the highest order, and he might have attained a commanding position as one of the most scientific physicians of the age in which he lived had he continued in his profession, but a nervous temperament, of such a peculiar and sensitive character as to unfit him in a great measure for the practical duties of a physician, led him to enter into other employments. In 1806, he was appointed Superintendent of the Salt Springs, and removed to Salina, New York, now the first ward of the City of Syracuse. In 1808, Dr. Kirkpatrick was elected to the House of Representatives, it being the last Congress under Jefferson's administration. Although not prominent as a public speaker, yet he was greatly respected at Washington as an intelligent, educated and high-minded man, and during that period formed an intimate acquaintance and friendship with many of the most distinguished men of the day. Dr. Kirkpatrick was a warm and earnest advocate for the making of the Erie Canal. At the close of his Congressional term, he was re-appointed Superintendent of the Onondaga Salt Springs in 1811, and held the office until 1831.

During the whole life of Dr. Kirkpatrick after removing to Salina, he continued to cultivate his literary taste by an intimate reading of all of the standard works of the day, and particularly of the English and Scotch Reviews; indeed to works of this character he devoted a large portion of his leisure time. At this time, when books were scarce, he possessed one of the largest libraries in Western New York. He was of a joyous and pleasant temperament, and delighted to sit down with literary friends and converse upon the current topics of the day. He was in mind, thought and feeling a gentleman. In manners he was dignified, easy, graceful and refined. Dr. Kirkpatrick died of cholera, September 2, 1832.

Timothy Treadwell Smith. I find no trace of Mr. Smith until 1801, when he was appointed Professor of the Greek and Latin Languages in Union College. He died in November, 1803.

David Stone was born in Bertie County, North Carolina, February 17, 1770. After graduating, he returned to North Carolina, and commenced the study of law under William R. Davie of the class of 1776. In 1790, he was admitted to the Bar, and from his assiduity in his profession, and his deep and varied acquirements, he soon rose to the highest ranks of the profession. Mr. Stone entered early into political life. From 1791 to 1794, he was in the State Legislature. From 1795 to 1798, he was Judge of the Supreme Court of the State. In 1799, he was elected to the House of Representatives of the United States; and in 1801 was transferred to the United States Senate. In this capacity he served until 1806, when he was again elected a Judge of the Supreme Court; this position he resigned in 1808, on being elected Governor of the State. In 1811, he was again in the Legislature, and in 1813, was again chosen United States

Senator. This was a most stormy period. The war which had been declared against Great Britain was at its height; parties were violently excited. Differing from his party in many important points, he resigned his seat November 21, 1814, and went into retirement. Mr. Stone never recovered his position with his party, or his influence in the State. He died in October, 1818.

Smith Thompson rose rapidly to distinction in New York, his native State. Having studied law with Judge Kent, he entered upon practice, and was soon appointed a District Attorney. In 1801, Mr. Thompson was appointed Judge of the Supreme Court of New York, two of his associates, Morgan Lewis and Henry Brockholst Livingston, being graduates of Princeton. The Reports of the Supreme Court are enduring monuments of the learning and ability of Brockholst Livingston and Smith Thompson. As a man of genius, Livingston was unquestionably the superior of Thompson; but for legal acumen, clearness of perception, and logical powers of mind, there are few if any men, in this or any other country, who excel Judge Thompson. In February, 1814, Chief-Justice Kent being appointed Chancellor, Judge Thompson succeeded him as Chief-Justice. In 1818, he was appointed by President Monroe Secretary of the Navy, and in 1823 was elected to the Bench of the Supreme Court of the United States. Judge Thompson was a man of great learning in his profession, and his private life was pure and exemplary. He died in 1843, aged 76.

Nicholas Vandyke represented the State of Delaware in Congress from 1807 to 1811; and again from 1817 to 1826. He died in May, 1826.

John Wells was born in Otsego County, New York. About the time of the massacre of Wyoming, the Indians, under the lead of the celebrated Brant, made an attack upon the settlements of Western New York, and the father, mother, uncle and aunt, and four brothers and sisters of John Wells, were murdered by the savages. He, being on a visit from home, escaped the fearful slaughter.

At college, Mr. Wells was distinguished for his habits of study and good conduct, and was pronounced the best Greek scholar and mathematician in the class. He was a great favourite with Dr. Witherspoon, who was in the habit of holding him up as an example of exemplary conduct, of industry, and of personal neatness.

He studied law in New York City, and was licensed as an Attorney in 1791, and admitted as a Counsellor in 1795. In 1797, he was appointed by Governor Jay one of the Justices of the Peace in a new court just established. He discharged the duties of this post with distinguished ability and impartiality.

In 1805, Mr. Wells first became prominent as an advocate in a number of libel suits, growing out of the duel between Hamilton and Burr. For some time previous to this he had been Editor of the *Evening Post*, and many of its ablest articles were from his pen. In 1807, Mr. Wells argued his first cause at the Bar of the Supreme Court, before the full Bench of Judges, and from that time to 1823, the year of his death, the Reports of the State bear abundant evidence of his extensive and varied practice, and of his research and profound learning.

On one occasion in an important case, after concluding his speech, his learned friend and illustrious rival at the Bar, Mr. Emmett, who had attended both the English and Irish Courts, observed, that it was the most able and finished argument he had ever heard. *Laudatus a laudato viro*—no higher praise could be bestowed. After its close, Mr. Wells went from court to his house, where his family, and some friends who had been listeners, overwhelmed him with compliments, He soon after retired, and was afterwards found kneeling in his chamber, and said that he had sought solitude to thank his God that he had enabled him to discharge his duty, and to pray for strength against the petty folly of vanity.

Mr. Wells died at Brooklyn, in September, 1823, of yellow fever, contracted in the cause of benevolence and humanity. All said that a great man had fallen. He was considered the pride of the New York Bar.

Mr. Wells possessed an acute, logical and investigating mind, improved by early discipline and culture. In his studies he possessed, in an eminent degree, the power of abstraction. He could pursue a train of thought amidst noise and conversation. Modesty formed a prominent trait in his character, and its deep tinge was perceptible throughout his whole life. The lofty integrity which adorned his character was founded in a deep sense of religion, and from a conviction arising from examination of its truth and holy uses. He was as eminent as a Christian as he was as a lawyer.

David Wiley received his license from the Presbytery of New Castle, and from 1794 to 1802 was pastor of Spring Creek and Cedar Creek Churches, in the State of Pennsylvania. He died in 1813.

1789.

William A. Anderson was admitted an Attorney of the Supreme Court of New Jersey, at the May Term, 1792.

Nathaniel Boileau was admitted to the Bar and practiced in Montgomery County, Pennsylvania. He was at one time Secretary of State of Pennsylvania. Mr. Boileau was for many years President of the Montgomery County Bible Society. He died at an advanced age in 1850.

Robert Hett Chapman was the son of Rev. Jedediah Chapman, the pioneer Presbyterian minister in Western New York. He spent the year after graduating at his father's house, devoting himself to general reading, undecided what profession to follow. But finally deciding upon the ministry, he pursued his studies, at the same time acting as an instructor at Queens College, New Brunswick, and was licensed by the Presbytery of New York, October 2, 1793, and immediately proceeded on a missionary tour through the Southern States. On his return from this tour he became pastor of the Presbyterian Church at Rahway, New Jersey, and was installed in 1796. In 1801 he became pastor of a Presbyterian Church in Cambridge, New York. In 1811 he was appointed President of the University of North Carolina, and entered upon his duties in 1812. He was eminently successful in elevating the tone of the college. Here he remained laboriously employed, not only in his college duties, but in preaching the Gospel, until 1817, when he resigned the Presidency, removing to the Valley of Virginia, where he became pastor of Bethel Church. He remained in Virginia for about ten years; then spent a year or two in North Carolina, and in 1830 removed to Tennessee, and settled at Covington. Here he was upon the frontier, and his influence for good was powerfully felt. As a teacher, he was faithful and diligent. As a preacher, he was highly evangelical. He died June 18, 1833.

Mr. Chapman published: A Sermon on Conscience; A Sermon on Regeneration.

John Collins. The ancestor of Mr. Collins came to this country from England in the seventeenth century, that he "might enjoy a purer worship of God and a more exact church discipline." Two of his distinguished sons are the subject of an article in Mather's "Magnalia," entitled "Gemini—The Life of the Collins's."

The subject of our sketch was born in Somerset County, Maryland, February 16, 1769. After graduating, he assumed the Presidency of Washington Academy, in his native county, at that time and long afterwards a most distinguished Seminary. He was licensed by the Presbytery of Lewes in 1791. In 1797 he purchased an estate in New Castle County, Delaware, whither he removed, and became and continued to be pastor of the Presbyterian Church in St. George's until his death, which occurred April 12, 1804. Acute disease claimed the victim, when in the vigour of his manhood—leaving a precious memory.

"Non annis, sed factis vivunt mortales."

Isaac Watts Crane, after graduating, studied law, and was admitted an Attorney of the Supreme Court of New Jersey at the September Term, 1797, and as Counsellor at the November Term, 1800. Mr. Crane was from Essex County, but practiced most of his life in Cumberland County, New Jersey. He died in 1856.

Mahlon Dickerson was from New Jersey. After

graduating, he read law and was admitted to the Bar by the Supreme Court of New Jersey in November, 1793. Soon after, he removed to Philadelphia, where he became Recorder of the City, and subsequently Quarter-Master-General of the State. Returning to New Jersey, he became a member of the Legislature, and then a Judge of the Supreme Court of the State. In 1815, he was elected Governor, which office he held until 1817, when he was chosen United States Senator, and continued in that position for sixteen years. In 1834 he became Secretary of the Navy under General Jackson, and held that Department until 1838, two years after the accession of Martin Van Buren. He died October 5, 1853.

David English resided in Georgetown, District of Columbia, after his graduation, probably engaged in teaching. In 1794 he was appointed tutor in the college, and held the post until 1796, when he took the management of the Seminary established at Baskingridge, New Jersey, by the Rev. Robert Finley. Here he remained for a few years, sustaining the high character of the institution. After retiring from this laborious position, he took up his residence again in Georgetown. Mr. English was a man of amiable manners and fine scholarship.

John Lyon Gardiner was the son of David Gardiner, the sixth proprietor of Gardiner's Island, Long Island. John Lyon was the seventh proprietor. After graduating, he resided upon his large estate, where he died November 22, 1816.

David Gardiner, a brother of the above, took up his residence in Flushing, Long Island, where he died April 6, 1815.

David Hosack was born in New York City, August 31, 1769. He was the son of a Scotchman who came to America with Lord Jeffrey Amherst. After graduating, he studied medicine, and received his degree at Philadelphia in 1791, and immediately proceeded to Europe, and pursued his studies in Edinburgh and London. A paper which he wrote on Vision, while in London, was published in the Transactions of the Royal Society in 1794. On his return to New York, he was appointed Professor of Botany and of Materia Medica in Columbia College. In the new College of Physicians and Surgeons he taught Physic and Clinical Medicine, in which branch he was especially eminent. From 1820 to 1828, he was President of the New York Historical Society. For more than thirty years Dr. Hosack was a prominent medical practitioner in New York. He exerted a wide and commanding influence in the community, and his Saturday evening parties, where he was accustomed to entertain the professional gentlemen of the city and distinguished foreigners, were widely known. In all prominent movements connected with the arts, the drama, medical and other local institutions, and the State policy of internal improvements, Dr. Hosack bore a part.

His Alma Mater is indebted to him for a Mineralogical Cabinet, containing about one thousand valuable specimens.

Dr. Hosack died suddenly December 23, 1835.

Dr. Hosack's publications are: Hortus Elginensis, 8vo. Facts relative to the Elgin Botanic Garden, 8vo. American Medical and Philosophical Register; editor. A Biographical Memoir of Hugh Williamson, M. D., LL.D., 1820, 8vo. Essays on Various Subjects of Medical Science, 1824–30; 3 vols. 8vo. Inaugural Discourse at the opening of Rutgers Medical College, 1826, 8vo. A System of Practical Nosology, 1829, 8vo. Memoirs of DeWitt Clinton, 1829, 4to. Lectures on the Theory and Practice of Physic, edited by Rev. Henry Ducahet, M. D., 1838, 8vo. He also published, A Paper on Vision in Philosophical Transactions (Royal Society), 1794. Medical Papers in Annals of Medicine, 1793, 1796. A Biographical Account of Dr. Benjamin Rush. Several Discourses.

Thomas Pitt Irving came to Princeton from Maryland. From about 1790 to 1812, he was the Principal of an Academy at Newbern, North Carolina, whence he was called to the double duty of presiding over the Academy, and officiating as Rector of the Church, at Hagerstown, Maryland. He was much distinguished as a teacher, and was regarded as one of the best Greek scholars and mathematicians of his day.

William Perry was a native of Talbot County, Maryland. From the best information I can obtain he died early in life.

Isaac Pierson belonged to an old New Jersey family. After graduation, he studied medicine, and was admitted a Fellow of the College of Physicians and Surgeons, New York. He followed his profession in Orange, New Jersey, where he continued to practice for nearly forty years. From 1827 to 1831, he was in the United States House of Representatives. He was a man of high Christian character. He died in 1841.

Charles Snowden was the youngest son of Isaac Snowden of Philadelphia, and the last of five brothers who graduated at Princeton. After graduating, he remained a few months as a tutor in the college, and pursued the study of theology. He was licensed to preach, and delivered one very eloquent and pathetic sermon, and that was all. Soon after, he became the proprietor of a newspaper in the City of New York; but the name of the paper, or how long he remained in New York, I have not been able to discover. After leaving New York, he removed to Pennsylvania, and engaged actively in the development of a coal property which he possessed, and in the building of a canal.

Ephraim King Wilson represented Maryland, his native State, in Congress from 1827 to 1831. He died in 1834. His son, William S. Wilson, graduated in the class of 1835, and was killed at the Battle of Sharpsburg in 1862, on the Confederate side. The family resided in Snow Hill, Maryland.

1789.

Silas Wood, after graduating, became a tutor, which position he held for nearly five years. He afterwards resided on Long Island, and was a Representative in Congress from the State of New York, from 1819 to 1829. He died March 2, 1847, aged 78.

He published: A History of Long Island.

1790.

Israel Harris, a son of Dr. Harris of Pittsgrove, Salem County, New Jersey, after graduating, pursued the study of law, and was admitted an Attorney of the Supreme Court of New Jersey, at the May Term, 1795. He practiced in Somerset County, New Jersey. Mr. Harris died young.

Robert G. Johnson was a son of Robert Johnson of an old family of Salem County, New Jersey. The father was a man of wealth and station, and the mother a descendant of early and wealthy settlers from England.

On one occasion the father of young Johnson complained bitterly to Dr. Witherspoon that his son had not been advanced as he expected. After bearing considerable reproach, the doctor broke out with the strong Scotch accent common when he was excited, "I tell you, sir, the boy wants capacity!"

Soon after graduating, Mr. Johnson became Captain of a troop of Cavalry, and soon rose to be Colonel. In 1794, he served in the army raised to quell the Whiskey Insurrection, as a paymaster.

Colonel Johnson was in his own right, and in the right of his wife, probably the largest land-owner in Salem County. In 1821, and from 1823 to 1825, he was a member of the Legislature of New Jersey. He was a man of truth and honour, but so fixed in his convictions as not always to be tolerant of those who differed with him. He was very hospitable and beyond question a true Christian, but owing to this peculiarity of temper was unpopular with many. Colonel Johnson was fond of historical research, and was Vice-President of the

New Jersey Historical Society from its foundation in 1845, till near his death, and furnished much historical matter; among other things, a Memoir of John Fenwick, the early proprietor of West Jersey. Colonel Johnson died at New Haven in October, 1850.

William Johnson studied law and settled in Charleston, South Carolina, where he rapidly rose to eminence. He was Associate-Justice of the Supreme Court of the United States. Judge Johnson was not only an able lawyer, but a man of cultivated tastes. He published a life of General Greene, that was deemed by General Henry Lee, the son of General Lee of the class of 1773, so unjust to his father's fame, and that of his brave Legion, that he resolved to defend both, which he did with success in an octavo volume, entitled "Campaigns of 1782 in the Carolinas." Judge Johnson besides his Life of General Greene, published, Essay to Philosophical Society; Nugæ Georgicæ, 1815; Eulogy on Adams and Jefferson, 1826. He received the honorary degree of Doctor of Laws from Princeton in 1818, and also from Harvard. Judge Johnson died in Brooklyn, New York, August 4, 1834.

John Ruan came from the Island of St. Croix. After graduating, he studied medicine, and practiced for many years in the City of Philadelphia. Dr. Ruan died in 1845.

John Taylor was born in South Carolina. He studied law, and was admitted to the Bar in 1793, but turned his attention chiefly to planting. He was a member of the South Carolina Legislature for a number of years, and represented that State in Congress from 1807 to 1809, and again from 1817 to 1821. From 1810 to 1816, he was in the United States Senate, and from 1826 to 1828 he was Governor of South Carolina.

He died in 1832.

1790.

George Spafford Woodhull was the son of Rev. John Woodhull of the class of 1766. After graduating, he studied law for two years, and medicine for one year; but determining to enter the ministry, he was licensed by the Presbytery of New Brunswick, November 14, 1797, and was ordained and installed as pastor of the Presbyterian Church, at Cranberry, New Jersey, June 6, 1798. Here he remained until 1820, when he was chosen pastor of the Church in Princeton. For twelve years he laboured here faithfully and successfully. In 1832 he resigned his charge, and spent the two last years of his life as Pastor of the Presbyterian Church at Middletown Point, New Jersey, where he died December 25, 1834. He was eminently blameless and exemplary in his life—eminently peaceful and happy in his death. Three of his sons graduated at Princeton; one in 1822, and two in 1828.

1791.

David Barclay, after leaving Princeton, studied theology, and was ordained by the Presbytery of New Brunswick, December 3, 1794, and installed as pastor of the Church at Bound Brook, New Jersey, where he remained until April, 1805, when, on account of some troubles, in June of that year, he removed, and became pastor of Knowlton, Oxford and Lower Mount-Bethel Churches, New Jersey. He continued here until 1811. Mr. Barclay was a man of decided ability; quick, earnest and energetic in his motions and his speech; of stout, athletic frame, but of an impetuous, imprudent temperament. Mr. Barclay had much trouble with his congregations, and one of his elders, Mr. Jacob Ker, published a volume of more than four hundred pages, entitled, "The Several Trials of David Barclay before the Presbytery of New Brunswick and Synod of New York and New Jersey." On the 25th of April, 1819, Mr. Barclay was dismissed to the Presbytery of Redstone, and took up his residence in Punxatawny, Pennsylvania, where he died in 1846.

Jacob Burnet was a son of Dr. William Burnet of the class of 1749. After graduating, he studied law for one year in the office of Richard Stockton, and afterwards with Elisha Boudinot. He was admitted to the Bar in 1796, and removed immediately to the North-west Territory, and settled at Cincinnati. He immediately rose to eminence in his profession. In these early times, Mr. Burnet was accustomed to travel on horseback from court to court, carrying his blanket and provisions; at night he camped in the woods, there being neither tavern, bridge, ferry nor even a road in his route.

After being a member of the Legislature of Ohio repeatedly, in 1816 Mr. Burnet retired from active practice, but in 1821 he was elected a Judge of the Supreme Court of Ohio, which position he filled with distinguished ability. From this position he was transferred to the Senate of the United States, where he exhibited the same traits of character for which he had always been remarkable—clearness and depth of understanding, sound reasoning, equable and happy temperament.

One of the founders of Ohio, Mr. Burnet lived to see the few early settlers of Cincinnati increased to one hundred and thirty thousand. At the age of eighty, he walked the streets erect, and he was yet interesting by his colloquial powers. Judge Burnet died May 10, 1853, aged 80.

He published, Notes on the North-western Territory, Cincinnati, 1847.

Joseph Caldwell was a native of New Jersey. During his whole collegiate course, he maintained the highest rank as a scholar. On the day of his graduation, he spoke the Latin Salutatory. For about a year he remained in Princeton as a tutor. In 1796 he was licensed by the Presbytery of New Brunswick, and was elected Professor of Mathematics in the University of North Carolina, being then only twenty-three years of age. Under his care, the prospects of the University speedily brightened and flourished; and in 1804 he was elected the First President. He continued to hold this office until 1812, when he returned to the Mathematical Chair, being succeeded by the Rev. Robert Hett Chapman, also an alumnus of Princeton of the class of 1789. In 1817 Dr. Chapman resigned, and Dr. Caldwell was again elected President. In 1824 he visited Europe for the purpose of purchasing books and apparatus for the University, and was absent about a year. The greatest good of the University, and, indeed, the general progress and intellectual improvement of the State, were ever the most engrossing objects of Dr. Caldwell's care, and with untiring perseverance and fidelity he presented the claims of education to the community, and appealed to the community for their support.

The degree of Doctor of Divinity was conferred upon him by his *Alma Mater* in 1816. He died January 24, 1835. North Carolina reveres his memory. Her most distinguished sons were his pupils, and cherish for him a truly filial affection; and the advance which that State made in intelligence and virtue, through the instrumentality of his labours, is an enduring monument of his power and wisdom.

Besides two or three occasional Sermons, Dr. Caldwell published A Compendious System of Elementary Geometry, in seven books: to which an eighth is added, containing such other Propositions as are Elementary. Subjoined, is a Treatise of Plain Trigonometry. He published also in one of the Raleigh newspapers, a series of articles called, "Letters of Carlton," which were designed to awaken a spirit of internal improvement in the State of North Carolina; and another series on Popular Education, or Free Schools. These were republished in a volume about the year 1825.

Samuel Sharpe Dickerson was a native of Talbot County, Maryland. After graduating, he became a physician, and representated his native county in the House of Delegates once or twice. He died about 1847 or 1848.

Maltby Gelston was the son of David Gelston, of New York, for some time a member of the Continental Congress, and afterwards Collector of the Port of New York. The son, after graduating, studied law, and was admitted to the Bar, but never entered actively into practice. When Mr. Monroe went as Minister to France, Mr. Gelston attended him as his private Secretary. For a number of years Mr. Gelston was President of the Manhattan Bank in New York. He was a man of sterling integrity and high character in the community. He died December 2, 1860.

1791.

Henry Hollyday was a native of Talbot County, Maryland, where his ancestors had lived for more than a hundred years. At one time he represented his county in the State Senate, and was never in public life except in that instance, having devoted himself thereafter to agricultural pursuits. He died in 1850.

Francis Markoe came to college from the Island of Santa Cruz. His ancestors were of Huguenot descent, and of high rank, the Duke of Sully being among them. After graduating, he returned to his native Island. Here, in the midst of luxury and wealth, he was, by a remarkable providence, converted to God. Finding the Island unsuited to his new feelings and new purposes, he removed to the City of Philadelphia about the beginning of the century, and entered into mercantile life. Here he was abundant in labour, especially in the instruction of the ignorant, in which was his great delight. Removing from Philadelphia to New York, he became an elder in the Mercer Street Presbyterian Church, of which Dr. Skinner was pastor. Here his Christian character shone forth pre-eminently. Dr. Skinner wrote of him: "Among contemporary Christians, so far as my acquaintance has extended, as complete and perfect pattern of holiness as he was, I have not seen; nor have I heard or read of many among saints of former times that seem to have more adorned, in all things, the doctrine of Christ."

A son of Mr. Markoe, Dr. Thomas M. Markoe, a distinguished surgeon of New York, graduated in 1836. Mr. Markoe died in triumph in New York, February 16, 1848.

Fredrick Stone came to Princeton from one of the Southern States. After graduating, he went to Philadelphia and entered upon the study of the law; but in 1793 the yellow fever appearing in the city, he repaired to Princeton, but was taken ill of the disease and soon died.

1791.

Elias Van Artsdale studied law, and was admitted to the New Jersey Bar at the September Term of the Supreme Court in 1795. He settled in Newark, New Jersey, and was long a distinguished lawyer. For many years he was President of the State Bank at Newark. He died in 1846, aged seventy-five.

1792.

Joseph McKnitt Alexander was the son of John McKnitt Alexander, famous for his connection with the Mecklenburg Declaration. After graduating with eclat, he returned to his native State and began the study of medicine. In due time he entered upon the practice of his profession, and acquired both reputation and wealth. He was distinguished for his practical judgment and plain common sense. For a time he was in great danger from the influence of French infidelity, which was then prevalent, but the truth triumphed, and in the meridian of life he became a worshipper of the God of his fathers, connected himself with the Presbyterian Church, and continued through life, until the infirmities of old age prevented, to be active in the promotion of its interests, in alleviating and ameliorating the condition of men. He died in 1841.

Nicholas Bayard was the youngest son of Colonel John Bayard of New Brunswick, New Jersey. After leaving college he studied medicine, and received his diploma in Philadelphia. He first commenced practice in New York City, but soon relinquished it for the drug business. After his marriage he removed to New Brunswick, but failing health led to his removal to Savannah, Georgia, in 1803, where he died, October 30, 1822.

George M. Bibb was a native of Virginia, but after graduating he studied law and was admitted to the Bar in Kentucky. Mr. Bibb was a Justice, and twice Chief-Justice of the Court of Appeals, and afterwards Chancellor of the State. For two years he was a member of the

State Senate. From 1811 to 1814, and from 1829 to 1835, he was in the Senate of the United States, from Kentucky. When Mr. Tyler became President of the United States, Mr. Bibb was appointed Secretary of the Treasury. On retiring from this office he took up his residence permanently in Washington, and until the close of life practiced his profession in that city. For a time he acted as an assistant to the Attorney-General of the United States. Until the last Mr. Bibb retained the ancient dress of broad-brimmed hat, small clothes, black silk hose and silver shoe-buckles. The personal appearance of Mr. Bibb, aside from his costume, was remarkable; he was a man of great physical vigour of constitution, as shown in his erect carriage and firm step after he had become an octogenarian. He was rather above the middle size, and his frame, like his mind, was compact and well knit together. He was a firm friend, a kind husband and an affectionate parent. His freedom and frankness with young people was especially remarkable and pleasing. One of his peculiarities was his great fondness for fishing. On one occasion in the Senate, it had been insinuated by the opposers of the administration, that some of the Senators, whose terms of office were about to expire, would be recipients of Presidential favours. "I deny this," said Mr. Bibb, at the conclusion of his speech, "so far as I am concerned. I have no personal object in view. I have no ambition. For myself, I prefer to sit with my rod and line on the banks of a pellucid stream enjoying the pleasure of calmness and contemplation, to any object that my ambition could achieve." A good story is told of him in this connection. One warm afternoon the officer in command at the Washington Arsenal observed Mr. Bibb sitting on a broken-down wharf hour after hour intently watching his float. At last he strolled down from the quarters to inquire, "What luck?" "None," replied Mr. Bibb. "I thought I had some bites two or three hours ago, but there is not a fish hereabouts, now, apparently."

"What is your bait?" asked the officer.

"A plump young frog, hooked through the fleshy part of his leg." Scarcely had he finished this reply, when the questioner, overcome with laughter, pointed to a log which was partly out of water, and there the fisherman saw his bait; the frog having got tired of swimming about, had jumped upon the log and was calmly enjoying the sun.

Mr. Bibb died in Washington, April 4, 1859.

He published, Reports of Cases at Common Law and in Chancery in the Court of Appeals of Kentucky, 1808–1817. 4 volumes, 8vo.

Peter Bleeker was a native of the City of New York. He died a few months after his graduation in 1793.

George Whitefield Burnet studied law and was admitted an Attorney of the Supreme Court of New Jersey, at the September Term, 1796. He settled and practiced in Newark, New Jersey; but subsequently removed to Cincinnati, Ohio, where he died in 1800.

James Chestnut was from South Carolina. After graduating, he returned to the South and engaged in Planting. His wife was Miss Cox, of Burlington, New Jersey, and was one of the company of young ladies who in 1789 strewed flowers in the path of Washington at Trenton, as he was on his way to his inauguration. A son of Mr. Chestnut graduated in the class of 1835, and was afterwards a United States Senator from South Carolina. Mr. Chestnut died in 1866.

William Chetwood, a native of New Jersey, was admitted to practice at the New Jersey Bar in 1798. During the Whiskey Insurrection, in Western Pennsylvania, he attended Major-General Lee, of the class of 1773, as Aid-de-camp. He was at one time a member of the upper house of the New Jersey Legislature, and during the administration of General Jackson was appointed to fill a vacancy in Congress. He was an able lawyer, and practiced his profession until his 70th year. He died December 18, 1857.

Peter Early was a Virginian by birth, but after graduating he removed to Georgia, and entered upon the practice of law. In 1802 he was elected to Congress, and soon became a leading member of that body. When the impeachment of Judge Chase was before Congress, he was associated with John Randolph and others in conducting the prosecution. His speech on this occasion is said to have been the ablest that was delivered on the side of the prosecution. He continued in Congress until 1807, when he was appointed Judge of the Superior Court in Georgia. In 1813 he was elected Governor of the State. In these critical times he acted with the greatest wisdom and firmness. His military arrangements were extremely judicious, and his administration of the government most able and patriotic. When some one suggested that the Union of the States might not be permanent, Governor Early replied, that if such a thing should happen, he had no wish that Georgia should survive the general wreck; he wanted to swim or sink together. He died August 15, 1817.

Jacob Ford was a brother of Timothy Ford of the class of 1783, and Gabriel Ford of the class of 1784. What became of him after his graduation, I have not been able to discover.

Charles Wilson Harris was a native of North Carolina. On his return to his home, he commenced the study of law, but in 1795 was appointed Professor of Mathematics in the University of North Carolina. He accepted the office only for one year, and declined renewing his term of engagement, wishing to follow his profession, in which he became eminent, being considered one of the best lawyers in the State.

1792.

William Hosack was a brother of David Hosack of the class of 1789. He never followed any business, but resided in the City of New York. He was intimate with Aaron Burr, and they were in Europe together about 1809.

Edmund Jennings Lee was the fifth and youngest son of Henry Lee of Prince William County, Virginia, and was born in that county, May 20, 1772. He was a brother of Henry Lee of the class of 1773, and of Charles Lee of the class of 1775. He married the daughter of Richard Henry Lee of the Continental Army. Mr. Lee was a lawyer by profession, and was, for many years, Clerk of the United States Court in Alexandria, when that county was part of the District of Columbia. He, however, continued to practice his profession in the Supreme Court of the United States, and in the courts of his native State. Mr. Lee died May 30, 1843.

In reply to the resolutions of respect on the occasion of his death, by the members of the Washington Bar, the Chief-Judge Cranch, said: "The Judges of this Court sympathize sincerely with the members of the Bar in the loss of one of its oldest, most respected and learned members. Mr. Lee, at the time of his death, was the only survivor of those who were counsellors of this Court at the time of its organization in 1801, and the Judges from their long association with him in the administration of justice, from their high respect for his character as a learned, able and upright advocate, as well as for the virtues which adorned his private life, cannot but greatly lament his loss, and uniting with the Bar in their sympathy with his bereaved family and friends, most willingly accede to the request that their proceedings be entered upon the minutes of the Court."

Mr. Lee died in the Communion of the Protestant Episcopal Church, of which he was a consistent and useful member for nearly half a century. In the history of that Church in Virginia since its revival, no name among the laity stands more conspicuous than his. He was one of the small number who, in 1814, gave their sanction to the call of the venerated Bishop Moore to the Episcopate of Virginia. From that period to the time of his death, he was elected annually a member of the Standing Committee of the Diocese. Bishop Meade wrote of Mr. Lee, "I not only knew Mr. Lee from my youth up, but I saw him in his last moments, and heard him with the truest humility speak of himself as a poor sinner, whose only hope was in Christ."

Mr. Lee left several children, most of whom are now living in Virginia.

George C. Maxwell after leaving college studied law, and was admitted an Attorney of the Supreme Court of New Jersey, at the May Term 1797, as a Counsellor at the May Term, 1800, and called as Sergeant-at-Law in 1816. Mr. Maxwell practiced in Hunterdon County, New Jersey. From 1811 to 1813, he was in the House of Representatives of the United States from New Jersey. He died at Flemington, New Jersey.

George Washington Morton was a brother of Jacob Morton of the class of 1778. After graduating, he entered upon the practice of law in New York City, but soon relinquished it for the mercantile business, and became a leading merchant in the St. Domingo trade. He died in 1810.

John C. Otto was the son of Bodo Otto, an eminent physician, and distinguished as a public character in the stirring periods of the Revolution. The son was born near Woodbury, New Jersey, March 15, 1774. After graduating, he entered the office of Dr. Rush, and in 1796 received his medical diploma from the University of Pennsylvania. Dr. Otto soon attained a highly respectable rank among his contemporaries, and in 1798 was elected one of the physicians of the Philadelphia Dispensary; an institution which he faithfully served for a period of five years. In 1813, he was appointed to succeed Dr. Rush, lately deceased, as one of the Physicians of the Pennsylvania Hospital. Here his untiring devotion to the sick, his sound medical knowledge, his matured judgment, and a deep sense of the responsibilities of the post, proved him to be the right man for the important position. Dr. Otto held this office during a period of twenty-two years.

His clinical lectures while connected with the hospital were models of conciseness, simplicity and truthfulness. One of his pupils, himself afterwards eminent as a physician, writes: "Who cannot look back with lively satisfaction and recall the slender and slightly-stooping frame of this venerable physician, as he passed around the wards of the hospital, stopping at each bed as he passed, kindly saluting his patient, making the necessary inquiries into his condition, and then, in the most unaffected, and yet impressive manner, addressing himself to the assembled class, and fastening upon their minds some valuable medical precept."

In addition to this responsible position, Dr. Otto was connected with several other public charities. During twenty years he served the Orphan Asylum, where he was much beloved by the children and by all connected with the institution. He was also physician during many years to the Magdalen Asylum, in the prosperity of which he took a deep interest. In 1840, Dr. Otto was elected Vice-President of the College of Physicians, a position which he occupied at the time of his death.

In social life Dr. Otto was remarkable for the simplicity and ease of his manners, and for the instruction which pervaded his conversation. He was a warm Presbyterian, but of a truly Catholic spirit. His religion was eminently vital and practical. He read the Scriptures morning and evening, and rarely passed a day without perusing a portion of Thomas à Kempis' Imitation of Christ. Dr. Otto died as he had lived, an humble and devout Christian, beloved and respected by all, June 26, 1844.

Dr. Otto published: Medical Papers in the New York Medical Repository, 1803; Coxe's Medical Museum, 1805; Eclectic Repository; North American Medical and Surgical Journal, 1828, 1830.

Joseph Reed, a son of General Joseph Reed of the class of 1757, was born in Philadelphia, July 11, 1772. After graduating, he studied law in Philadelphia, and was admitted to the Bar. Mr. Reed was for a number of years Recorder of the City. He died March 4, 1846.

Mr. Reed published: The Laws of Pennsylvania, 1822–1824. Five volumes, 8vo.

William Ross became a lawyer and practiced in Orange County, New York. At one time he was quite prominent in politics. In 1812, he was an active member of the Lower House of the Legislature of New York, and in 1814, a member of the State Senate, where he remained for many years.

James Ruan was from St. Croix, and was probably the brother of John Ruan of the class of 1790. I cannot find a trace of him after his graduation.

Robert Russell was ordained by the Presbytery of New Brunswick in 1795, and about 1797 he joined the Presbytery of Philadelphia, and settled as pastor of the Presbyterian Church at Allen Township (now Allentown), Pennsylvania, succeeding the Rev. Francis Peppard, a graduate of the class of 1762. Here Mr. Russell laboured for more than a quarter of a century. He died in 1827.

John J. Sayres was a native of New York. He was admitted to Deacon's and Priest's Orders by Bishop Clagget of Maryland. In January, 1799, he entered on the charge of Durham Parish, Charles County, Maryland. After remaining here about a year, in consequence of feeble health, he removed to Georgetown, District of Columbia, where he supported himself by teaching and preaching as strength would permit. He was Chaplain to the United States Senate in 1806 and 1807. He died in 1808. Mr. Sayres is remembered as a faithful and excellent minister, and was much beloved by his people.

William B. Sloan came to Princeton from Lamington, New Jersey, of which place he was a native. He studied theology with Dr. John Woodhull, of Freehold, New Jersey, and was licensed by the Presbytery of New Brunswick, May 31, 1797, and in 1798 was ordained by the same Presbytery, and installed as pastor of the United Congregations of Greenwich and Mansfield. For seventeen years he served both congregations, and then became the pastor of Greenwich only; when, through increasing infirmities, he was compelled to resign his charge in October, 1834.

Mr. Sloan was a man of noble presence — above the medium height, erect, slender, but well formed; his features finely chiselled, yet manly and dignified in expression; his eye, a clear expressive blue; his gait and bearing stately yet unconstrained. His talents were respectable, though not great; his style simple and unaffected. He was not a very vigorous thinker, but was an earnest and affectionate preacher. He died July 3, 1839.

Jacob S. Thompson read law and was admitted an Attorney of the Supreme Court of New Jersey, at the November Term, 1796, and practiced in Sussex County, New Jersey. In February, 1800, he was appointed by the Governor Clerk of that county; and in October of the same year was reappointed by the Legislature, and held office till 1805.

William Morton Watkins, after graduating, returned to Virginia and studied law, but never practiced his profession, but engaged in planting. He was, at one time, a member of the Legislature. Mr. Watkins was a man of considerable talent. He died at an advanced age in 1865.

George Willing was the son of the Honourable Thomas Willing, of Philadelphia; and was born in that city, April 14, 1774. It is probable that he received his earlier instruction from teachers there; and it was a high testimony to the reputation in that day of Princeton College that his father, so closely identified with the reputation and people of Philadelphia, and a man of the highest discernment and sagacity, should have given him his later education at Nassau Hall. On leaving college, he entered the counting-house of his father; he afterwards went to India on commercial business of the house of Willing & Francis. A disposition not inclined to the activities of business, and the possession of an ample fortune, induced him to retire from commerce in early life; and during part of the year, at his country residence of Richland, near Philadelphia, he devoted himself a good deal to the occupations of elegant agriculture. He was a member of the Society for the Promotion of Agriculture, which, under the presidency of his near connection, the Honourable Richard Peters, of Belmont, Philadelphia, attained reputation many years ago, and still preserves it. He died December 22, 1827, and is buried in the grounds of Christ Church, Philadelphia, where many of his ancestors lie.

1793.

Dow Ditmars, the son of Abraham Ditmars, of Jamaica, Long Island, was born June 12, 1771. After graduating, he studied medicine, and settled at Hellgate (now Astoria), Long Island, where he continued to reside until his death.

Manuel Eyre, after graduating, became a successful merchant in Philadelphia. One of his sons graduated in the class of 1838.

John Gibson, a brother of James Gibson of the class of 1787, was a well known merchant in Philadelphia. He was also a fine classical scholar. Mr. Gibson never married. He died about 1824, and is buried at St. Peter's Church, Philadelphia.

John Henry Hobart was descended from an ancient New England family, and was born in Philadelphia, September 14, 1775. Soon after graduating, he entered a counting-house in his native city, but finding the employment repugnant to his tastes and habits, and a tutorship at Princeton being offered to him, he left Philadelphia and entered upon his new duties in the college in January, 1796. Here he prosecuted his theological studies under the direction of the President, Dr. Samuel Stanhope Smith. Having remained in Princeton two years, he repaired to Philadelphia and completed his theological course under the direction of Bishop White, and in June, 1798, was admitted by him to the Order of Deacons. He was first settled in the neighbourhood of Philadelphia, but in 1799, accepted an invitation to Christ's

Church, New Brunswick, New Jersey. Here he remained for one year, when he took charge of St. George's Church at Hempstead, Long Island. He had scarcely become settled there, when he was offered the Rectorship of St. Mark's Church, New York, which he promptly declined; but in September, 1800, he became Assistant Minister of Trinity Church, New York, and shortly after was ordained Priest by Bishop Provost. In 1811 he was elected Assistant Bishop of the Diocese of New York. Here his labours were immense. On the death of Bishop Moore in 1816, Dr. Hobart became Diocesan of New York. There was scarcely any subject in which Bishop Hobart felt a deeper interest than the proper education of the clergy, and the incipient efforts which he put forth on the subject at that early period may be said to have formed the germ of the Theological Seminary which was located in New York in 1819. About 1821 Dr. Hobart was appointed to the chair of Pastoral Theology and Pulpit Eloquence in that institution. He discharged the duties of his professorship so as effectually to secure the affection, gratitude, and admiration of his pupils. In 1823 he visited Europe, on account of his health, which had become impaired, where he remained until September, 1825. On his return he addressed himself to his duties with renewed zeal and energy. He died September 10, 1830. As a preacher Dr. Hobart was rapid and business-like, earnest in his manner, and perfectly natural in his delivery. His voice, though not strong, was clear, and his tones varied. His attachment to his own church was very strong, and led him to the most vigorous efforts for the promotion of its interests.

Bishop Hobart was a voluminous writer, and published much that was ephemeral. His principal publications are:

The Companion for the Altar. 1804. The Companion to the Book of Common Prayer. 1805. The Clergyman's Companion. 1806. A Collection of Essays on the Subject of Episcopacy. 1806. The Christian's Manual of Faith and Devotion. 1814. Mant and D'Olyly's Bible, with Notes.

1823. Besides these, Bishop Hobart published between twenty and thirty Pastoral Charges, Pastoral Letters, Sermons, Addresses, etc.

Nathaniel Hunt was a native of New Jersey. After graduating, he lived and died upon a farm about two and a half miles from Princeton. Mr. Hunt taught a country school for some years before his death, which occurred in 1805 or 1806.

Robert Hunt studied law and was admitted an Attorney of the Supreme Court of New Jersey at the February Term, 1799, and practiced in Trenton, New Jersey. He was a son of Abraham Hunt, a merchant of that city. He died in October, 1802.

John Neilson, a son of John Neilson of New Brunswick, New Jersey, became a Physician of great eminence, and practiced during a long life in the City of New York, where he was respected and honoured by the whole community. He died in 1857.

Robert Ogden was admitted an Attorney of the Supreme Court of New Jersey, at the September Term, 1797. He was a nephew of Governor Aaron Ogden of the class of 1773, and was born September 16, 1775. After his admission to the Bar, Mr. Ogden settled in Newbern, North Carolina, where he practiced for a time, and then removed to Charleston, South Carolina. In 1821 he removed to Louisiana, and in 1825 was appointed Judge of the Parish of Concordia. Mr. Ogden died at Greenville, Louisiana, in 1857.

Charles Tennent was a native of South Carolina, and a son of the Rev. William Tennent of the class of 1758. I can learn nothing of his history after his graduation.

Isaac Van Doren was a native of New Jersey. After graduating, he studied theology with Dr. Theodore Dirck Romeyn, and completed his studies with Dr. Livingston. He was licensed by the Classis of New York, and was ordained about 1798. In 1800 he became pastor of the Reformed Dutch Church at Hopewell, Orange County, New York, where during a pastorate of twenty-three years he was blessed with eminent success. Leaving his charge, he removed to Newark, New Jersey, and was for four years Principal of an Academy in that place; after which, with his eldest son, he established the Collegiate Institute on Brooklyn Heights. From thence he removed to Lexington, Kentucky. After spending several years in teaching in the West, he returned to New Jersey. His latter years were passed happily and usefully among his children. Mr. Van Doren was eminently social, given to hospitality, the gifted counsellor of young clergymen and of all who sought his advice. He was not a brilliant man, but was remarkable for sound common sense, of a cheerful disposition, unspotted integrity, and unostentatious piety. He died at Perth Amboy, August 12, 1864.

Mr. Van Doren's only publication was a Tract entitled, "A Summary of Christian Duty," compiled from the Douay Bible.

Joshua Madox Wallace, son of Joshua Madox Wallace, Esq., was born at Philadelphia, September 4, 1776. The capture of the city soon after by the British forces, caused the retirement of the family of the parents of Mr. Wallace to a seat of theirs on the Raritan, Somerset County, New Jersey, called Ellerslie, after the ancestral estate in Scotland, from which country, Mr. John Wallace, the grandfather of the subject of our notice, came. The elder Mr. Wallace, himself a scholar, instructed his son during more tender years, at his own home. He was afterwards placed with a younger brother, John Bradford (of whom more hereafter), under the care of the Rev. William Frazer, a particular personal friend of the elder Mr. Wallace, and a most exemplary clergyman of the Church of England and minister of the Episcopal Church at Amwell, not very far from the country seat of Mr. Wallace. On the close of the war, the elder Mr. Wallace having established his residence in Burlington, New Jersey, this son in due time was entered at Princeton College; an institution in which the father had always taken great interest, and of which, from 1798, till his death in 1819, he was an active and efficient Trustee. We have no particular record of his studies and progress there. It seems to have been satisfactory. His younger brother was placed there a year or two afterwards. President Samuel Stanhope Smith writes to their father, March 27, 1792: "It gives me singular pleasure to be able to say of the good morals, diligence and talents of your sons, every thing that the fondest and worthiest parents can wish, and I anticipate the satisfaction which you must have in their company when they return home after their examination; and you will allow me to say I sincerely participate in it."

After his graduation, Mr. Wallace was placed in the counting-house of Mr. William Cramond, an English merchant of high standing in Philadelphia, with a view to entering on commercial pursuits. A few years afterwards, he was sent abroad, visiting the Island of Madeira, and passing some time in Great Britain and Ireland, and making what was then called the "grand tour" of the Continent. He married, as appears by Sir Bernard Burke's "Visitation of Seats and Arms" (where an account of the family is given, vol. i., p. 32), "Rebecca daughter of William McIlvaine, of Burlington, in New Jersey, M.D.," and died at his country residence near Philadelphia, January 7, 1821. A son of Mr. Wallace graduated at Princeton in 1833, and an only surviving son, Ellerslie Wallace, M.D., a well-known physician of Philadelphia, is now a Professor in one of the principal medical colleges in that city.

1794.

Thomas M. Bayly, a Virginian by birth, entered into public life in 1798, and continued therein until 1830. He served in both branches of the Virginia Legislature, and was a member of the State Constitutional Convention of 1830. From 1813 to 1815, he was in the House of Representatives of the United States. It was said of Mr. Bayly that he never lost an election. He died in 1834.

James M. Broom was a member of Congress from Delaware, from 1805 to 1807. He died in 1850.

George Washington Campbell entered the profession of the law. He was a member of Congress from Tennessee from 1803 to 1809, serving during the two last terms as Chairman of the Committee of Ways and Means. He was afterwards appointed Judge of the United States District Court of Tennessee. In 1811, he was elected to the United States Senate, but resigned on being appointed Secretary of the Treasury in 1814. The following year he resumed his seat in the Senate, and served till 1818, when he was appointed Minister to Russia, where he remained until 1821. He died February 7, 1848.

Edmund Elmendorf acted as a tutor for several months after graduating. He studied law and was admitted an Attorney of the Supreme Court of New Jersey, at the September Term, 1799; and as a Counsellor at the May Term, 1800. Mr. Elmendorf removed to the City of New York, where he engaged in practice. For a number of years he was Clerk in Chancery. He died in 1856.

1794.

Nicholas Everett was a nephew of the wife of Walter Minto, Professor of Mathematics and Natural Philosophy in the College at Princeton. He studied law and practiced in New York City. He was at one time a Justice of one of the City Courts. Mr. Everett was a laborious, active man, but not at all brilliant.

William B. Ewing became a Physician. He was a member of the Legislature of New Jersey, and at one time Speaker of the Lower House. He died in 1866.

James G. Force was ordained by the Presbytery of New York, November 30, 1796, and installed as pastor of New Providence, New Jersey. He was dismissed from this charge October 6, 1802. He died in 1849.

Moore Furman was a son of Moore Furman, a prominent citizen of Trenton, New Jersey. He entered no profession, and died at Lawrenceville, New Jersey, April 18, 1804.

John White Furman, a brother of the above, after his graduation, resided on a farm at Pittstown, Hunterdon County, New Jersey. He was killed by falling from his horse. He died April 28, 1802. It was no doubt the intention of the two brothers to follow agriculture, as their father was a large landed proprietor, but their premature death defeated their plans.

Richard M. Green was a brother of Charles D. Green of the class of 1787. He never entered a profession, but followed the bent of his inclinations in agricultural pursuits. He died in 1853.

John Sylvanus Hiester, son of Joseph and Elizabeth Hiester, was born in Berks County, Pennsylvania, July 28, 1794. He began the study of law with Attorney-General Bradford, but upon the death of that eminent lawyer in 1795, he passed into the office of Jared Ingersoll, under whose direction he finished that study. Mr. Hiester never practiced law, but upon Thomas McKean becoming Governor of Pennsylvania, he was appointed Prothonotary of the Common Pleas, and Clerk of the Criminal Court of Berks County. He held this position for nine years. For many years he was Cashier of the Farmers' Bank of Reading. He died March 7, 1849.

Thomas Yardley How studied law, and was admitted an Attorney of the Supreme Court of New Jersey in May, 1799. A few years later, he took orders in the Episcopal Church, and was for a time Rector of Grace Church in the City of New York. He had a share in the celebrated Church Controversy with Hobart, Linn, Beasley, Mason, Miller and others, in the early part of the present century.

In 1812, he received the honorary degree of Doctor of Divinity from Columbia College, New York. It is said that Dr. How afterwards relinquished the ministry, and returned to the law, removing to one of the Western States, where he probably died.

Holloway Whitefield Hunt received license from the Presbytery of New Brunswick about 1792, and on the 17th of June, 1795, was ordained and settled as pastor of the Churches at Newton and Hardiston, New Jersey. In 1804, he removed to Hunterdon County, and took charge of the United Churches of Kingwood, Bethlehem and Alexandria. He was a tall, portly man, of a very fair complexion, and in later years his hair white with age. He was a man of fair abilities, and in his prime was a popular preacher. His manners were bland and attractive, and he had the faculty of attaching the people of his charge very strongly to him. In the latter years of his life, Mr. Hunt gave up the active duties of the ministry on account of increasing infirmities. He died in Hunterdon County, New Jersey, in 1858.

Titus Hutchinson. I presume that Mr. Hutchinson was a native of Vermont, where he practiced law and rose to distinction. In October, 1825, he was appointed a Judge of the Supreme Court of the State, in which position he remained until 1830, when he was appointed Chief-Justice.

Mr. Hutchinson died in 1857.

Henry Kollock, a son of Shepard Kollock, of Elizabethtown, New Jersey, spent three years following his graduation at his father's house, reviewing his college studies. In 1797 he was appointed tutor, John Henry Hobart being his colleague, between whom and Kollock there sprang up a most intimate and ardent friendship, which lasted during life. At this period there was in the college a Literary Association called the "Belles Lettres Society," consisting of the officers of the college and the resident graduates. They met once in two weeks, and the exercises consisted in reading an essay, followed with remarks or criticisms by the members, and then a debate on some political, literary, moral or religious question. The subject was selected several weeks before it was taken up, and all were expected to come prepared. On one of these occasions, the subject selected was the exclusive right of Bishops, in the Episcopal sense of the term, to ordain to the office of the gospel ministry; and our two young tutors were the combatants. Great interest was excited, not only by the nature of the subject, but also by the known talents of the debaters. Each, of course, took the side of the church to which he belonged, and brought all his ability to the defence of it. It was Saturday afternoon, and many of the under-graduates, who were not permitted to enter the room, abandoning their usual walks and amusements, collected, some around the library door, where the debate was held, and others on the outside of the building, so that, through the open windows, they might catch something of what was said. There they stood fixed for two or three hours. The debate was ably and eloquently conducted on both sides; and the Presbyterians who were present did not think their cause suffered in the hands of Mr. Kollock. To the honour of the disputants, this exciting debate did not, for a moment, interrupt their kindly feelings towards each other. In 1800, Mr. Kollock was licensed to preach by the Presbytery of New York, still holding his position as tutor, and preaching to the congregation in Princeton, where his eloquence made a profound impression.

After leaving the college, he became pastor of the Presbyterian Church in Elizabethtown, where he remained for three years. His fame was not confined to his own State. He received calls from many important churches. In 1803, the Trustees of the College appointed him Professor of Theology, and the Congregation of Princeton invited him to be their pastor. Accordingly, in the autumn of that year, he returned to Princeton in the double character of professor and pastor. But he was not permitted to remain here long. After repeated solicitations, he was prevailed on to accept a call from the Independent Presbyterian Church in Savannah, Georgia, and in 1806 he removed to his new field of labour.

In 1810 he was called to the Presidency of the University of Georgia, which he declined. While in Savannah his labours were abundant, especially among those ill with the yellow fever; and although he was not attacked by the fever, yet his health finally gave way, and he was compelled, for a time, to leave his charge, making a tour through Europe. On his return in 1817 he entered again into the same exhausting course of labour; but in less than two years he broke down again, and died December, 29, 1819.

Dr. James W. Alexander says of Mr. Kollock that he was "one of the most ornate yet vehement orators whom our country has produced."

A collection of Dr. Kollock's Sermons was published in Savannah in 1822, in 4 volumes 8vo.

Paul Paulison, after graduating, studied theology, intending to enter the ministry of the Reformed Dutch Church, but he was never ordained. He passed his whole life in Hackensack, New Jersey, his native town, where he died in 1832. Two of his sons graduated at Princeton, one in 1822 and the other in 1834.

Henry Polhemus, a native of Somerset County, New Jersey, was licensed by the Classis of New York in 1798, and settled as pastor of the Reformed Dutch Churches of Harlingen and Nashanic, New Jersey, in 1798, where he remained until 1809, when he became pastor of the Church at English Neighbourhood, New Jersey. Mr. Polhemus continued in this charge until 1813, when he became pastor of the Church at Shawangunck, New York, where he remained until his death, which occurred in 1816.

Edwin Reese was probably the son of Dr. Thomas Reese of the class of 1768. After his graduation, he returned to the South, and became Principal of a flourishing Academy in Pendleton District, South Carolina.

John N. Simpson was born in Bucks County, Pennsylvania, April 6, 1770. After graduating, he married a daughter of Dr. Wiggins, of Princeton, and settled upon a farm near that place. After a few years he removed to Baskingridge, and represented the County of Somerset in the Legislature of New Jersey. In 1811 he removed to New Brunswick and entered largely into mercantile business, having a partner in a large house in New York. He was again elected to the Legislature, and represented Middlesex County for a number of years; he was also at one time Judge of the Court of Common Pleas of that county, and was for a long time Cashier of the Bank of New Brunswick. Mr. Simpson was a great friend of education and internal improvement. Perhaps no person in the State did more to develope the resources of the State. When the project was first spoken of, for a canal to unite the Delaware and Raritan, by Mr. Simpson, in the Legislature of New Jersey, it was considered impracticable. He drew up the first bill that was ever presented for a charter for a company to make the said canal, but did not live to see it completed.

It was owing mainly to his influence that the State of New Jersey was stimulated to take the part she did in promoting the cause of common school education.

A few years before his death, Mr. Simpson edited a paper in Princeton called the *Princeton Courier*. He was a great friend of his *Alma Mater*, and, after his death, there was found among his papers a subscription-list in behalf of rebuilding the college, drawn up by him, while it was in flames, and headed by him with a subscription of five hundred dollars; and it is said that, before the flames were extinguished, he had a subscription-list of five thousand dollars.

Mr. Simpson was an elder in the Presbyterian Church in New Brunswick. He died in Princeton, May 13, 1832.

John Brown Slemons received his license to preach from the Presbytery of New Castle in 1797, and was installed pastor of Monokin and Wicomico Churches in Maryland in June, 1799. He remained in this charge until 1821, when he retired to a farm which he owned, and spent the remainder of his days in retirement. Mr. Slemons was a man of more than ordinary powers, and was said to have been a Boanerges. He was pointed and often blunt. His delivery was not esteemed equal to his sermonizing powers. An anecdote of Benjamin Dashiel, an Episcopalian and lawyer, contemporary of Mr. Slemons, who set a pretty high estimate upon his own oratorical powers, is a very good illustration of the estimate put upon Mr. Slemons's Sermons. Mr. Dashiel is handed down to have said, "Let Parson Slemons *write* the sermon, let *me* preach it, and big Billy Handy set the Psalm, and we will convert the devil."

John Bradford Wallace was a brother of Joshua M. Wallace of the preceding class. He was born at Ellerslie, his father's seat, August 17, 1778. His course at Princeton was manly and exemplary. He was invariably diligent, patient and accurate in his studies. The vigour and precision of his memory was one of the results of his regularity and care, and, in connection with a delightful voice and enunciation, was such that President Smith used often to say, "It was indeed a pleasure to hear Mr. Wallace's recitations."

Mr. Wallace was admitted to the Pennsylvania Bar in 1797, and before long was acknowledged to stand in its most dignified ranks. Strength, discrimination and directness were the characteristics of his understanding. In 1822 Mr. Wallace fixed his residence in Meadville, Pennsylvania. He was soon elected to the Legislature of the State, which position he held for three successive years, when he removed to Philadelphia.

Mr. Wallace was a warm and active member of the Episcopal Church. His piety was bright and remarkably practical. A fervid and delightful sentiment, it inspired in his own heart both love and confidence. After his graduation Mr. Wallace assumed the middle name of Bradford, after his mother's family. He died in Philadelphia, January 7, 1837.

William R. Williamson was admitted an Attorney of the Supreme Court of New Jersey, at the May Term, 1799, and practiced in Essex County, New Jersey.

John R. Witherspoon was from South Carolina. He studied medicine and practiced in his native State, but afterwards removed to Alabama, where he died in 1850. He published a description of a Latin Bible in his possession. Dr. Witherspoon was widely known and highly respected throughout the South.

1795.

James Agnew was the son of Daniel Agnew, an Irishman, an Elder in the Presbyterian Church of Princeton, and for some time Steward of the College. After graduating, Mr. Agnew studied medicine, and was rising to prominence as a physician at Pittsburg, Pennsylvania, when he died in 1800.

John A. Boyd studied law, and was admitted an Attorney of the Supreme Court of New Jersey, at the November Term, 1799, and settled at Hackensack, Bergen County, New Jersey. Mr. Boyd was Surrogate of Bergen County from November, 1803, till his death in 1828.

David Comfort was licensed by the Presbytery of New Brunswick in 1798, and soon after became pastor of the Presbyterian Church at Kingston, New Jersey, where he laboured during a long life, honoured and beloved by all. From 1816 until his death in 1853, he was a Trustee of the College.

Silas Condit was a native of Newark, New Jersey. He represented New Jersey in Congress from 1831 to 1833; and was a member of the State Convention which formed the Constitution in 1844. Mr. Condit was a man highly esteemed, and held offices of trust in his native town. He died November 29, 1861.

George R. Cuthbert belonged to an influential family in Canada. After graduating, he returned to Canada.

1795.

Josiah Harrison, a native of New Jersey, after his graduation studied law, and was admitted to the Bar at the February Term of the Supreme Court of New Jersey, in 1800. He practiced for many years in Gloucester and Burlington Counties, and was for a number of years Law Reporter of the Supreme Court. He died in 1865.

Mr. Harrison published: Laws of New Jersey, 1820–1833; Camden, 1833, 8vo. New Jersey Supreme Court Reports, 1837–1842, 4 vols., 8vo, 1839–1843.

Samuel Hayes was from Newark, New Jersey. He studied medicine with Dr. J. R. B. Rodgers of the class of 1775. In 1799, he was appointed "Apothecary of the New York Hospital." In 1800, he sailed to India as Surgeon of the ship "Swan." In 1803, he was in the drug business in New York for a few months, and in 1804, he became associated with Dr. Cyrus Pierson in the practice of medicine in Newark, New Jersey. Dr. Hayes was a man of acknowledged skill. He was a good scholar and faithful to the interests of his patients. He ever maintained a high Christian character. He died July 30, 1839.

Elbert Herring, the sole living representative of the graduates of the eighteenth century, bears about with him the burden and the honours of ninety-five years. He is still sound in body and in mind. He was born the year after Independence was declared. He entered college when Dr. Witherspoon was President, and was present at his funeral the next year, and the impression made by the appearance of that noble form as it lay in the coffin, has never been obliterated. Seventy-three years after that event, Judge Herring sat with his classmate Joseph Warren Scott upon the stage, and witnessed the inauguration of another eminent Scotchman, who like his great compeer, has infused new life into the venerable body of our beloved *Alma Mater*.

After graduating, Mr. Herring entered upon the practice of the law in New York, his native city. In 1805, he was appointed Judge of the Marine Court, which position he held for three years; and was again appointed to the same office a few years later. Judge Herring was a confidential friend of De Witt Clinton, and was by him appointed the first Register of the City and County of New York. In 1831, he was appointed by General Jackson the first Commissioner of Indian Affairs, which position he held for about five years. Judge Herring long since retired from the active duties of life, but not from the public duties of a living Christian. His seat in the church and the prayer-meeting is seldom vacant.

Patrick Houstoun was a son of Richard Houstoun of Georgia, and was a grandson of Sir Patrick Houstoun, and a nephew of Governor John Houstoun of Georgia. After graduating, he returned to Georgia.

George W. Woodruff of the class of 1783, married a sister of Patrick Houstoun.

Richard Rayhold Keene was a native of Dorchester County, Maryland. While in college he was a scholar of respectable standing. After graduating, he established himself as a lawyer in Baltimore, and married the daughter of Luther Martin of the class of 1766. Mr. Keene afterwards removed to New Orleans, and made quite a figure in the political world as District Attorney of the United States for the Orleans Territory, and was a conspicuous character in the disputes which grew out of the Burr Conspiracy. He afterwards resided several years in Spain, where, during the war with Napoleon, he bore the rank of Colonel in the Spanish service. Mr. Keene's second wife was a native of Spain. The life of Mr. Keene was checkered by many and singular turns of adverse and prosperous fortune, and he closed his career possessed of little of this world's wealth.

He died at St. Louis while on a visit to Colonel Richard R. Keene, in 1839.

Mr. Keene published: "A Memorial to the Spanish Government," which made some noise at the time.

Eleazer W. Keyes returned to his home in Connecticut after graduation, and became quite prominent as a lawyer. Mr. Keyes married the daughter of General Ethan Allen of Revolutionary fame.

Elias Riggs received his license to preach from the Presbytery of New York in March, 1802, and for some time supplied the Presbyterian Church at Perth Amboy, New Jersey. On the 2d of August he was ordained. In the month of October, 1806, he removed to New Providence, New Jersey, and was installed pastor of the Presbyterian Church in that place, June 10, 1807. He continued in this pastoral charge to the end of his life. He died February 25, 1825. Mr. Riggs was eminently a godly man and a faithful pastor, and commanded by his exemplary life and conversation, the affections of his people and respect of the community. He entailed upon the world a well-trained family that does honour to his name, and has done good to the Church and the world. Mr. Riggs left a family of two sons and four daughters, both of his sons becoming Presbyterian ministers, the younger one being the distinguished missionary at Constantinople, the Rev. Elias Riggs, D.D., LL.D.

Joseph Warren Scott, a son of Dr. Moses Scott of New Brunswick, New Jersey, after graduating, studied medicine for a short time with his father, and also paid some attention to theology, a science congenial to his intellect and early education. On one occasion he attended court in New York and became greatly interested in the able argument of one of the lawyers, and this was the incentive that led him to adopt the law as his profession. He was admitted an Attorney of the Supreme Court of New Jersey, at the February Term, 1801, and a Counsellor, February, 1804, and was called Sergeant at Law, at the February Term, 1816. In criminal cases he showed great power and almost resistless eloquence. He argued his last case at the age of eighty, and spoke for several hours without much weariness, considering his years. Hon. Hamilton Fish, Secretary of State of the United States, on hearing of his death writes to a friend, "Genial and bright in intellect and wit, four score and ten years had not, when last I met him, quenched the ardour of his warm and impulsive nature; and I shall ever remember Colonel Warren Scott as one of the most attractive talkers and agreeable companions whom it has been my fortune to meet." Colonel Scott died April 27, 1871, having, with the Hon. Elbert Herring of the same class, long outlived all his contemporaries.

John Sergeant, a native of Philadelphia, was a son of Jonathan Dickinson Sergeant of the class of 1762, and a great grandson of President Dickinson. After leaving college, Mr. Sergeant was for a short time a clerk in a mercantile house, but this not suiting his tastes, he studied law and was admitted to the Bar in 1799. For several years he was Prosecutor for the Commonwealth of Penn'a. Mr. Sergeant was a member of the House of Representatives from 1815 to 1823, from 1827 to 1829, and from 1837 to 1842. He was especially famous for his part in the great Missouri Compromise of 1820. He was selected by President Adams to represent the United States in the Panama Congress. The measures of international law which were proposed to be settled in that Congress, were deemed so important that Mr. Clay, the Secretary of State, had filled eighty pages of instructions to Mr. Sergeant on the subject. In 1832 he was a candidate for Vice-President of the United States on the same ticket with Mr. Clay. In 1840 President Harrison tendered to him the mission to England, which he declined. Mr. Sergeant was for half a century known and honoured for his extraordinary ability in his profession of the law, for his habitual courtesy, his liberal fairness, and his undoubted integrity. In the cause of charity he was never appealed to in vain; and for many years before his death took an active interest in all the public affairs of his native city. He received the honorary degree of Doctor of Laws from Union College in 1822, from Dickinson College in 1826, and from Harvard in 1844.

Mr. Sergeant's Select Speeches were published in 1832; and a number of Addresses appeared separately.

Edward Darrell Smith studied medicine and became Professor of Chemistry and Mineralogy in the College of South Carolina. He died near St. Louis, Missouri, August 17, 1819.

Dr. Smith published, Translation of Desault's Surgical Works, two volumes, 8vo. 1814. Inaugural Dissertation on the Circulation; Philadelphia, 1800.

John Witherspoon Smith, a son of President Samuel Stanhope Smith, studied law and removed to St. Louis, where he became Judge of the United States District Court of St. Louis.

Robert Johnstone Taylor was born at Belfast, Ireland, in December, 1777. He was the son of Captain Jesse Taylor and Elizabeth Johnstone. On the 29th of September, 1779, his father, with his entire family, consisting of his wife and eight children, of which the subject of this notice, then not two years old, was the youngest, embarked in a vessel, of which he was the sole owner, mounting fourteen guns, bound for Philadelphia. After a long and stormy passage of thirteen weeks, and being compelled to throw ten of his guns overboard, his ship, by stress of weather, was driven ashore at the mouth of James River, in Virginia, got amongst the ice, and with a cargo of salt, then estimated to be worth ten "hard dollars" per bushel, was totally lost. After the loss of his vessel, he went with his family to Williamsburg, and remained there until May, 1780, when he removed to Alexandria.

1795.

The subject of this sketch was prepared for college by the celebrated Dr. James McWhirr, who predicted for his pupil a brilliant career. Mr. Taylor graduated at the head of his class, and immediately commenced the study of law at Alexandria, in the office of Colonel Charles Simms, and was admitted to the Bar in 1798. On the fly leaf of his note book, under the date of November, 1795, in his own handwriting, is the following quotation from "Johnson's London:"

> "But thou, should tempting villany present,
> All Marlbro hoarded, or all Villiers spent,
> Turn from the glittering bribe thy scornful eye,
> Nor sell for gold what gold can never buy;
> The peaceful slumber, self-approving day,
> Unsullied fame and conscience ever gay."

Practicing on the principles inculcated in these noble lines through a long, useful and active life, he secured the confidence and respect of every one who knew him, and at the time of his death stood in the front rank of his profession, side by side with those great Virginia lawyers of his day, Chapman Johnson, Henry St. George Tucker, Benjamin Watkins Leigh, and Robert Stannard. From the year 1813 to 1830 his practice was large in the Supreme Court of the United States, but he was compelled to relinquish it, his practice in the courts of his State having become so extensive and onerous as to leave him no time for any thing else. At the Bar of the Supreme Court he ranked as a lawyer with Pinckney, Wirt, Walter Jones, and his class-mate, John Sergeant of Philadelphia, whom he frequently encountered in the argument of important cases, and who all recognized in him "a foeman worthy of their steel." It was after an able argument in one of these cases, that Chief-Justice Marshall paid him the highest compliment probably ever paid to a lawyer, when he said that he was the only lawyer he had ever known in all his experience at the Bar and on the Bench, who never said a word too much or a word too little for the cause he advocated. Mr. Taylor died at Alexandria on the 4th of October, 1840, universally beloved, esteemed and lamented.

A son of Mr. Taylor graduated in the class of 1835, and is now an eminent lawyer in Alexandria.

Abraham Ten Eyke was from Albany, New York, to which city he returned after graduation and commenced the practice of law.

James Tilton was a native of Delaware, and a son of Nehemiah Tilton, a Colonel in the Revolutionary army, and otherwise employed during his life in government service. After his graduation he studied medicine and commenced practice in Wilmington. He afterwards removed to the western country.

Matthew G. Wallace studed theology with the Rev. Nathan Grier, and removed immediately to Ohio. Mr. Wallace was among the first Presbyterian Ministers who settled in Ohio. About the year 1802 he became pastor of the First Presbyterian Church in Cincinnati, which had been founded in 1790 by Rev. David Rice of the class of 1761. Afterwards he preached at Springfield, Hamilton and other places in Ohio. He was in the ministry nearly sixty years, and in the latter part of his life resided in Terre Haute, Indiana, without charge, where he died at the age of eighty, August 12, 1854.

Clayton Wright was a native of Queen Ann County, Maryland, and was killed early in life in a duel.

1796.

William T. Anderson, a Jerseyman by birth, studied law, and was admitted an Attorney of the Supreme Court of New Jersey at the September Term, 1801. Mr. Anderson pursued his profession in Sussex County, New Jersey, for many years. He was a man of high standing and character, and of considerable legal attainments. He died in 1850.

Henry Axtell, a son of Henry Axtell, a farmer and a revolutionary officer, was born at Mendham, New Jersey, June 9, 1773. After his graduation, he taught school for several years at Morristown and Mendham. In 1804 he removed to Geneva, New York, where he was for several years more at the head of a flourishing school. On the 1st of November, 1810, he was licensed to preach by the Presbytery of Geneva, and, after preaching in various places, he was, in 1812, installed as colleague pastor with the Rev. Jedediah Chapman, at Geneva. Here he remained during his life. The degree of Doctor of Divinity was conferred upon him by Middlebury College in 1823. Dr. Axtell was a bold and faithful preacher, and sometimes very powerful. He was both practical and argumentative, and eminently scriptural in his preaching.

In stature, he was rather above the average, of a broad, athletic form. He died in the utmost peace, February 11, 1849.

Dr. Axtell published a Sermon preached at the ordination of Julius Steele, 1816.

George C. Barber was admitted an Attorney of the

Supreme Court of New Jersey at the February Term, 1801. He practiced in Elizabethtown, and was for some time Clerk of the Borough. Mr. Barber was an elder in the Presbyterian Church. He married a daughter of Governor Aaron Ogden of the class of 1773. He died in 1828.

John Macpherson Berrien. The ancestors of Mr. Berrien were Huguenots. His grandfather was John Berrien, one of the Judges of the Supreme Court of New Jersey. The father of Mr. Berrien removed in early life to Georgia, and during the Revolutionary struggle was an officer in the American Army, and was very conspicuous at the Battle of Monmouth. His mother was a sister of John Macpherson of the class of 1766.

The subject of our sketch was born in New Jersey during a temporary residence of his parents, August 23, 1781. After graduating, he returned to Georgia, and read law in the office of Joseph Clay, a graduate of the class of 1784, and was admitted to the Bar before he was eighteen. He now applied himself to his profession with great industry. His books were his delight, and to his studious habits, in the early stages of his legal career, may doubtless be attributed the great success which he afterwards met with, and which placed him in time among the first lawyers in America. In November, 1809, he was elected Solicitor of the Eastern District of the State of Georgia, and the following year Judge of the same district. This office he held for twelve years, being re-elected every three years. During this period, the war of 1812 occurred, and the excitement of the public mind added, in no small degree, to the responsibilities of his station; but he administered the laws with prudence, firmness and impartiality.

In 1822 and 1823 he was in the Legislature, and in 1824 was chosen to the United States Senate. During his term in the Senate, there was not a subject of general interest with which he did not display consummate knowledge. His speeches were always listened to with profound attention, and acquired for him the reputation of being one of the most gifted orators and able statesmen in our country.

In 1829 Mr. Berrien was appointed Attorney-General of the United States, in consequence of which he resigned his seat in the Senate. This office he resigned in 1831. In 1840 he was re-elected to the Senate. This period will long be remembered for the important and delicate questions which agitated the counsels of the nation. In them Mr. Berrien took a prominent part, and added to the fame he had already acquired. He resigned his seat in the Senate in May, 1852, and retired to private life. In 1830 Princeton conferred upon him the degree of Doctor of Laws, on the occasion of his delivering an address before the literary societies. Mr. Berrien died January 1, 1856.

His publications consist of a few Addresses and Speeches.

Elias Boudinot Caldwell, a son of James Caldwell of the class of 1759, was for many years Clerk of the Supreme Court of the United States, but is especially known for the prominent part he took in the cause of African Colonization. In honour of him the managers of the Society gave the name of Caldwell to a town in their African colony. While living in Washington, Mr. Caldwell obtained a license from the Presbytery, and was accustomed to preach to the ignorant and degraded in that city. He died in May, 1825.

A Speech of Mr. Caldwell's, on African Colonization, was published in 1817.

Moses I. Cantine entered college from the State of New York, and, after graduating, studied law and settled in Catskill. In 1814 he was elected to the State Senate from the Middle District, his colleague from the same District being William Ross of the class of 1792. In 1820 he became one of the proprietors and editors of the *Albany Argus*. Mr. Cantine was a brother-in-law of Martin Van Buren. He was frank, generous and kind in his social intercourse, and, although not brilliant, was a man of highly respectable talents.

John Starke Edwards was a son of the Hon. Pierpont Edwards of Connecticut, and grandson of President Edwards. After graduating, he returned to New Haven and commenced the study of law, and attended the lectures at the law school of Tapping Reeve at Litchfield. He was admitted to the Bar as Attorney and Counsellor in 1799; and in the same year removed to Ohio—to what was then known as the Western Reserve. In 1800, he was appointed by Governor St. Clair, Recorder of Trumbull County. He was admitted to practice by the General Court of the Territory North-west of the Ohio River, in October of the same year. In 1812, he was commissioned as Colonel of one of the regiments in the Fourth Division of Ohio Militia, then under command of General Elijah Wadsworth, a distinguished Revolutionary patriot; and after General Hull's surrender at Detroit, August 15, 1812, by which the whole north-western frontier was thrown open to invasion by the enemy, he took an active part with other patriotic citizens of the country in concerting measures of defence.

In October, 1812, he was elected to Congress from the Sixth District of Ohio, but he never took his seat, for in January, 1813, on a visit to the army on the north-western frontier, he was seized with camp fever, and died on the 29th of that month.

The social and professional standing of Mr. Edwards was all that the most ambitious and aspiring could desire, and his prospects of future distinction in public and private life were bright and flattering in the highest degree.

Mr. Edwards was a man of fine appearance, and in stature about six feet in height, stoutly built, of florid complexion, and commanding presence. He was not an easy and fluent speaker, and therefore not distinguished as an advocate; but his fine legal attainments, his candour, honourable bearing and undoubted integrity, won the confidence and respect of his professional brethren of the court and of the jury, and he was eminently a successful lawyer.

Wilhemus Eltinge received his license to preach in 1798, and from 1799 to 1850, was pastor of the Reformed Dutch Church at Paramus and Saddle River, New Jersey, and other churches gathered in the vicinity. Called at the early age of twenty-one to the ministry, he remained for fifty-one years in a single charge; at times, however, adding to this a neighbouring congregation. He was a man of great firmness and decision. It was difficult to change his opinion when once formed. He was a pointed preacher. He neither courted the favour nor feared the frowns of men. During the first three years of his ministry, he was blessed with a great revival, about three hundred being added to his churches. He was a ready debater, and always active in ecclesiastical bodies. He lived almost forty years on a farm of his own, ten miles from his charge; and would start on Saturday morning, lecture in some house in the evening, preach on Sabbath morning, and lecture again in the evening on his way home. He often quoted to young ministers, when urging them to diligence in the Master's work, "*Juniories ad labores! Seniores ad honores!*" He received the honorary degree of Doctor of Divinity from Rutgers College in 1839. He died in 1851.

John Fitzgerald, a native of South Carolina, died the year after his graduation.

Robert M. Forsyth was the eldest son of Major Forsyth, the first Marshal of Georgia, and brother of Governor John Forsyth of the class of 1799. He pronounced the Valedictory Oration at the time of his graduation, and was considered the best public speaker who had been in the college for many years, and he has not, perhaps, often been since surpassed. He was distinguished for his remarkable scholarship while in college, as well as for every moral grace and virtue. Mr. Forsyth died of the yellow fever at Savannah in the autumn of 1797, the year after his graduation.

William Gaston was a native of Newbern, North Carolina. His father, Dr. Alexander Gaston, was a man of letters, and a determined patriot. Mr. Gaston was first sent to the Catholic College at Georgetown, District of Columbia, but his health failing, he returned home, and in 1794, entered Princeton. He graduated with the highest honours of his class. "The proudest moment of my life," he once said, "was when I communicated the information to my mother that I had not only graduated, but with honour." And he has often been heard to say, that whatever distinction he had attained in life, was owing to her pious counsel and faithful conduct, Mr. Gaston studied law with François Xavier Martin, and was admitted to the Bar in 1798.

In 1800, when only twenty-two years of age, he was elected to the Senate of North Carolina. But his small patrimony demanded his close attention to his profession, and he did not again appear in public life until 1808, when he was elected a member of the House of Commons, of which body he was chosen Speaker. In 1813, he was elected a Member of Congress; and again in 1815. Here he attracted the attention of the whole country by his eloquence and manly boldness. At the end of his second term, he declined re-election, and devoted himself to his profession. In 1827, he was again returned to the House of Commons. In 1834, Mr. Gaston was elected Judge of the Supreme Court of North Carolina. In 1840, he was solicited to accept the post of United States Senator, but he declined, and devoted himself with new ardour to the duties of his Judgeship. The manner in which he discharged his important duties; his profound and varied literature; his extensive legal knowledge; his severe and patient research; his polished and clear composition, render his opinions not only monuments of legal learning, but models of elegant literature. He died January 23, 1844. Judge Gaston received the honorary degree of Doctor of Laws from Princeton, on the occasion of his delivering an address before the literary societies of the College in 1835; from the University of Pennsylvania in 1819; from Harvard in 1826, and from the University of New York in 1834.

French F. McMullen was born in Delaware, and after his graduation studied law, and resided near Dover, Delaware. He never became distinguished in his profession.

John Moody, a native of Pennsylvania, after leaving college, studied theology, and was licensed by the Presbytery of Carlisle in 1801. He was soon after ordained by the same Presbytery and settled as pastor of Middle Spring Presbyterian Church, Pennsylvania, where he remained until his death in 1857. During the latter years of his life he was, through the infirmity of age, unable to perform ministerial work.

He was a laborious, faithful and successful pastor. He received the degree of Doctor of Divinity from Marshall College in 1849.

Henry W. Ogden, a son of Mathias Ogden of Elizabethtown, New Jersey, after graduating, removed to New Orleans, where he continued until his death.

Philip Clayton Pendleton was from Virginia. He studied law, and rose to some eminence in his profession. He was the United States District Judge for the

Western District of Virginia for some years. He died in 1863.

Nathaniel Venable, a brother of Samuel W. Venable of the class of 1780, returned to Virginia and followed planting. Mr. Venable was one of the first Trustees of Hampden Sidney College.

1797.

William and Martin Agnew were twins—the sons of Daniel Agnew of Princeton, and brothers of James Agnew of the class of 1795. William became insane, but continued to reside at Princeton until his death at an early age. He wore a long beard, a very uncommon thing in those days. Martin became a farmer, and died at a very advanced age in Hunterdon County, New Jersey, in 1857.

Thomas Bayley was a native of Somerset County, Maryland. He represented his native State in Congress from 1817 to 1823.

Fredrick Beasley was born in North Carolina. During his college course he contracted an intimate friendship with John Henry Hobart and Henry Kollock, which was terminated only by death. After graduating, Mr. Beasley studied theology with President Samuel Stanhope Smith, acting at the same time as tutor in the college. In 1801 he was ordained Deacon by Bishop Moore of New York, and Priest by the same, in 1802. In September, 1802, he became Rector of St. John's Church, Elizabethtown, but the next spring he resigned his charge, and accepted a call to the Rectorship of St. Peter's Church, Albany. He remained here until 1809, when he removed to Baltimore and became Rector of St. Paul's Church in that city. In 1813, his health being delicate, and feeling the need of a position where lighter service would be required, he resigned his charge and accepted the office of Provost of the University of Pennsylvania, a place that admirably suited his intellectual tastes and habits, and its duties he discharged with acknowledged ability and fidelity for fifteen years. Dr. Beasley resigned this post in 1828, and in 1829 became Rector of St. Michael's Church, Trenton, New Jersey, where he remained until 1836. His health becoming very much impaired, he gave up his charge at Trenton and removed to Elizabethtown, where he spent the remainder of his days, dying November 1, 1845. He received the honorary degree of Doctor of Divinity from Columbia College and from the University of Pennsylvania in 1815.

Dr. Beasley was a man of slight frame, below the ordinary height, and was very easy and rapid in his movements. He was remarkably social and frank in all his intercourse. His acquirements in literature were very considerable, and in these pursuits was his chief delight. His sermons were terse, well written, and cogent as to reasoning. His studies lay mainly in the direction of Mental Philosophy. He had no relish for the Scotch Philosophers, but admired John Locke above all others.

Dr. Beasley published: A Discourse before the Ladies' Society, instituted for the Relief of Distressed Seamen in the City of Albany. 1808. Inaugural Sermon in St. Paul's Church, Baltimore. 1810. A Sermon on Duelling. 1811. An Anonymous Pamphlet, entitled Serious Reflections addressed to Episcopalians in Maryland, on the State of their Church generally, but more particularly on the Pending Election of a Suffragan Bishop. 1813. A Sermon before the Diocesan Convention of Pennsylvania. 1815. American Dialogues of the Dead. 1815. A (second) Sermon on Duelling. 1822. A Search of Truth in the Science of the Human Mind; Part I., one volume, 8vo. 1822. [He left in MS. Part II. complete.] A Vindication of the Argument *a priori* in proof of the Being and Attributes of God, from Objections of Dr. Waterland. 1825. Review of Brown's Philosophy of the Human Mind. 1825. A Vindication of the Fundamental Principles of Truth and Order in the Church of Christ, from the Allegations of Rev. William E. Channing, D.D. 1830. An Examination of No. 90 of the Tracts for the Times. 1842. Dr. Beasley edited the two volumes of Dr. Samuel Stanhope Smith's Posthumous Sermons, and wrote the Memoir of his Life prefixed to the first volume. He also contributed largely to the periodical literature of the day.

Richard L. Beatty, a native of Monmouth County,

New Jersey, after graduating, studied law, and was admitted an Attorney of the Supreme Court of New Jersey at the November Term, 1802. Mr. Beatty lived and died at Allentown, New Jersey.

James W. Clarke was a native of Bertie County, North Carolina. In 1802 and 1803, he represented his native county in the House of Commons; and was again a member from Edgecombe County in 1811. From 1812 to 1814 Mr. Clarke was a member of the Senate of North Carolina. In 1815 he was elected to the House of Representatives of the United States; he served out his term and declined re-election. In 1828 he was appointed Chief Clerk in the Navy Department at Washington, which post he soon resigned. Mr. Clarke died in 1843, esteemed and loved by all who knew him.

Aaron Coe studied law and was admitted an Attorney of the Supreme Court of New Jersey at the November Term, 1801. He died in 1857.

Daniel Crane was from Essex County, New Jersey. In 1803 he was licensed by the Morris County Presbytery, and the year following was ordained by the same Presbytery and settled as pastor of the Presbyterian Church at Chester, New Jersey. He remained in this charge until 1808, when he became pastor of the Church at Fishkill, New York, June 7. Here he laboured with great zeal and success for thirteen years. In July, 1821, he took charge of the First Congregational Church in Waterbury, Connecticut, still retaining his connection with the Presbytery. In 1825 he returned to Fishkill and taught in a select school for two years, and then accepted a call to his old charge in Chester, New Jersey. He was installed July 18, 1827, and continued there until September 14, 1831, when he resigned. The remainder of his life was passed in preaching and doing good, as health and opportunity permitted. He died April 1, 1861.

1797.

Henry Waggaman Edwards was a brother of John Starke Edwards of the class of 1796, and a grandson of President Edwards. He studied law at Litchfield under Tapping Reeve, and commenced practice in New Haven. He was a Representative in Congress from 1819 to 1823, and United States Senator from 1823 to 1827, and a member of the State Senate of Connecticut from 1828 to 1829. In 1830 he was Speaker of the Connecticut House of Representatives, and was Governor of the State in 1833, and from 1835 to 1838. Upon his recommendation a Geological Survey of the State was taken. Mr. Edwards received the honorary degree of Doctor of Laws from Yale in 1833. He died July 22, 1847.

William Clark Frazer, a native of White Hall, New Castle County, Delaware, after graduating, studied law, and practiced for some years in the City of New Castle. Having married a lady in Lancaster, Pennsylvania, he took up his residence in that place, and in 1836 was appointed, by General Jackson, Judge of the Eastern District of Wisconsin Territory. He filled his judgeship a very brief period, dying at Milwaukee, October 18, 1838, aged 62 years.

Abraham Harrison, a native of New Jersey, after his graduation, followed agricultural pursuits and resided in Orange, New Jersey. Mr. Harrison was for many years an officer in the Presbyterian Church, and a leading man in the community where he resided. He died in 1851.

Thomas Edgar Hughes came to Princeton from York County, Pennsylvania. He was licensed to preach by the Presbytery of Ohio, October 17, 1798. On the 27th of August, 1799, he was ordained and installed pastor of the Church of Mount Pleasant, Beaver County, Pennsylvania, where he laboured successfully for upwards of thirty years. He afterwards removed to Wellsville,

Ohio, and was pastor of a Presbyterian Church in that place for three years. He died May 2, 1838. He was the first minister of the gospel who settled north of the Ohio River. He performed, at least, two missionary tours to the Indians on the Sandusky River, and in the neighbourhood of Detroit.

Alexander S. Kerr, a native of Pennsylvania, died in 1798, the year after he graduated.

Peter Le Conte was a son of the Rev. Jedediah Chapman, of Orange, New Jersey, and afterwards of Western New York. He dropped the name of Chapman in order to preserve the name of his mother. He studied law as a profession, and rose to eminence at the Bar in Western New York. Mr. Le Conte was for many years an elder in the Presbyterian Church at Ovid, New York. His conversation and life bear witness that he was acquainted with God, and lived in daily communion with him. He was a man of sound judgment, punctual in the performance of duty, and employed his talents in the service of Christ. He died September 17, 1836.

Charles Fenton Mercer. In 1798, while a student of law, Mr. Mercer tendered his services to General Washington for the defence of the country against a threatened invasion by the French, and received from him a commission as First Lieutenant of Cavalry, and soon after that of Captain, which he declined, not intending to devote his life to the military profession. In 1803, after spending a year in Europe, he commenced the practice of the law in Virginia, his native State. From 1810 to 1817 he was a member of the General Assembly ot that State. In 1811 he was again called to military service by the General Government; and, in 1813, was appointed aid to the Governor, and rose to the rank of Brigadier-General of Militia, having command of the forces in Norfolk. In 1816, while in the Legislature, as

Chairman of the Committee of Finance, he devoted his time to the promotion of internal improvement, and was chief supporter of the measure for the Chesapeake and Ohio Canal, and was appointed President of the Company. From 1817 to 1840 he represented his State in Congress. In 1853 he visited Europe for philanthropic motives, and used his efforts for the entire abolition of the slave trade. Mr. Mercer received the honorary degree of Doctor of Laws from Princeton in 1826. He died May 4, 1858.

Edmund Morford was born in New Jersey. He removed to South Carolina after graduating, and became editor of the Charleston *Courier*. Mr. Morford afterwards established the Charleston *Mercury* and became its editor. He was very prominent as a political writer. He died in 1833.

Jacob S. Otto, a brother of John C. Otto of the class of 1792, became a merchant in the City of Philadelphia.

Matthew La Rue Perrine belonged to a large and influential family in Monmouth County, New Jersey. He studied theology under Dr. John Woodhull, of Freehold, and was licensed to preach by the Presbytery of New Brunswick, September 18, 1799. On the 24th of June, 1800, he was ordained, and for four months acted as a Missionary in Western New York. On the 15th of June, 1802, he was installed as pastor of the Presbyterian Church at Bottle Hill, New Jersey. In 1809 he made another missionary tour, and on the 31st of October, 1811, was installed as pastor of the Spring Street Church, New York. Here he continued till the summer of 1820, when, by his own request, the pastoral relation was dissolved. In 1821 he was elected to the Professorship of Ecclesiastical History and Church Polity in the Auburn Theological Seminary. He continued actively engaged in the discharge of his various duties till near the close of his life. He received the honorary degree of Doctor of Divinity from Allegheny College in 1818.

The personal appearance of Dr. Perrine was altogether agreeable. His countenance indicated great mildness and benignity, mingled with thoughtfulness and intelligence; his manners were urbane and winning; his temper amiable and benevolent. He was naturally of a speculative and metaphysical turn. In theology, he harmonized with Dr. Emmons. As a preacher, he was always instructive and interesting, but could not be called popular. His style was correct and perspicuous, but, in a great measure, unadorned. There was great charm in the mellow and gentle tones of his voice. He had the reputation of being an accurate and thorough scholar. He died February 11, 1836.

Dr. Perrine published: Letters concerning the Plan of Salvation, addressed to the Members of the Spring Street Church, New York, 1816. A Sermon before a French Missionary Society in New York, 1817. An Abstract of Biblical Geography, 1835.

John Howe Peyton was the son of John Rowzee Peyton, of Stafford County, Virginia. Being admitted to the Bar, he settled at Staunton, Virginia, where he was long eminent.

Dennis De Berdt Reed was a son of the distinguished General Joseph Reed of the class of 1757. Mr Reed died at sea, January 5, 1805.

Richard Rush was the son of Dr. Benjamin Rush, and grandson of Richard Stockton—both signers of the Declaration of Independence, and both graduates of Princeton. He studied law with William Lewis, Esq., then one of the leaders of the Philadelphia Bar, and was admitted to practice in 1800. For the next seven years he was devoted to the study of his profession. In 1808, he became prominent by his defence of Colonel Duane, editor of the *Aurora*, the Democratic organ in Philadelphia.

In January, 1811, he was appointed by Governor Snyder, Attorney-General of Pennsylvania. In November of the same year, he was appointed by Mr. Madison First Comptroller of the Treasury. When the war of 1812 commenced, Mr. Rush by his pen and in public addresses, entered warmly into the defence of Mr. Madison and his policy. In 1814, when but thirty-three years of age, he was offered the post either of Attorney-General, or Secretary of the Treasury. He chose the first, which he held until 1817, discharging its important duties with eminent success. After the inauguration of Mr. Monroe, in 1816, John Q. Adams, then Minister to England, was appointed Secretary of State, but for about six months previous to his return, Mr. Rush acted in that capacity. In October, 1817, he was appointed Envoy Extraordinary and Minister Plenipotentiary to the Court of Great Britain, holding this high position until 1825. In 1825, he entered upon the office of Secretary of the Treasury, to which he had been previously appointed by Mr. Adams, and served during the continuance of that Administration. In 1828, Mr. Rush was nominated on the same ticket with Mr. Adams for the office of Vice-President of the United States, and received the same number of electoral votes. Mr. Rush warmly sympathized with General Jackson in his administration. In March, 1847, he was appointed by President Polk, Minister to France. This was the last public position held by him. The closing years of his life were spent in retirement at the paternal estate of Sydenham, in the suburbs of Philadelphia. He died in Philadelphia, July 30, 1859.

The publications of Mr. Rush are: Narrative of a Residence at the Court of London from 1817 to 1825, 8vo, London and Philadelphia, 1833. In 1845, he published a new and enlarged edition of the same work under the title of "Memoranda of a Residence at the Court of London, comprising incidents, Official and Personal, from 1819 to 1825; including negotiations on the Oregon Question and other unsettled questions between the United States and Great Britain." Oration delivered at Washington, July 4, 1812. Letters on Free Masonry, Philadelphia, 1831. Report against the Bank of the United States, 1834. Whilst Attorney-General of the United States, he superintended the publication of a new edition or codification of the Laws of the United States, issued in 1815 in 5 volumes. Washington in Domestic Life; from original Letters and Manuscripts. 1857. Occasional Productions, Political, Diplomatic and Miscellaneous. 1857. He also occasionally contributed to periodical literature.

John Strawbridge was a native of Pennsylvania. After graduating, he entered mercantile life, and was for many years a merchant in Philadelphia. He died at Germantown, Pennsylvania, April 4, 1858.

Stephen Thompson received his license from the Presbytery of New York, October 9, 1800, and was ordained and installed pastor of the Church at Connecticut Farms, New Jersey, June 15, 1802. In 1834, he removed to Indiana, where he died, May 31, 1856.

George McIntosh Troup was born in Georgia. On his return from college he studied law. In 1801, he was a member of the Legislature of Georgia, and was re-elected in 1802 and 1803. In 1806, he represented his State in Congress, holding the position until 1815. In 1816, he was elected to the United States Senate, where he remained two years. In 1823, he was elected Governor of Georgia, from which post he retired in 1827, with a popularity equal to that of any former Chief Magistrate. In 1828, he was returned to the United States Senate, and held the position until 1834. In the Senate his feebleness of health forbade his participation in debate. Governor Troup was a great advocate for State Rights and State Sovereignty. He died in 1856.

John Vancleve studied medicine, and practiced during his life in Princeton. He was a man of high attainments and great skill in his profession. He was a Trustee of the College from 1810 to the day of his death in 1826. Dr. Vancleve was a native of Hunterdon County, New Jersey.

1797.

John Watson, probably the most remarkable man in a most distinguished class, was a native of Western Pennsylvania; but being left an orphan at an early age, he was received into the house of a friend of the family. When about six or seven years old, a copy of the "Vicar of Wakefield" fell into his hands, and from that time his desire to obtain knowledge was insatiable.

The lady who had taken him into her house after the death of his parents, had a handsome collection of books, and especially of novels, of which she was a great reader. She soon discovered that Watson was, at every leisure moment, reading these books, and she peremptorily forbade him the use of them. He wished to be obedient, but he could not resist his desire to read. He secretly took her books, and concealing them in a private place, read them by stealth. The stratagem being discovered, the book-case was locked and the key securely laid away; but he finding a key which unlocked the case, continued to read until he had devoured every book in the library. When about nine years old, he lived with a man who kept a tavern and a retail store, and under his instruction became proficient in writing and arithmetic. He was employed in the store and in the bar-room as circumstances required. About this time he fell in with a copy of Addison's Spectator, which he read with great delight, and the Latin sentences prefixed to each number, excited in him an intense desire to learn Latin. He soon got possession of a copy of Horace and an old Latin dictionary, and without the help of a grammar or other aids, he soon became familiar with the greater part of that difficult author.

While he was thus employed, Judge Alexander Addison of Western Pennsylvania, while attending court, stopped at the public-house where Watson lived, and returning late one night found the young bar-keeper reading Horace by the light of the fire. From the Judge he received the first encouraging word that he had received since the death of his father. He remained in this place until he was nineteen, keeping bar and studying the classics and various branches of literature and science.

About this time his proficiency became known to Rev. John McMillan, D.D., who appointed him an assistant teacher in the Academy at Cannonsburg. Here he remained eighteen months, when he entered the College at Princeton. Here he was pre-eminent for scholarship, unblemished morals and unaffected piety.

On returning to his native State, he was immediately chosen Principal of the Academy at Cannonsburg; and soon after, by an able and powerful appeal to the Legislature, he obtained the Charter of Jefferson College, of which he became the first President. In 1798, he was licensed to preach, and took charge soon after of a small congregation near Cannonsburg, and continued its pastor in connection with his college duties, until a short time before his death, which occurred November 31, 1802.

Mr. Watson's scientific and literary attainments were equally extensive and exact. He was a good French, Spanish and Italian scholar, and was familiar with the Hebrew and Arabic. In a word, he was one of the most remarkable men of the day.

1798.

Charles Ewing was the son of James Ewing, a distinguished citizen of New Jersey. He took the first honour in his class; and, after graduation, studied law in Trenton, New Jersey, and was admitted to practice in 1802. In October, 1824, he was appointed Chief-Justice of the State of New Jersey, and re-appointed in 1831. Judge Ewing may be justly reckoned among the greatest ornaments of the New Jersey Bar. His acquaintance with his own department of knowledge was both extensive and profound, closely resembling that of the English black-letter lawyers. In a very remarkable degree he kept himself abreast of the general literature of the day, and was even lavish in regard to the purchase of books.

He was an elder in the Presbyterian Church in Trenton, and was an active and earnest Christian. He was eminently conservative in Church and State; punctual in adherence to rule and precedent, incapable of being led into any vagaries, sound in judgment, tenacious of opinion, indefatigable in labour, and incorruptibly honest and honourable, so as to be proverbially cited all over the State. Judge Ewing received the honorary degree of Doctor of Laws from Jefferson College in 1830. He died at Trenton, August 5, 1832.

Daniel Eliot Huger came from South Carolina, to which State he returned after graduating. For nearly half a century he was identified with the public service of his State as a member of the Legislature, State Senate and Judge of her Courts. From 1843 to 1846 he was in the Senate of the United States. He died in August, 1854.

1798.

George Washington Reed, the youngest son of General Joseph Reed, was born in Philadelphia, May 26, 1780. After graduating, he entered the navy as a midshipman, and was soon promoted. In 1804 he was in command of the "Nautilus," and was in the engagement at Tripoli, where he showed great heroism. When the War of 1812 broke out, Mr. Reed, then a Commander, was placed in command of the sloop-of-war "Vixen." On the 12th of November, 1812, his vessel was captured by the British frigate "Southampton." Soon after the capture, both vessels were wrecked on the Bahama Keys, at the Island of Conception. The frigate's crew became mutinous from intoxication, and the property which was saved from both wrecks was retrieved by the generous and indefatigable exertions of the American sailors. Captain Reed himself was as actively engaged in the direction and encouragement of the men as any of the British officers, and received the public acknowledgment of the British Commander, accompanied by an offer of his parole to return home. But such were the noble sentiments by which he was ever actuated, that he would not leave his officers and men, preferring to remain with them in an unhealthy climate, to which they were taken; he became a victim to an obstinate fever, brought on by the anxieties and fatigues to which, by his unpleasant situation and his unremitting attentions to the comforts of his men, he was necessarily exposed. His interment was attended by the British officers and a detachment from the garrison, and his funeral obsequies were accompanied by those honours due to his rank, and seldom withheld from each other by brave and generous enemies. He died at Jamaica, West Indies, January 4, 1813.

Henry Sergeant, a brother of John Sergeant of the class of 1795, resided, after his graduation, in Philadelphia, where he pursued a mercantile life.

Thomas Sergeant, a brother of the preceding, became eminent for his legal knowledge; and from 1834 to 1846 was Judge of the Supreme Court of Pennsylvania, and filled many other public stations with high reputation. He died May 5, 1860.

The publications of Judge Sergeant are: Treatise upon the Laws of Pennsylvania relative to the Proceedings by Foreign Attachment; Philadelphia, 1811, 8vo. Constitutional Law, 1822, 8vo. View of the Land Laws of Pennsylvania, etc., 1838, 8vo. Reports, etc. Sketch of the National Judiciary Powers.

In early life Judge Sergeant was a contributor of prose and poetical articles to the periodicals.

Joseph Holmes Van Mater, of Monmouth County, New Jersey, never studied a profession, but engaged largely in agricultural pursuits. He died in 1860.

1799.

John Alston, after graduating, returned to South Carolina, his native state, and was occupied in planting cotton.

William A. Alston, a brother of the above, never studied a profession, but, like his brother, was engaged in planting in South Carolina.

Eleazer Burnet received his license to preach from the Presbytery of New York in 1804; and was ordained and installed at Newburg on the 20th of November, 1805; and died at New Brunswick, New Jersey, November 22, 1806. He was labouring under a pulmonary disease at the time of his ordination. Mr. Burnet was distinguished for a quiet, amiable and devout spirit.

John Forsyth was born in Fredericksburg, Virginia, but removed with his father to Georgia when he was but four years old. He was prepared for college by the Rev. Mr. Springer, a graduate of Princeton of the class of 1775. After graduating, he returned to Georgia, and read law in the office of John Y. Noel, of Augusta, a graduate of the class of 1777. Soon after his admission to the Bar he was appointed Attorney-General of the State, and in this office attained great distinction. In 1811 he was elected to the House of Representatives of the United States. In 1818 he was transferred to the United States Senate, where he remained until 1819, when he was appointed Minister to Spain, where he remained several years engaged in adjusting the differences between that country and the United States. While in

Spain he was again elected to the House of Representatives, in which body he took his seat in 1823. In 1827 he was elected Governor of Georgia. At the expiration of his term of office in 1829, he was again elected to the United States Senate, where he remained until 1834, when he succeeded Mr. M'Lean as Secretary of State. During no period since the War of 1812, had our foreign relations involved questions more important; and the honour and success with which they were conducted were owing, in a great degree, to the talents and firmness of Mr. Forsyth. He died in Washington City, October 21, 1841.

In person he was upright and finely proportioned. As a speaker, he never failed to attract attention. He was always courteous and complimentary to his antagonist. He used little gesture, and his most emphatic passages were always in an under tone, which never failed to produce a deep impression. In a still small voice he poured out heart and soul and feeling, charming his audience into silence.

Mr. Forsyth was not a hard student, but he was a deep thinker. He mastered the contents of a book whilst others would be turning over its leaves. His knowledge was extensive, and whatever he knew was always at command. As an off-hand debater, he had no superior.

William Jenkins, the youngest son of David Jenkins, Esq., was born in Lancaster County, Pennsylvania, in 1779. After completing the study of the law, he soon became prominent at the Lancaster Bar, and second to none among famed contemporaries, who made that Bar so distinguished. Mr. Jenkins was an able jurist and ripe lawyer, a safe counsellor and most eloquent advocate, winning his way to the hearts of a jury with a resistless power, and presenting to the court the strong law points of his case with a tact and energy that seldom failed in its effects. His mind was eminently legal, and a superior knowledge of law was his distinguishing characteristic.

A son graduated at Princeton in 1835. Mr. Jenkins died in the City of Lancaster in 1853, universally respected for his social and high moral qualities.

James Cathcart Johnson, a native of North Carolina, after leaving college studied law in his native State, but never practiced. His whole time was taken up in managing his large estates.

Fredrick Nash was the son of Abner Nash, the second Governor of North Carolina under the Constitution. He became a distinguished lawyer. In 1804, 1805, he was in the House of Commons of North Carolina. In 1818 he was elected a Judge of the Superior Courts of Law and Equity, which he resigned in 1819. In 1827, 1828, he was again in the House of Commons. In 1836 he was elected a Judge of the Superior Court, from which he was transferred in 1844 to the bench of the Supreme Court, which he occupied with great satisfaction to the State and credit to himself.

James Rogers was born in Milford, Delaware, and was a son of Governor Daniel Rogers of that State. He studied law with Nicholas Ridgley, afterwards Chancellor of Delaware, and after admission to the Bar settled in New Castle, where he followed his profession. He married a daughter of the Hon. James Booth, Chief-Justice of the Court of Common Pleas of Delaware, and held for twenty years the office of Attorney-General of Delaware. Mr. Rogers ranked with the first lawyers of his day, was a leading man of the Federalists, and was respected and esteemed by all. He was a communicant, trustee and vestryman of Immanuel Church, New Castle, for many years. Relinquishing the practice of the law, he retired to his seat, Boothhurst, about a mile and a half from New Castle, and resided there till his death, May 12, 1868, aged eighty-eight years. He was erect, and retained his powers of mind and body remarkably to his decease. He is universally spoken of as a perfect gentleman in dress, manners and character. Four sons survive him ; two of them lawyers in San Francisco, California.

Henry G. Wisner was a son of Henry Wisner, a man of note in Orange County, New York. After studying law he settled at Goshen, New York, where he rose to the highest eminence in his profession.

1800.

James Carnahan, the son of Major Carnahan of the Revolutionary army, was born in Carlisle, Pennsylvania, in 1775. He graduated with the highest honours, speaking the English Salutatory at Commencement. For one year after his graduation he studied Theology under Dr. McMillan at Cannonsburg, Pennsylvania, after which he returned to Princeton, becoming tutor in the college, and pursuing his theological studies under President Smith. In April, 1804, he was licensed by the Presbytery of New Brunswick, and supplied the vacant churches in the bounds of that Presbytery for some time. On the 5th of January, 1805, he was ordained pastor of Whitesborough and Utica Churches in New York, where he remained until 1814, when, on account of the state of his health, he resigned his charge, and, after teaching for a short time at Princeton, New Jersey, removed to Georgetown, District of Columbia, and opened a Classical Academy, which soon became quite prosperous. In 1821 he received the honorary degree of Doctor of Divinity from Hamilton College.

In 1823 Dr. Carnahan was elected President of the college, Dr. Green having resigned the year before. He remained in this eminent post for thirty years, presiding with dignity and honour. But in 1853 failing health, and the increasing infirmities of age, compelled him to resign. He remained a member of the Board of Trustees till his death. He died at his son-in-law's, in Newark, March 3, 1859. The time during which Dr. Carnahan presided over the college was the period of its greatest prosperity.

Dr. Carnahan published a number of Baccalaureate

Addresses and Sermons, and some articles in the earlier numbers of the *Princeton Review;* he also edited the Life of the Rev. John Johnson, of Newburg, New York, in 1856. Though a forcible writer, with great perspicuity of style, he was very reluctant to appear as an author, so much so, that he expressly stated in his will that none of his lectures or other manuscripts should be published. His funeral took place in Princeton, and his dust mingles with the dust of the mighty dead of Nassau Hall.

Arthur Rose Fitzhugh, a native of Stafford County, Virginia, took the second honour of his class, and delivered the Valedictory. He returned to Virginia and read law, but did not practice his profession. He died at the early age of forty-two in the year 1823. Mr. Fitzhugh was a man of remarkable talent; and was celebrated for his handsome person and address.

Jacob Lindly came to college from Western Pennsylvania in company with his classmate James Carnahan. Lindly had a fine horse which he would ride for five or ten miles, and then tie him by the road side and proceed on foot; his friend, Carnahan, coming up, would mount the horse and ride on. Thus alternating they at last reached Princeton. How little did the young men imagine, while they were "riding and tying," that both would in course of years become Presidents of Colleges; the one of his *Alma Mater*, the other of a college in what was then a far western Territory.

Mr. Lindly became the first President of Ohio University at Athens, about 1804. Whether he was ever settled after he left the University, I have not been able to discover. He died in 1856.

Benjamin Morgan Palmer was the grandson of the Rev. Samuel Palmer of Barnstable, Massachusetts, and a son of Job Palmer who emigrated from Massachusetts to Charleston, South Carolina, previous to the Revolution. The subject of our sketch was born in Philadelphia, September 25, 1781, his parents having been driven there by the storm of the Revolution. He was licensed to preach on the 7th of June, 1803, by the "Congregational Association of Ministers" in South Carolina, and ordained and installed pastor of the Church at Beaufort, South Carolina, April 28, 1804. Here he laboured with much fidelity until 1813, when he removed to Charleston, and became pastor of the Circular Church, where he continued until 1835, when his health failed, and he resigned. The honorary degree of Doctor of Divinity was conferred upon him by the College of South Carolina in 1815. He died October 9, 1847.

The great charm of Dr. Palmer's character was transparent simplicity. His mind was saturated with the meaning, spirit and language of the Bible. His thoughts in the pulpit were, therefore, always fresh. His prayers were most remarkable. He was of medium stature; though a spare habit and an erect figure added to his apparent height. He was pre-eminently composed in manner, and dignified in his carriage; his voice was deep and sonorous. In the midst of society he was often sunk in deep reverie, wrapped up in the seclusion of his own thoughts.

Dr. Palmer published: Believing Baptism, no Argument against Infant Baptism; a Sermon preached in Beaufort, 1809. Gratitude and Penitence recommended from the united consideration of national judgments; a Sermon delivered on a day appointed for Humiliation, Thanksgiving and Prayer in Charleston, 1814. The Signs of the Times discovered and improved; two Sermons delivered in the Independent Church, Charleston, 1816. The Dejected Christian Encouraged; two Discourses preached in the Independent Church, Charleston, 1816. A Charge at the Ordination of Rev. Jonas King and Alfred Wright, the former of whom was ordained a City Missionary in Charleston, among the Seamen and others; the latter as a Missionary to the Choctaw Indians; 1819. A Sermon on the Anniversary of the Sabbath School Association in Charleston, 1819. Importance of the Ministerial Office; a Sermon preached in the Independent or Congregational Church in Charleston at the Ordination of five young men as Evangelists, 1821. Religion Profitable; a Sermon with a special reference to the case of Servants, delivered in the Circular Church, 1822. The three following were published in the *Southern Preacher*, 1824. The Reasons which Christians have for mourning the sudden removal of men who have been distinguished for the excellence of their characters, and the usefulness of their lives; a Sermon delivered on the death of Dr. David Ramsay. A Sermon on the Consequences of Unbelief. A Sermon on the Admonition administered to Elijah. Good men the Protection and Ornament of a Community; a Sermon delivered in the Circular Church, Charleston, on the death of Josiah Smith, Esq., eldest Deacon of the Church, 1826. The Children of professing believers God's Children; or, The Right of the Children of God's people to the initiating seal of the Covenant asserted and maintained; a Sermon delivered in the Circular Church, 1835. A Sermon published in the *National Preacher*, entitled, "The Sinner Arraigned and Convicted," 1836. The Family Companion, with an Appendix containing a Sermon delivered on the Sacramental occasion that terminated his pastoral relation to his people in July, 1835.

Robert F. Smith was a son of John Blair Smith of the class of 1773. He was settled for some time over a Presbyterian Church at Snow Hill, Maryland, where he died in 1824.

INDEX.